Puritans and Roundheads

by

Jacqueline Eales

HARDINGE SIMPOLE PUBLISHING

Hardinge Simpole Publishing,
1/R, 50 Leven Street,
Glasgow G41 2JE,
Scotland.

Transferred to Digital Printing in 2002

First published in Great Britain by
Cambridge University Press, 1990
in the series
Cambridge Studies in Early Modern British History
ISBN 0-521-36512-0

ISBN 0-9513757-1-7

For Gwenda Pearson and
Jessica Saraga

They are grown exceeding rude in these parts. Every Thursday some of Ludlow, as they go through the town, wish all the puritans of Brampton hanged, and as I was walking one day in the garden (Mr Longley and one of the maids being with me), they looked upon me and wished all the puritans and Roundheads at Brampton hanged.

Lady Brilliana Harley to Sir Robert Harley, mid-June 1642 (BL Loan 29/72)

CONTENTS

FIGURES

PREFACE

The most enduring description of the causes and effects of the English Civil War is contained in S. R. Gardiner's unequalled history of England between 1603 and 1656, first published in the latter years of the nineteenth century. Gardiner saw the war as part of a deepening political and religious struggle, which spanned the reigns of James I and Charles I and which had far-reaching consequences in the formation of a constitutional monarchy and the spread of religious toleration.[1] This analysis had much in common with the 'Whig' interpretation of history, which equated the 'destinies of the English people' with the fortunes of the Whig political party and strove to locate the origins of that party in a mounting opposition to the first two Stuart Kings culminating in the Civil War.[2] Gardiner, however, consciously sought to avoid such a one-sided explanation and his profound knowledge of the documentary sources combined with meticulous scholarship ensured that his narrative would dominate the efforts of his predecessors and contemporaries alike. His conclusions about the nature of the Civil War have also had a lasting influence on successive historians from both sides of the Atlantic.[3]

Yet the constitutional bias of Gardiner's work has not gone unchallenged. The formulation of economic and social ideas about the origins of the English Civil War, most notably by R. H. Tawney, Max Weber and Christopher Hill amongst others, has considerably widened understanding of the cross current of forces, which, in the words of Christopher Hill, 'prepared men's minds for revolution' in the 1640s.[4] It must be emphasised, however, that Marxist-

[1] S. R. Gardiner, *History of England, 1603–1642*, 10 vols. (1883–4); *idem, History of the Great Civil War, 1642–1649*, 4 vols. (1893); *idem, A History of the Commonwealth and the Protectorate, 1649–1660*, 4 vols. (1903). At his death Gardiner had only taken his narrative as far as 1656 and the work was continued by C. H. Firth, whose *The Last Years of the Protectorate, 1656–1658* appeared in 1909.

[2] R. C. Richardson, *The Debate on the English Revolution* (1977), 1–60 *passim*.

[3] See, for example, J. E. Neale, *Elizabeth I and her Parliaments, 1584–1601* (London, 1957), 436; W. Notestein, *The Winning of the Initiative by the House of Commons*, The Raleigh Lecture on History, 1924 (reprint, 1971), 48.

[4] R. H. Tawney, *Religion and the Rise of Capitalism* (London, 1926); M. Weber, *The Protestant Ethic and the Spirit of Capitalism* (London, 1930); C. Hill, *Intellectual Origins of the English Revolution* (Oxford, 1965), 6.

influenced theories, which explained the war in terms of class conflict between a waning aristocracy and a burgeoning bourgeoisie, have been less than convincing and do not fit the complexities of allegiance that led to the formation of the royalist and parliamentarian parties.[5]

More recently there has been a shift towards the argument that the conflict was the outcome of short-term phenomena more closely linked with the specific aims and policies of Charles I. Revisionist attacks on Whig and Marxist interpretations of the war have come from many quarters and are linked primarily by a rejection of hindsight and the desire to see the events of the war within the context of the society which produced it. Thus some of the county historians, influenced in particular by the work of Alan Everitt, have seen local matters, rather than central politics, as the prime concern of the gentry in the early seventeenth century.[6] Those who took issue with the State or the Church are seen as a minority, whose opposition was at odds with the more general desire for consensus and harmony, and was emphatically not a part of a wider bid for political and religious freedoms. Historians of central institutions have echoed these ideas. Professor Elton has queried the belief that events in the early Stuart Parliaments constituted a 'High Road to Civil War' and Professor Russell, in a seminal article, has argued that 'before 1640, Parliament was not powerful, and it did not contain an "opposition" '. Elsewhere Russell has further suggested that Charles I was not 'facing a profoundly alienated country before the outbreak of the Scottish troubles in 1637' and that the advent of war against Scotland in 1639 placed an intolerable strain on royal finances which had not kept pace with inflation over the previous century. This and other immediate problems facing the crown helped to provoke a state of civil war in 1642.[7]

Revisionist historians have, however, tended to underestimate the effects of political and religious divisions in the early Stuart period.[8] Nevertheless,

---

[5] R. H. Tawney, 'The Rise of the Gentry, 1558–1640', *Economic History Review*, 1st Series, XI (1941), 1–38; H. R. Trevor-Roper, 'The Gentry, 1540–1640', *Economic History Review Supplements*, 1 (1953); L. Stone, *The Crisis of the Aristocracy, 1558–1641* (Oxford, 1965). For an overview of this debate see L. Stone, *The Causes of the English Revolution, 1529–1642* (London, 1972), 26–43.

[6] A. M. Everitt, *Suffolk and the Great Rebellion, 1640–1660*, Suffolk Record Society, III (1960); *idem, The Community of Kent and the Great Rebellion* (Leicester, 1966); *idem, Change in the Provinces: the Seventeenth Century* (Leicester, 1969); *idem, The Local Community and the Great Rebellion*, Historical Association, General Series 70 (1969). See also J. S. Morrill, *Cheshire, 1630–1660: County Government and Society during the English Revolution* (Oxford, 1974) and *idem, The Revolt of the Provinces: Conservatives and Radicals in the English Civil War, 1630–1650* (London, 1976).

[7] G. R. Elton, 'A High Road to Civil War?' in *Studies in Tudor and Stuart Politics and Government: Papers and Reviews, 1946–1972*, II (1974), 164–82; C. Russell, 'Parliamentary History in Perspective', *History*, LXI (1976), 3; *idem, Parliaments and English Politics, 1621–1629* (Oxford, 1979), 426; *idem, 'Why Did Charles I Fight the Civil War?', History Today*, XXXIV (June, 1984), 31–4.

[8] T. K. Rabb and D. M. Hirst, 'Revisionism Revised; Two Perspectives on Early Stuart

their work has had the invaluable effect of reducing our reliance on hindsight and has restated the importance of contemporary opinions in the search for explanations of the origins and causes of the Civil War. Both sides were convinced that their opponents were extremists, who aimed at the destruction of customary religious and political institutions. The parliamentarians believed that a catholic faction had been gaining increasing influence and power at court throughout the reign of Charles I, a belief which was sustained by his marriage in 1625 to Henrietta Maria, a French catholic princess, and by the growing number of catholics and crypto-catholics who had been openly tolerated at court in the 1630s.[9] The Long Parliament activists argued that only sweeping reforms could fully root out these papist influences, which had infiltrated both the State and the Church. In contrast the King rejected the charge of a 'catholic plot' outright, regarding the demands made by Parliament for control of the militia and for a voice in choosing his privy councillors as an attempt to usurp vital prerogative powers of the crown. As for the proposed religious reforms, he viewed any criticism of the established Church as evidence of dangerous extremism designed to undermine royal authority. For these reasons Charles refused to negotiate a compromise with Parliament, finding it difficult to believe that his opponents had any legitimate grievances. His supporters were similarly motivated by the desire to defend what they saw as familiar forms of worship and the rule of law.[10]

In a sense both sides were victims of a conspiracy theory, but the emergence of such theories rested on conflicting ideologies about both the nature and exercise of political power and what constituted right religion, which had been developing over a lengthy period of time. Politics and religion were inextricably linked, as Sir John Eliot noted in the course of the 1625 Parliament when he declared that 'religion it is that keeps the subject in obedience'. It was 'the common obligation among men; the tie of all

Parliaments', *Past and Present*, XCII (1981), 55–99; C. Hill, 'Parliament and People in Seventeenth Century England', *Past and Present*, XCII (1981), 100–24; P. G. Lake, 'Constitutional Consensus and Puritan Opposition in the 1620s: Thomas Scott and the Spanish Match', *Historical Journal*, XXV (1982), 805–25; D. Underdown, *Revel, Riot and Rebellion* (Oxford, 1985); J. P. Sommerville, *Politics and Ideology in England, 1603–1640* (London, 1986); R. P. Cust, *The Forced Loan and English Politics, 1626–1628* (Oxford, 1987); P. G. Lake, 'Calvinism and the English Church, 1570–1635', *Past and Present*, CXIV (1987), 32–76; R. Cust and A. Hughes, eds., *Conflict in Early Stuart England* (London, 1989).

[9] C. Hibbard, *Charles I and the Popish Plot* (Chapel Hill, 1983), *passim*.

[10] These comments are based on my reading of the public messages which passed between the King and Parliament from the time of the Grand Remonstrance until the start of the war; see E. Husbands, ed., *An Exact Collection of All Remonstrances, Declarations, Votes, Orders, Ordinances, Proclamations, Petitions, Messages, Answers and Other Remarkable Passages between the King's Most Excellent Majesty, and His High Court of Parliament Beginning at His Majesty's Return From Scotland, Being in December 1641, and Continued Until March 21 1643* (1643).

friendship and society; the bond of all office and relation; writing every duty in the conscience, the strictest of all laws'. The need for uniformity in religious belief was paramount, and Eliot concluded that 'where there is division in religion, there are distractions among men'.[11] In this he was stating a commonplace belief that religious uniformity was a prerequisite for political unity. During Elizabeth's reign, for example, William Cecil had believed, according to his contemporary biographer, that 'there could be no government where there was division; and that State could never be in safety where there was toleration of two religions. For there is no enmity so great as that for religion, and they that differ in the service of God cannot agree in the service of their country.'[12] Behind the religious divisions which Eliot discerned in the kingdom in 1625 there also lay opposing political ideologies for, as the work of Dr Sommerville has emphasised, in the early Stuart period there was 'no unity on the questions of the nature and limitations of royal authority, the relationship between the law and the King, and the role of Parliament in Church affairs'.[13]

This present study of the Harleys of Brampton Bryan aims to demonstrate the ways in which an individual family was affected by these competing religious and political ideologies in the years before and after the outbreak of the English Civil War. The Harleys, headed by Sir Robert Harley KB (1579–1656), were the only major gentry family in Herefordshire to give their wholehearted support to Parliament throughout the war. Their stand against the King led to the eclipse of their traditional influence in the county from 1642 until the defeat of the royalists in 1646. The Harleys' subsequent reassertion of their local power at the end of the First Civil War was shortlived, however, as they opposed the execution of the King in 1649 and withdrew from public life under the Commonwealth, only fully regaining their former status after the death of Cromwell. Much of the surviving information about the background and course of the Civil War in Herefordshire is contained in the personal papers of the Harleys, and the letters and other documents collected by the family form the basis of this book.[14]

[11] Eliot is quoted in J. Forster, *Sir John Eliot: A Biography, 1592–1632* I (London, 1872), 146–7.

[12] Cited in C. Russell, 'Arguments for Religious Unity in England, 1530–1650', *Journal of Ecclesiastical History*, XVIII (1967), 209.

[13] Sommerville, *Politics and Ideology*, 4.

[14] A detailed description of the Harley Family papers is to be found in the Documentary note, pp. xvii–xviii, and in the Select bibliography at the end of this study.

ACKNOWLEDGEMENTS

I would like to thank the archivists and librarians of the various institutions which I have visited whilst working on this study. They have helped to overcome many of the problems which I encountered and have considerably eased the path of my research. I am also particularly grateful to Mr Christopher Harley, of Brampton Bryan, who has generously allowed me to consult and to cite manuscripts in his possession.

During the preparation of this book I have received invaluable advice and support from Richard Cust, Kenneth Fincham, David Hebb, Ann Hughes and Mark Kishlansky. I am also indebted to the editors of the *Cambridge Studies in Early Modern British History* for their comments, especially to Professor Anthony Fletcher for his encouragement and guidance in preparing the final draft. I owe particular gratitude to Professor Conrad Russell, who first suggested the Harleys as a fruitful topic for research and who has commented on numerous earlier versions of this work. Penelope Corfield provided similar help when I was writing my thesis on the Harleys and has encouraged me throughout all the stages of publication.

My greatest debt in the completion of this book lies with Peter Lake and Richard Eales, who have discussed specific points and problems with me, and who have read and commented upon draft chapters. They have both been unfailingly generous with their time and expertise, and have helped to sustain my enthusiasm for the sometimes difficult process of historical research.

ABBREVIATIONS

Add. Mss.	Additional Manuscripts
BL	British Library
BIHR	*Bulletin of the Institute of Historical Research*
Commonplace Book	The Commonplace Book of Brilliana Conway, 1622, University of Nottingham Library, Mss. Department, Portland Mss., London Collection
CCAM	M. A. E. Green, ed., *Calendar of the Committee for Advance of Money, 1643–1656*, 3 vols., 1881
CCC	M. A. E. Green, ed., *Calendar of the Committee for Compounding with Delinquents, 1643–1660*, 5 vols., 1888–92
CJ	*Journals of the House of Commons*
CSPD	*Calendar of State Papers Domestic*
1628 Debates	R. C. Johnson, M. F. Keeler, M. Jansson Cole and W. B. Bidwell, eds., *Proceedings in Parliament, 1628*, 6 vols., New Haven, 1977–83
D'Ewes (C)	W. H. Coates, ed., *The Journal of Sir Simonds D'Ewes from the First Recess of the Long Parliament to the Withdrawal of King Charles from London*, New Haven, 1942
D'Ewes (N)	W. Notestein, ed., *The Journal of Sir Simonds D'Ewes from the Beginning of the Long Parliament to the Opening of the Trial of the Earl of Strafford*, New Haven, 1923
DNB	*Dictionary of National Biography*
Grosvenor Diary	Transcript of the 1626 Parliamentary Diary of Sir Richard Grosvenor, Yale Center for Parliamentary History
Harl. Mss.	Harleian Manuscripts, British Library
HMC	Historical Manuscripts Commission

JBS	*Journal of British Studies*
JEH	*Journal of Ecclesiastical History*
JMH	*Journal of Modern History*
LJ	*Journals of the House of Lords*
Nicholas Diary	Transcript of the 1624 Parliamentary Diary of Edward Nicholas, Yale Center for Parliamentary History
PRO	Public Record Office
SP	State Papers
Spring Diary	Transcript of the 1624 Parliamentary Diary of Sir William Spring, Yale Center for Parliamentary History
TRHS	*Transactions of the Royal Historical Society*
TSANHS	*Transactions of the Shropshire Archaeological and Natural History Society*
TT	*Thomason Tracts*, British Library
TWNFC	*Transactions of the Woolhope Naturalists' Field Club*
Whitelocke Diary	Transcript of the 1626 Parliamentary Diary of Bulstrode Whitelocke, Yale Center for Parliamentary History

Fig. 1 Map of Herefordshire

THE HARLEY PAPERS:
A DOCUMENTARY NOTE

This study is based primarily on the private papers of Sir Robert Harley KB (1579–1656) and of his third wife, Lady Brilliana Harley (c. 1598–1643). Following Sir Robert Harley's death these papers descended to the Harley's eldest son, Sir Edward Harley KB (1624–1700), and thence to his eldest son, Robert Harley, 1st Earl of Oxford (1661–1724).

The reader should be aware that the private papers of the Harley family are quite distinct from the Harleian Collection of Manuscripts, which is now held by the Manuscripts Department of the British Library.[1] The Harleian Manuscripts were collected by the 1st Earl of Oxford and his son, Edward, the 2nd Earl of Oxford (1689–1741). After the death of the 2nd Earl, his wife, Henrietta, and daughter, Margaret (1715–1785), sold the Harleian Manuscripts to the nation in 1753.

Some of the Harleys' private papers were retained at their family home, Brampton Bryan in Herefordshire. Other personal Harley papers entered the possession of the Dukes of Portland as a consequence of the marriage of Margaret Harley to William Bentinck, 2nd Duke of Portland, in 1734.[2] Some Harley papers were subsequently detached from the Portland holdings following the marriage in 1759 of Lady Elizabeth, the eldest daughter of the 2nd Duke of Portland, to Thomas Thynne, 3rd Viscount Weymouth. These papers are now held at Longleat and have been calendared by the Historical Manuscripts Commission.[3] Microfilm of these papers is available for consultation at the Institute of Historical Research and in the Manuscripts Department of the British Library.

In recent years many Harley family papers have been deposited, along with other manuscripts belonging to the Dukes of Portland, in the Nottingham

---

[1] See *A Catalogue of the Harleian Manuscripts in the British Museum*, 4 vols. (1808–12).

[2] *DNB*, VIII, 1289, 1279–80.

[3] Historical Manuscripts Commission, *Calendar of the Manuscripts of the Marquess of Bath Preserved at Longleat, Wiltshire*, vol. I (1904), v. Volume I of this series covers the manuscripts cited in this present work. This calendar is very reliable and most citations given here are of the calendar rather than to the less generally accessible documents at Longleat.

County Record Office, in Nottingham University Library and in the British Library. Handlists of some of the Portland Manuscripts now held at Nottingham County Record Office and at Nottingham University are available for consultation at the National Register of Archives.

The Harley papers amongst the Portland Manuscripts in the British Library (BL Loan 29) fall into two categories, bound and unbound material. The bound volumes are arranged chronologically and have been calendared by the Historical Manuscripts Commission.[4] The foliation of these bound volumes is extremely erratic and is only a rough finding aid within each volume. In citing from BL Loan 29 I have endeavoured to give both a description and the date of individual documents as a surer guide to location. It should be noted that the British Library intends to reclassify Loan 29 documents as Additional Manuscripts in due course. A concordance will be available to convert Loan 29 references to the new Additional sequence.

Other private papers relating to the Harleys have also been acquired by the British Library and other repositories separately from the Portland deposits. These collections are described in greater detail by Clyve Jones in his article 'The Harley Family and the Harley Papers', *British Library Journal*, XV (1989).

I would like to express my gratitude to Maija Jansson at the Yale Center for Parliamentary History for enabling me to consult YCPH transcripts of the parliamentary diaries of Edward Nicholas, Sir William Spring, Sir Richard Grosvenor and Bulstrode Whitelocke. In quoting from these transcripts I have cited the day of debates in order to facilitate comparison with the original manuscripts. A full list of these transcripts and the location of the original diaries are given in the Select bibliography, below.

I would also like to acknowledge the help which I received from Clyve Jones in preparing the Documentary note and in compiling the genealogical table of the Harley family (fig. 2).

All quotations from manuscripts and from contemporary printed sources have been modernised in respect to both spelling and punctuation. Dates are given Old Style, with the year regarded as beginning on 1 January in the text; in the footnotes the form 1641/2 has generally been adopted in citing from original sources.

---

[4] Historical Manuscripts Commission, Fourteenth Report, Appendix, part 2, *The Manuscripts of His Grace the Duke of Portland Preserved at Welbeck Abbey*, 10 vols. (1891–1931). Volume III of this series covers the manuscripts cited in this present work.

Introduction

The symbolic start of the English Civil War came on the afternoon of 22 August 1642, when Charles I raised his standard at Nottingham and rallied his troops against the forces of Parliament. Fears that a civil war was imminent had been widespread since the beginning of the year and military preparations had already been under way for some months. Since January propaganda from both sides had been circulating in England and Wales, which set out two opposing accounts of the causes of the conflict, and in March Parliament had openly accused the King of being the instigator of the coming war. In the localities distinct parties had begun to form as people read and reacted to the declarations and orders promulgated both by the Crown and by Westminster, and in the counties armed clashes had broken out in the summer months, several weeks before the King's formal act at Nottingham.[1]

The course of the hostilities varied in intensity from region to region and for this reason the growing number of county-based histories of the seventeenth century have greatly increased our knowledge of why the war started and how it progressed. Such studies demonstrate that at its outset the war cannot be categorised as a class struggle, although it would later take on some of the dimensions of such a conflict. In origin it was essentially a religious and political cleavage amongst the leaders of English society.[2] Herefordshire is recognised as an area where the tensions between royalists and parliamentarians erupted at an early date, well before the declaration of war.[3] Moreover, the discord between the two parties there was exceptionally well

---

[1] The most succinct account of events leading to the outbreak of the war is still contained in Gardiner, *History of England, 1603–1642*, X; for an excellent synthesis of more recent research into this period see A. J. Fletcher, *The Outbreak of the English Civil War* (London, 1981); for Parliament's declaration of March 1642 see Husbands, *Exact Collection*, 99.

[2] Amongst the best of the county studies are A. J. Fletcher, *A County Community in Peace and War: Sussex, 1600–1660* (London, 1975) and A. Hughes, *Politics, Society and Civil War in Warwickshire, 1620–1660* (Cambridge, 1987); see also J. S. Morrill, 'Introduction' in J. S. Morrill, ed., *Reactions to the English Civil War, 1642–1649* (London, 1982), 9–12.

[3] Fletcher, *Outbreak of the English Civil War*, 302; R. Hutton, *The Royalist War Effort, 1642–1646* (London, 1982), 3–4.

1

documented by the Harleys of Brampton Bryan, who were alone amongst the major gentry in the county in their support for Parliament.

The Harleys, headed by Sir Robert Harley from the death of his father in 1631 until his own death in 1656, ranked amongst the wealthiest and most politically powerful families in Herefordshire. They belonged to the gentry elite, which governed local society through service as deputy-lieutenants, sheriffs, and justices of the peace. Members of Parliament were also chosen from the highest echelon of this select body. By the early seventeenth century the Harleys were long established just below the county leaders, outranked only by the Scudamores of Holme Lacy, the Crofts of Croft Castle and the Coningsbys of Hampton Court. They had been living at Brampton Bryan for three centuries, inter-marrying with other families in the area and working with the county gentry in governing the local community.[4] In the early 1620s Sir Robert was at last able to make the final push into the highest level of gentry society and his newly acquired prominence was achieved largely as a result of three judicious marriages, which not only increased his network of influential relatives and friends, but crucially also brought him three cash dowries within the space of two decades. In 1623 Sir Robert, then in his mid-forties, married for the third and last time; his new bride was Brilliana, the daughter of the Secretary of State, Sir Edward Conway of Ragley Hall, Warwickshire. This marriage offered Harley a valuable personal connection with the court, for in the 1620s Conway was becoming increasingly indispensable to King James and later to King Charles, through the influence of his patron and royal favourite, the Duke of Buckingham.[5]

Yet there were more personal reasons for Sir Robert's decision to marry Brilliana, and in particular there was a great religious sympathy between the couple. Both Sir Robert and Lady Brilliana were supporters of extreme reformed protestantism and they were aware that they were regarded as puritans by many of their contemporaries.[6] In the 1640s, when the Harleys broke from the rest of the county elite, which they had previously sought so hard to dominate, their adherence to Parliament would be expressed primarily in terms of their religious opposition to the Stuart regime.

In October 1640 Sir Robert was returned as senior knight of the shire to the Long Parliament, where he was one of the most active critics of the royal

---

[4] W. R. Williams, *The Parliamentary History of the County of Hereford* (Brecknock, 1896), 41–4; Royal Commission on Historical Monuments, *Herefordshire: An Inventory of the Historical Monuments*, III (1934), 20.

[5] Sir Robert's marriages and his relationship with Secretary Conway are discussed more fully in chapter 2, below. For Conway see *DNB*, IV, 975–6, and R. Lockyer, *Buckingham: The Life and Political Career of George Villiers, First Duke of Buckingham, 1592–1628* (London, 1981), 113–14, 127, 209, 235, 255–66, 268.

[6] PRO SP16/320/13, 334/41; T. T. Lewis, ed., *Letters of the Lady Brilliana Harley*, Camden Society, 1st Series, LVIII (1854), 40.

government. He retained his seat in the Commons throughout the fighting in the First Civil War of 1642 to 1646 and the Second Civil War of 1648, but was expelled from the House during Pride's Purge in December 1648, along with his eldest sons Edward and Robert, because he opposed the trial and execution of King Charles.[7] As an MP in the 1640s Sir Robert was in correspondence with some of the leading activists involved on both sides of the conflict in Herefordshire and his papers reveal the deeply held beliefs which separated parliamentarians from royalists at the onset of the war and also indicate the degree to which local people were aware of political developments at Westminster. The leading gentry and a number of local clergy in the county were clearly well informed and were beginning to take sides during the months before the outbreak of war, and other sections of the county population were equally partisan in the spring and summer of 1642.

Lady Brilliana Harley was herself one of the most energetic supporters of Parliament in Herefordshire, and endured great physical hardship in its cause, remaining at the family home throughout the opening phase of the war, and commanding the defence of Brampton Bryan Castle against a royalist siege in the summer of 1643. The siege was lifted in just under seven weeks, but then Lady Harley's health gave way completely and she died in the autumn, in her mid-forties, from what appears to have been pneumonia. The demands of civil war forced many women to perform unaccustomed acts of valour and Lady Harley's brave defence of her home was matched by two royalist ladies who repulsed parliamentarian sieges. At Corfe Castle in Dorset Lady Mary Bankes led the defence against repeated parliamentarian attack between 1643 and 1648, while in Lancashire the Countess of Derby success-fully defended Lathom House throughout a three-month siege in 1644. Accounts of the events at Corfe and Lathom have much in common with the siege of Brampton and all three ladies were highly regarded by con-temporaries for showing courage in the face of real physical danger; even their opponents did not fail to respect these women who displayed such laudable strength of character. In early August 1642, just before the declar-ation of war, Lady Brilliana was visited by Sir William Croft, one of the most active of the Herefordshire royalists, who addressed her as 'my Lord Conway's daughter, my Lord Conway's sister and Sir Robert Harley's wife, and a woman of a great spirit'. In an account of the siege of Brampton, Lady Brilliana was later described with similar esteem by Priam Davies, a parliamentarian Captain, who helped to defend the castle against the royalist attack. He recorded that 'her gallant resolution, her admirable wisdom in government, her earnest zeal in religion, her care of all our preservations, her encouragements in greatest difficulties, had so drawn all our hearts to the

---

[7] D. Underdown, *Pride's Purge: Politics in the Puritan Revolution* (Oxford, 1971), 147.

admiration and honour of her perfections, that her commands carried us into the cannon's mouth'.[8]

Lady Harley's moral and physical determination also brings to mind the spirit demonstrated by Lucy Hutchinson, the wife of Colonel John Hutchinson, who was the governor of the parliamentarian garrison at Nottingham. We know of the Hutchinsons' lives primarily through Lucy's *Memoirs* of her husband, written after his death in 1664. This work was not intended for the general public and was first published in 1806, but it was obviously designed to justify the Colonel's actions during the wars and the Interregnum, and was written many years after the events it described.[9] In contrast, most of what is known about Lady Harley is derived from contemporary documents, largely her own letters, which reveal her immediate thoughts and actions and which also contain the most detailed information that we have about the outbreak of the Civil War in Herefordshire. The majority of the letters were addressed to her husband at Westminster and to her eldest son Edward, who joined Sir Robert in 1640 and enlisted in the parliamentarian army in 1643. During those years Lady Harley vividly recounted the growing tensions in Herefordshire and, where it is possible to check her comments against other sources, it is clear that she was sending her family accurate news.[10]

Although over 400 of Lady Brilliana's letters have survived, the replies from Sir Robert and Edward Harley are apparently lost. It is quite possible that Lady Brilliana deliberately destroyed them herself at the onset of the siege of Brampton, for she had sufficient political sense to realise that such letters should not fall into the hands of the royalists. Any study of Sir Robert Harley is further hampered by the fact that there are major gaps in the county records for Herefordshire in the early Stuart period. There are no surviving assize, quarter sessions or lieutenancy papers for Herefordshire until after the Restoration. The problems posed by such lacunae can be overcome to a certain extent, however, by a consideration of the Harleys' experiences in the 1620s and 1630s. Sir Robert's speeches in the Parliaments of the 1620s and his work as a local governor, in conjunction with private papers, such as Lady

---

[8] HMC, *Manuscripts of the Marquess of Bath*, I, 1–33; G. Bankes, *The Story of Corfe Castle* (London, 1853), 180–93, 210–19; E. Halsall, *A Journal of the Siege of Lathom House* (London, 1902). Lady Brilliana to Harley, 11 August 1642, BL Loan 29/174ff.305r–304v; HMC, *Manuscripts of the Marquess of Bath*, I, 28. Lathom was besieged by troops under the command of Sir Thomas Fairfax, who had married Anne Vere, first cousin to Lady Harley; for this family relationship between the Harleys and Fairfax see Lewis, *Letters of the Lady Brilliana Harley*, xiii.

[9] J. Sutherland, ed., *Lucy Hutchinson's Memoirs of the Life of Colonel Hutchinson* (Oxford, 1973).

[10] Lady Brilliana's letters to her husband are to be found amongst the Portland Papers in the British Library, see BL Loan 29/72 and 29/172–4 *passim*. (Volumes 172–4 have been calendared, see HMC, *Manuscripts of His Grace the Duke of Portland*, III, 17–117 *passim*). The letters to her son were published by the Camden Society in 1854, see n.6 above.

Brilliana's commonplace book dating from 1622, illustrate the development of the principles and beliefs which led the Harleys to side with Parliament against their monarch, and which separated them from the other leading gentry in their county in the 1640s.[11]

Much recent debate on the causes of the Civil War has centred on whether the opposition to King Charles was triggered largely by the specific conditions of the late 1630s, or whether its origins can be traced to competing ideologies about the nature of kingly power, or to fundamental religious divisions, which were of more long-term significance.[12] The Harleys' religious views, which can be traced back to the early 1620s, if not earlier, certainly included criticism of the established Church, but during the reign of King Charles Sir Robert and Lady Brilliana were greatly alarmed by the growing influence of Arminianism in the English Church, which was encouraged by royal patronage and protection. This did not mean that the Harleys were automatically political opponents of the Stuart regime, and Sir Robert was consistently able to combine a successful career as a local magnate with his unorthodox religious views in the years before the meeting of the Long Parliament. In 1642 he was in his early sixties and had served the crown locally since 1603, when he was first appointed to the magistracy in Herefordshire. Sir Robert had also been elected to six of the early Stuart Parliaments, including the two Parliaments of 1640, and when he spoke in the Commons he did so as an experienced local governor, well aware of the strains which frequently arose between central policies and the expectations of the people he represented.[13] Harley and other men of his standing were responsible for integrating the demands of the centre and the responses of the locality, and in this respect they were the servants both of the crown and of the local community, but during the reign of Charles I certain royal policies served to make this an overwhelmingly difficult task.[14]

The ideal course was to be seen to steer even-handedly between these two arenas of political activity. Thus, during the 1626 Parliament when Sir Robert sat as senior knight for his county, the rector at Brampton Bryan,

[11] Lady Brilliana's commonplace book is now held at Nottingham University Library Manuscripts Department as part of the London Collection of the Portland Manuscripts. It is referred to as 'commonplace book' throughout this study.

[12] For this debate see the Preface, n.8, above.

[13] PRO, C66/1662; Harley served for Radnor borough in 1604, for Herefordshire in 1624 and 1626, for the borough of Evesham in 1628, and for Herefordshire again in the Short and Long Parliaments; see *Return of the Names of Every Member Returned to Serve in Each Parliament*, I (1878) 448, 458, 469, 479, 481, 489. *DNB* omits Harley's service in 1626 and 1628 and further states that Harley served in 1614, but I have found no evidence to support this, see *DNB*, VIII, 1282. I am grateful to Maija Jansson of the Yale Center for Parliamentary History for providing information about the 1614 Parliament.

[14] E.g. T. G. Barnes, *Somerset 1625–1640: A County's Government During the 'Personal Rule'* (Cambridge, Mass. 1961); Cust, *Forced Loan* also contains much valuable information about the integration of national and local demands.

Thomas Pierson, wrote privately to warn his patron of the 'two dangerous temptations between which you now stand, viz. the applause of prince and people'. A much more public statement of the same sentiment is to be found on the monument to Sir Dudley Digges, the Master of the Rolls, who died in 1639 and was buried at St Mary's church, Chilham in Kent, where it is recorded that he was 'unbiased by popular applause, or court hopes'. The increasing political and religious divisions of the 1620s and 1630s made such ideal integrity all the more difficult to achieve, however, and Digges in fact suffered brief periods of imprisonment for his conduct in Parliament, including his speech on the impeachment of the Duke of Buckingham in 1626, whilst also seeking court office, which he attained in 1636.[15]

Like Digges, and indeed most gentlemen of his rank, Harley also cultivated court contacts. The patronage of the court was desirable in itself, but it also reinforced Harley's status in the county. In 1626 he was rewarded with appointment as Master of the Mint, gained through the influence of his father-in-law, Secretary Conway. Harley was forced to forfeit this post in 1635, ostensibly because the previous Master still had a legal interest in the position, but his puritanism and the death of his patron Conway in 1631 were clearly important factors as well.[16] In the 1630s the King was consciously excluding men from his patronage if their religious and political outlook differed from his own and there is a parallel between Harley's dismissal and that of Sir Robert Heath, who like Harley spoke out against Arminianism and was removed from his post as Lord Chief Justice of the Common Pleas in 1634.[17]

Despite his own loss of place at court, Harley continued to serve as both a justice of the peace and as a deputy lieutenant in Herefordshire. In the 1630s the crown had urgent need of such experienced and loyal men, when unfamiliar taxes and the demands of war combined to create an escalating level of hostility towards royal policies in the English counties. The burden of taxation caused from 1634 onwards by ship money and later by levies to finance the Scottish war was unwelcome throughout England, while the war

---

[15] Thomas Pierson to Harley, 24 March 1625/6, BL Loan 29/121; *DNB*, V, 973–4.

[16] The full background to Harley's term as Master of the Mint is given in G. E. Aylmer, *The King's Servants: The Civil Service of Charles I, 1625–1642* (London, 1974), 372–9, although I would disagree with Professor Aylmer's description of the Harleys as 'enemies' of a number of local families, including the Crofts, before the war; see J. S. Levy, 'Perceptions and Beliefs: the Harleys of Brampton Bryan and the Origins and Outbreak of the First Civil War' (University of London, Ph.D. Thesis, 1983), 112–15. Harley received his final annual payment of £500 as Master of the Mint in 1635, see PRO E407/78/5 f.5v (I am grateful to Professor Russell for this reference). Harley was reinstated as Master by order of Parliament in 1643 and resigned in 1649 after the execution of the King, *CJ*, III, 69, 72, 73; VI, 210.

[17] R. Cust, 'Charles I and a Draft Declaration for the 1628 Parliament', *Historical Research*, forthcoming. See also P. Kopperman, *Sir Robert Heath, 1575–1649*, Royal Historical Society Studies in History, forthcoming.

itself, which started in 1639, was disliked partly because of the expense and the disruption which it caused and partly because many people felt sympathy for the Scots as a fellow protestant nation.[18] Sir Robert Harley's papers, read in conjunction with state documents, reveal just how difficult it had become for local officials to implement unpopular policies in the 1630s, though Harley and his colleagues did as well as they could, given the unfavourable climate of local opinion.[19]

The letters written by Lady Brilliana similarly reveal a great deal about the role of the Harleys amongst the leading local gentry before the 1640s. Lady Brilliana wrote about the family and the estates; but she was also very conscious of the status of her family in the county and of the position which they held in local politics and was therefore careful to keep Sir Robert and Edward Harley aware of local affairs and attitudes. She was also keenly interested in news of national importance and frequently recorded her comments on events outside the county borders. As a frequent member of Parliament in the 1620s Sir Robert was concerned by and informed about public events; while Lady Brilliana undoubtedly owed her obvious interests in these matters to her own family background. These factors were duly acknowledged by Secretary Conway in mid-1629 when he apologised for being unable to send any news of consequence:

I know that you my son Harley, having been so long versed in Parliament affairs, cannot but long after the contingent things to it, and you, my daughter, born in a strange land, the daughter of an ambassador and a councillor, will be out of countenance if you be not able to know what the neighbour princes do, and what we think to do.[20]

The Harleys were by no means atypical, for there is ample evidence that the circulation of news in general was becoming more sophisticated in the 1620s and 1630s in order to satisfy a growing demand. The early 1640s witnessed a further rapid expansion in the availability of news about national affairs and in November 1641 the first printed book of English domestic news appeared. During the course of the following year at least thirty distinct diurnals were

---

[18] Barnes, *Somerset, 1625–1640*, 276–7; Morrill, *Revolt of the Provinces*, 24–30; the standard work on ship money is still M. D. Gordon, 'The Collection of Ship Money in the Reign of Charles I', *TRHS*, 3rd Series, IV (1910), 141–62; see also P. G. Lake, 'The Collection of Ship Money in Cheshire During the Sixteen-Thirties: A Case Study of Relations Between Central and Local Government', *Northern History*, XVII (1981), 44–71; J. Fielding, 'Opposition to the Personal Rule of Charles I: The Diary of Robert Woodford, 1637–1641', *Historical Journal*, XXXI (1988), 781–2.

[19] Herefordshire lieutenancy papers 1640, BL Loan 29/123/42; PRO SP16/459/86; Lewis, *Letters of the Lady Brilliana Harley* 18, 48, 49.

[20] See, for example, Lady Brilliana to Harley, 24 February 1625/6, BL Loan 29/72; Lewis, *Letters of the Lady Brilliana Harley* 12, 30, 45, 46, 49, 51–5, 56, 57, 58; Viscount Conway to Harley, 28 July 1629, BL Loan 29/202 f.254r.

on sale, and gentry correspondence for the period reveals how eagerly these and other publications were sought after.[21]

Such a high degree of concern with national events is at odds with the idea of the inward-looking 'county community', which has been a major theme in many studies of the early Stuart period. This concept relies heavily upon tracing the personal and official links of county society in order to demonstrate that the gentry were intensely localist in outlook, an approach which has been rightly criticised on two counts: first, because it concentrates almost exclusively on the experiences of the gentry, rather than on the lives of other members of the community and secondly, because it deliberately emphasises localism, whilst ignoring evidence to the contrary.[22] These are valid objections, but they do not invalidate the methodology of the best of the county studies. The definition of gentry relationships, which underpins the notion of the 'county community', is a valuable analytical tool, which can, however, demonstrate ties outside a county as well as within it. The Harley papers are full of examples of the varied ways in which the gentry were linked together. Kinship, friendship, and the shared responsibilities of public office all helped to create strong sympathies between the Harleys and other gentry families, both within Herefordshire and beyond the county boundaries. The connections forged by the Harleys were all-important in an age when people expected to receive patronage of various forms from a wide network of relatives, friends, and acquaintances, and they generated a feeling of what might best be termed 'gentry community', rather than 'county community'. There is a very strong sense of common feeling with other gentry families in Lady Brilliana's letters, which was based partly on shared social rank as well as on personal contacts and was clearly not governed by geographical boundaries.[23]

This common feeling may have been reinforced by the fact that Herefordshire was less insular than many other counties, including some like Kent and Sussex, which have been the subject of detailed study.[24] Unlike those two counties Herefordshire is completely landlocked and in the early seventeenth century was encircled by the English counties of Shropshire, Worcestershire

---

[21] R. Cust, 'News and Politics in Early Seventeenth-Century England', *Past and Present*, CXII (1986), 60–90; F. S. Siebert, *Freedom of the Press in England, 1476–1776* (Urbana, 1965), 203–4; P. Zagorin, *The Court and the Country: The Beginning of the English Revolution* (London, 1977), 203–6; Fletcher, *Outbreak of the English Civil War*, xxvii–xxix.

[22] C. Holmes, 'The County Community in Stuart Historiography', *JBS*, XIX (1979–80), 54–73.

[23] L. Stone, *The Family, Sex and Marriage in England, 1500–1800* (1977), 124–9; R. Houlbrooke, *The English Family, 1450–1700* (1984) 46–7; Lewis, *Letters of the Lady Brilliana Harley*, 21, 25.

[24] Everitt, *Community of Kent*, 20–55; Fletcher, *A County Community in Peace and War*, 3–21.

and Gloucestershire, and the three Welsh counties of Monmouthshire, Brecknockshire and Radnorshire (fig. 1). The county was also linked with Wales administratively by the jurisdiction of the Council of Wales, which covered the thirteen counties of Wales and the four English marcher counties of Herefordshire, Gloucestershire, Worcestershire and Shropshire. Between 1604 and 1614 many of the prominent gentry in the four marcher counties, led by Sir Herbert Croft, pressed to have the powers of the Council restricted solely to Wales. Their objections centred on the interpretation of the word 'marches', the powers of the King and what they saw as the excessive fees and unjust decisions of the Council. The Council was part of the spread of royal power to the localities which had taken place under the Tudors; and the opposition of the gentry was based partly on the threat which they felt that this posed to their local powers and prestige. The Harleys were not involved in the attacks on the jurisdiction of the Council in these years and in 1623 Sir Robert himself became a member of the Council. He was, however, drawn into the more muted opposition of the 1620s and in the Long Parliament he was an active member of the committee designed to examine the foundation and powers of the Council, whose work contributed to the collapse of the Council's authority in 1641.[25]

As a marcher county, Herefordshire was open to considerable Welsh influence since Hereford lay on the main road running from London to Aberystwyth, and the county experienced a seasonal influx of Welsh labourers seeking employment during the summer harvest. This type of contact may help to explain why in 1641 Sir Robert's local puritan circle expressed their deep concern about the problems associated with education and with religion in Wales, where, according to a petition preferred to the Commons in that year, there were not thirteen 'competent preachers which preach twice, or preach and expound the catechism every Lord's day in the Welsh tongue in their own cure'. As a result of being unable to hear the word of the Lord in their native tongue, the 'people perish and the ignorance and superstition, and the excess of all sin is very lamentable'. Sir Robert was clearly deeply concerned by the problems created by this language barrier and in October 1641 he wrote to the vicar of Llanbister in Radnorshire, at the request of some of the parishioners, asking him to allow a Welsh speaker to preach to them on the sabbath, 'in regard many of them understand not

---

[25] C. A. J. Skeel, *The Council in the Marches of Wales* (London, 1904); P. Williams, *The Council in the Marches of Wales under Elizabeth I* (Cardiff, 1958); P. Williams, 'The Attack on the Council in the Marches, 1603–1642', *Transactions of the Honourable Society of Cymmrodorion* (1961), 1–22; R. E. Ham, 'The Four Shire Controversy', *Welsh History Review*, VIII (1976–77), 381–99; R. E. Ham, *The County and the Kingdom: Sir Herbert Croft and the Elizabethan State* (Washington, D.C., 1977), 164; HMC, *Thirteenth Report, Appendix, part 4, Dovaston Manuscripts* (1892), 270; *CJ*, I, 684, 767; *1628 Debates*, III, 473–4; *CJ*, II, 57, 216; Sir William Croft to Harley, 1 January 1640/1, BL Loan

English, whereby your ministry must needs be less effectual with that people, though your endeavours may be not the less painful'.[26]

Sir Robert's own reputation as a godly magistrate stood highest in the border region and this is clearly reflected in the numerous pleas for help which he received at the start of the Long Parliament from puritans in Hereford-shire, Shropshire, Worcestershire, Wales and as far afield as Lancashire. At Sir Robert's funeral in 1656 the sermon was delivered by Thomas Froysell, the vicar of Clun, whose parish lay across the county border in Shropshire. Froysell compared Harley with two southern Shropshire gentlemen, Richard More of Linley, who died in 1643, and Humphrey Walcot of Walcot, who died in 1650. These three were, said Froysell, 'the triangles of our country; and whilst they lived were special friends, and of one heart for God in the concernment of his gospel'.[27] Froysell's use of the term 'country' is note-worthy, indicating not the county, nor even part of one county, but the border area straddling Herefordshire and Shropshire, which had long been renowned as a centre of godly worship under the leadership of Sir Robert Harley and his fellow puritan gentry.[28]

The Harleys' distinctive religious outlook drew them into a network of like-minded laity and ministers which had little to do with geographical

29/173 f.7r; Edward Martyn to the Earl of Bridgewater, 22 November 1641, Shropshire Record Office, Bridgewater Mss., 212/364.

[26] J. Ogilby, *Britannia, Volume the First: Or an Illustration of the Kingdom of England and Dominion of Wales* (1675), plates 1–3; J. N. Jackson, 'Some Observations upon the Here-fordshire Environment of The Seventeenth and Eighteenth Centuries', *TWNFC*, XXXVI (1958–60), 37; Corpus Christi Ms. 206 f.12v; 'petition from many in the principality of Wales', BL Loan 29/124/69; *D'Ewes (N)*, 366; draft letter from Harley to Mr Hansard, Vicar of Llanbister, 7 October 1641, BL Loan 29/27 part 1.

[27] T. Froysell, *The Beloved Disciple, or a Sermon Preached at the Funeral of the Honourable Sir Robert Harley, Knight of the Honourable Order of the Bath; at Brampton Bryan in Herefordshire December 10 1656* (1658), 120; Froysell also preached at Walcot's funeral: see T. Froysell, *The Gale of Opportunity. Or, a Sermon Preached (at Lidbury-North) at the Funeral of the Worshipful Humphrey Walcot, of Walcot, esq: June 8th 1650* (1652). The sermon at More's funeral was dedicated to Sir Robert Harley as a 'bosom friend' of the deceased: see H. Hardwick, *The Saints Gain by Death, and their Assurance Thereof. Sermon Preached at the Funeral of that Worthy Patriot Richard More, Esquire, late one of the Burgesses in this Present Convention of Parliament for the Town of Bishops-Castle in the County of Salop*(1644). For the role played by More and Walcot as godly magistrates in Shropshire see P. G. Lake, 'Puritanism, Arminianism and the Decapitation of Enoch ap Evan's Mother', forthcoming. Sir Robert's contacts with puritan ministers at the start of the Long Parliament are outlined in chapter 5, below.

[28] Alan Everitt equates the use of the term 'country' firmly with the county and has written: 'when people like Mary Hyde and Henry Oxinden spoke of their "country", they did not mean England, but Wiltshire or Kent': Everitt, 'The Local Community and the Great Rebellion', 6, see also *idem, Community of Kent*, 13. In other contexts the term 'country' was used in contrast to the term 'court'; the literature on this contrast is extensive, but see particularly Zagorin, *The Court and the Country, passim*; Cust, *The Forced Loan and English Politics*, 223–4, 303; R. Cust and P. G. Lake, 'Sir Richard Grosvenor and the Rhetoric of Magistracy'. *BIHR*, LIV (1981); and Lake, 'Constitutional Consensus and Puritan Opposition in the 1620s', 805–25.

boundaries. Furthermore, the Harleys and other puritans identified the national interest with the cause of right religion and their sympathy for the reformed Churches of western Europe also gave their religious beliefs an internationalist dimension. The lives of the Harleys thus provide an example of how a family could be part of a county community while simultaneously maintaining interests and ties which cut across county and even national boundaries. By 1640 both Sir Robert and Lady Brilliana had spent large portions of their lives outside Herefordshire. Sir Robert had matriculated at Oxford university in 1597 and had completed his studies at the Middle Temple in London. He was first elected to the Commons in 1604 and his time as a 'Parliament man' gave him the opportunity to meet people from all over England and Wales.[29] Later, his achievement of court office meant that Harley spent further time in London, where he could meet relatives, friends, and other court officials and also cultivate contacts with the puritan clergy of London.

When she married Harley in 1623, Lady Brilliana was herself an outsider in Herefordshire. Her unusual christian name was an adaptation of Brill, the Dutch town where she was born (most probably in 1598), and where her father was governor at the turn of the century.[30] After her marriage Lady Brilliana maintained close contact with her relatives in Warwickshire, Oxfordshire, Lincolnshire, London and elsewhere, and from his first two marriages Sir Robert had developed strong family connections outside Herefordshire, most notably in Shropshire and Kent. Such links provided a system of communication and influence which was separate from county life; but in this respect the Harleys were typical of the leading gentry in Hereford-shire, many of whom had relatives living outside Herefordshire or owned land in other counties and also left the county to further their education at the universities or the inns of court in London. Before the 1640s the Harleys were accepted as part of the governing class in Herefordshire, not only on an official level but also on a personal level, and they were on reasonably friendly terms with many of the leading gentry, including men who would later be royalists, such as Sir William Croft, Viscount Scudamore, and Sir Walter Pye the younger.[31]

The one respect in which the Harleys differed greatly from their fellow gentry in the county has already been briefly mentioned. The Harleys were the

---

[29] J. Foster, *Alumni Oxonienses: The Members of the University of Oxford, 1500–1714* (Oxford, 1891–2), 651; H. A. C. Sturgess, ed., *Register of Admissions to the Honourable Society of the Middle Temple*, I (1949), 75; *Return of the Names of Every Member*, I, 448.
[30] Lewis, *Letters of the Lady Brilliana Harley*, xiii; PRO SP9/95 f.188a, v; *DNB*, IV, 975–6.
[31] The Harleys' family connections are discussed more fully in chapter 2; for the connections of the Herefordshire gentry see G. McParlin, 'The Herefordshire Gentry in County Government, 1625–1661' (University College of Wales, Aberystwyth, Ph.D. Thesis, 1981) and Levy, 'Thesis', 38–40.

only leading Herefordshire gentry who were puritans and it was their puritanism, more than anything else, which separated the Harleys from other magnate families in their county. The exact nature of puritanism is a subject which has attracted much debate. Some authorities have stressed the reforming nature of puritanism, arguing that puritans saw the Elizabethan Church Settlement as incomplete, others deny that puritanism centred on Church reforms and argue instead that it can only be defined as 'a certain style of evangelical protestantism'.[32] Very broadly puritanism combined a desire for plain worship with an intense emphasis on the godly behaviour of the individual. It could encompass non-conformity, since puritans consciously attempted to follow the spirit of God's law as they understood it and they were not afraid to criticise or even break earthly laws in the process. There was thus an inherent tension in the puritan position between the rhetoric of obedience to God's laws on the one hand and the insistence of some individuals on non-conformity on the other. Some puritans, including the Harleys, were also in favour of Church reforms, such as a more rigorous observation of the sabbath and a better-paid and well-regulated ministry, but we should be aware that they shared these views with a broad spectrum of the population, not all of whom were puritans.[33]

The difficulties we encounter in defining puritanism stem partly from the fact that contemporaries themselves did not agree on what they meant when they used the word 'puritan'. It was certainly used to describe critics of the established Church, but usage also spilt over into the secular sphere and the term could denote those who opposed the crown's domestic and foreign policies. Such was the resulting confusion that in the early 1620s there were demands for an official definition to be given by the King or by Parliament 'so that those who deserve the name may be punished and others not calumnated'.[34] As part of this debate Sir Robert Harley himself penned

---

[32] B. Hall, 'Puritanism: The Problem of Definition', in G. J. Cuming, ed., *Studies in Church History*. II (1965), 283–96; P. Christianson, 'Reformers and the Church of England under Elizabeth I and the Early Stuarts', and P. Collinson, 'A Comment: Concerning the Name Puritan', *JEH*, XXXI (1980), 463–88; H. C. Porter, *Puritanism in Tudor England* (1970), 9; H. Davies, *The Worship of the English Puritans* (Glasgow, 1948), 11; P. G. Lake, 'Matthew Hutton – A Puritan Bishop?', *History*, LXIV (1979), 202.

[33] *1628 Debates*, II, 383; III, 587, 431. On the wide diffusion of sabbatarian beliefs see, for example, C. Hill, *Society and Puritanism in Pre-Revolutionary England* (1964), 146–218; and K. L. Parker, *The English Sabbath: A Study of Doctrine and Discipline from the Reformation to the Civil War* (Cambridge, 1988). It should also be noted that both James I and Archbishop Laud were in favour of restoring impropriated tithes to give the clergy better stipends, a scheme which was put briefly into action by the puritan feoffees for impropriations between 1625 and 1633; see J. Wormald, 'James I and VI: Two Kings or One?', *History*, LXVIII (1983), 203; and C. Hill, *Economic Problems of the Church* (Oxford, 1956) 245–74. For Sir Robert Harley's contacts with the feoffees, see below, p. 66.

[34] Quoted in Hill, *Society and Puritanism*, 19; see also pp. 13–29.

several pages of notes in 1621, giving his own thoughts on the controversy for Sir Horace Vere, the commander of the English volunteer force in the Palatinate. Harley's ideas covered a wide range of topics, including non-conformity and the characteristic puritan emphasis on the importance of the conscience of the individual, but he did not arrive at a simple all-embracing definition.[35]

From the mid-1620s onwards, however, religious opinions in England became increasingly divided as the Arminians began to exercise growing influence within the established Church. Led by such luminaries as Arch-bishops Laud and Neile, and Bishops Montagu, Wren and Harsnett, the Arminians vigorously pursued Church policies which clashed violently with puritan ideals. While the puritans favoured plainly adorned churches, which would not distract the minds of the worshippers, the Arminians strove to introduce church decorations, such as stained glass and elaborate wood carvings, which would remind the congregation of the 'beauty of holiness'. The most intense area of debate, however, lay in the Arminian rejection of the Calvinist theology of predestination, the belief that God had irrevocably predestined the soul of every man and woman to heaven or to hell and that nothing a man did on earth could alter his ultimate fate.[36]

The Harleys and many others were thus convinced that the Arminians were spear-heading an attempt to reintroduce catholic ceremony and theology into England, and by the meeting of the Long Parliament the activities of the Arminians were widely interpreted as part of a concerted catholic conspiracy against Church and State. During the first session of that Parliament the Harleys and other future parliamentarians became convinced that only a restraint on the powers of the bishops, or alternatively the abolition of episcopacy altogether, could safeguard the Church against catholic corrup-tion. In Herefordshire many people shared this desire to check the excesses of the Laudian episcopate, but believed that the removal of newly introduced ceremony and ornamentation from the churches and the dismissal of certain bishops would be sufficient reform, and they were not prepared to alter the structure of Church government. The fate of episcopacy was thus an important element in the split between royalists and parliamentarians both in Herefordshire and in other counties.[37]

---

[35] Sir Robert Harley's holograph notes endorsed 'P', BL Loan 29/27 part I – these notes are discussed at greater length below, see pp. 46–7.

[36] N. Tyacke, *Anti-Calvinists: The Rise of English Arminianism, c. 1590–1640* (Oxford, 1987); *idem*, 'Puritanism, Arminianism, and Counter-Revolution', in C. Russell, ed., *The Origins of the English Civil War* (1973), 119–43; C. Russell, 'The Parliamentary Career of John Pym', in P. Clark, A. G. R. Smith and N. Tyacke, eds., *The English Commonwealth, 1547–1640: Essays in Politics Presented to Joel Hurstfield* (Leicester, 1979), 159–64; Lake, 'Calvinism and the English Church, 1570–1635', 32–76.

[37] Hibbard, *Charles I and the Popish Plot*, *passim*; Fletcher, *Outbreak of the English Civil War*, 91–321, *passim*.

During her husband's absence as a member of the Long Parliament, Lady Brilliana maintained Brampton's reputation as a haven for puritans, and at the start of hostilities the castle was used as a refuge by local people who opposed the King essentially on religious grounds. Brampton was fortified against attack and became a parliamentarian garrison, resisting one royalist siege in 1643, but succumbing after Lady Brilliana's death to a second siege at Easter 1644. Parliamentarian influence in Herefordshire was then almost extinguished until December 1645 when Colonel John Birch seized Hereford for Parliament. The Harleys then found themselves vying with new men, such as Birch, in their attempts to regain their traditional influence in the county.[38] The end of the First Civil War in 1646 brought success to Parliament, but also presented the victors with the problems of concluding a Church settlement and disbanding an army, which felt cheated both of arrears of pay and of political recognition. Sir Robert and his eldest son Edward favoured disbandment, or the dispersal of the troops to Ireland, and at the height of the crisis over the fate of the troops Edward Harley was one of the eleven MPs whom the army wanted to impeach. The execution of King Charles I marked Sir Robert's withdrawal from public life as he and his sons refused to acknowledge the establishment of the Commonwealth in 1649.[39]

The experiences of the Harleys touch upon many of the major debates about the origins of the English Civil War and illustrate the complex interrelationships of social, political and religious sympathies which guided people to choose sides in the course of the conflict. The Harleys were chiefly influenced by their religious beliefs and believed that they were involved in a war to establish true religion in the face of a catholic inspired plot against Church and State. It was this perception which compelled the Harleys to abandon their traditional loyalties both to the monarchy and to the local community and which sustained their defiance of the King during the Civil War and its immediate aftermath.

[38] HMC, *Manuscripts of the Marquess of Bath*, I, 1–33; G. E. Aylmer, 'Who Was Ruling in Herefordshire from 1645 to 1661?', *TWNFC*, XL (1970–2), 373–87; McParlin, 'Thesis', 86–227.

[39] The history of the Harley family after the death of Lady Brilliana in 1643 is discussed more fully in chapter 8, below.

2

The Harley family

Sir Robert Harley married his third wife, Brilliana Conway, in July 1623 at Greenwich, the site of a favourite royal palace. The choice of Greenwich was significant for, in marrying Brilliana, Harley had secured a vital link with the court. His new father-in-law was a prominent courtier, trusted by two successive monarchs and by their favourite, the Duke of Buckingham. Thomas Gataker of Rotherhithe officiated at the Harleys' wedding and took as the text of his sermon Proverbs, chapter 18, verse 22 – 'he that findeth a wife, findeth good, and obtaineth favour of God'.[1] It was an apt choice, for the family was firmly regarded as the principal unit of social organisation by protestant Englishmen in the early seventeenth century. Other social divisions, such as the estate, the parish, village, town and county, were seen as strong influences, but it was the concerns of the family which were believed to dominate the activities of most individuals.

Sir Thomas Smith in his famous work *De Republica Anglorum* of 1583 followed the model laid down by Aristotle, when he described the family as the source of civil society: 'the naturalest and first conjunction of two toward the making of a further society of continuance is of the husband and of the wife after a diverse sort each having care of the family'. This was a commonplace of English political thinking in the early Stuart period and can be found in such varied sources as the *Commons Journals* or the writings of the puritan John Winthrop, governor of Massachusetts. The ideal image of the family was patriarchal, in which the wife was subject to her husband, the children to their parents, and servants to their masters. Good order within the family was thus linked by many writers to good order within the state: 'care in superiors, and fear in inferiors, cause a godly government both private and public, in family, church, and commonwealth', wrote Richard Greenham in his *Works*, first published in 1599.[2]

The word 'family' has three quite distinct, but overlapping meanings, when applied to this period of English history. First, the term can mean the

---

[1] PRO SP84/113/98; T. Gataker, *A Wife in Deed* (1623), 1.
[2] T. Smith, *De Republica Anglorum* (1583), 12; T. A. Sinclair (trans.), Aristotle, *The Politics* (1962), 27; Hill, *Society and Puritanism*, 459–62.

immediate 'nuclear' family of parents and children. It was this smaller grouping which exerted the greatest influence over the lives of most people in the early Stuart period. Recent research indicates that the nuclear family 'was a common feature of seventeenth-century England', probably the majority of households consisting of this elementary unit. At the higher reaches of society the family would also live with a number of domestic servants, who formed part of the household, and the head of the family was responsible for the well-being and good behaviour of the servants as well as of the family members themselves.[3]

Secondly, the family existed as an historical entity consisting of a long line of ancestors as well as living members of the family, and future descendants not yet born. This notion of the 'historical' family had greatest relevance for the propertied classes, the inheritors of wealth and land, which had been accumulated by their forebears. This inheritance would be used to support those in current possession, but it also had to be carefully husbanded and handed on to subsequent generations. Along with wealth it was also possible for the historical family to acquire social prestige, indeed in most cases the two were inseparable. A family which lost wealth could expect to sink in the social hierarchy, while a family which gained wealth could expect to rise, and the ownership of land was the unrivalled symbol of status, because it was the basis for political power.[4]

Thirdly, the term 'family' can also be applied to the widespread network of living individuals linked by blood and by marriage. The members of this 'extended' family were commonly referred to as 'cousins', 'kindred', or 'kinsmen' in the seventeenth century. A cousin was often someone with very remote ties of kinship, who might or might not be interested in the welfare of other members of the family group. Yet even very distant family links were carefully cultivated, since kinsfolk were a potential source of help in both private and public life.

THE NUCLEAR FAMILY

Sir Robert Harley was born at Wigmore Castle, in Herefordshire, and the parish register shows that he was baptised on 1 March 1579. He was the sole surviving child of the union between Thomas Harley and his first wife Margaret Corbet of Moreton Corbet, Shropshire. Sir Robert spent the first year or so of his life at Wigmore, where his father was steward to the Earl of Shrewsbury, and the family probably moved to Brampton Bryan at the death of Robert's grandfather, John Harley the younger, in 1582. John had been a catholic and throughout his life had refused to accept the new protestant

[3] Houlbrooke, *English Family*, 10, 19.
[4] Stone, *Crisis of the Aristocracy*, 41.

religion; in 1577 he had come to the notice of the Church authorities because of his eccentric habit of reading loudly from a 'Latin, popish primer' during divine service at Brampton Bryan. The Harleys had not then acquired the right to choose the incumbent at Brampton and the rector must have been sorely tried by the antics of his powerful neighbour. According to a much later family tradition, John Harley had also sheltered the Jesuit priests, Campion and Parsons. This is quite plausible, for it ties in with the known movements of Parsons in 1580 when he visited Gloucester, Hereford and Worcester, and Brampton would certainly have been a suitably isolated hiding-place, since it is situated in the far north-west of Herefordshire some twenty miles from the county and diocesan centre of Hereford (fig. 1).[5]

At least two of John's children followed his religious example. His son William and his daughter Jane were both catholic recusants. Jane Harley married the catholic Roger Mynors of Treago and in 1609 was described as one of the principal women recusants in Herefordshire. Her brother Thomas was no catholic, but nor did he embrace extreme reformed protestantism, despite the fact that his wife Margaret came from a family where the practices of the reformed religion were openly encouraged. Her father, Sir Andrew Corbet, had delegated his rights as patron of Moreton Corbet to the parishioners, and in 1573 the puritan non-conformist, William Axton, had been chosen for the living by the parish. Margaret was most probably the earliest puritan influence in young Robert Harley's early life, but her religious guidance was abruptly cut short by her death and in 1589 Thomas Harley married for the second time. His new wife gave Thomas another son, who was baptised James.[6]

There is scant information about the lives of Robert and James until they were sent to Oxford university, where their father had received his own education in the 1570s. Robert entered Oriel College in April 1597 and graduated with a BA in July 1599. At Oxford he was under the care of a Welsh tutor, Cadwallader Owen, who probably provided a further major puritan influence in the young man's life. James Harley arrived at Oxford some eight years later and was admitted to his father's old college, Brasenose, in 1607, and supplicated for his BA in the summer of 1611. After their time at the university, the lives of the two brothers took very different courses. On

---

[5] Lewis, *Letters of the Lady Brilliana Harley*, vi; HMC, *A Calendar of the Shrewsbury and Talbot Papers*, II (1971), 161; Sir James Croft to Thomas Harley, 9 April 1582, BL Loan 29/202 before f.38; PRO SP12/118/7 (i) (I am grateful to Janet Hammond for this reference); Anonymous Life of Sir Robert Harley, undated, BL Loan 29/122/23; *DNB*, XV, 412.

[6] For William Harley see J. H. Matthews, *Collections Towards the History and Antiquity of the County of Hereford in Continuation of Duncumb's History*, Hundred of Wormelow, Upper Division, part II (Hereford, 1913), 117; for Jane Mynors see PRO SP14/48/138; P. Collinson, *The Elizabethan Puritan Movement* (1967), 139; Marriage Settlement, 16 September 1589, Brampton Bryan, Harley Mss., Bundle 67.

leaving Oxford Robert set about the pursuit of a public career and in 1599 went to study at the Middle Temple, where he remained until at least February 1603.[7] An education at the inns of court was regarded as essential for country gentlemen, not to fit them for careers as lawyers, but to stand them in good stead in their future roles as justices of the peace. There were also other practical considerations to be borne in mind. As landowners the gentry needed to know the legal ins and outs relating to the transfer and inheritance of land. Disputes over land could also embroil gentlemen in lengthy law suits and a working knowledge of English law could prove to be most useful in the maintenance of property rights. Robert remained in London after his studies had ended and in 1603 was made a Knight of the Order of the Bath at the coronation ceremony of James I. This was a signal honour for Harley and he may have had some patron at court who had recommended him for inclusion in the list of 62 new creations. It was widely rumoured at the time that some of the new knights had paid for entry to the order, but there is no reason to believe that Harley was amongst them. Sir Robert's knighthood was the prelude to his burgeoning public career. In the spring of 1604 he was returned to his first Parliament as burgess for Radnor and at about the same time was admitted to the bench of justices in Herefordshire.[8]

In contrast, James Harley settled down to the life of a minor country gentleman, as befitted a younger son who did not stand to inherit much from his father. In 1610 he married Ann Gardiner, a local girl from the Brampton estate and they lived on an income provided by Thomas Harley. James and his wife were both to die within a month of each other in the summer of 1618 and their daughter died in the following year; while Sir Robert Harley's own first attempts to start a family were almost as traumatic. In February 1603 he married Ann, the daughter of Charles Barrett of Belhouse, Essex, but on 1 December she died from the complications of childbirth. She was buried with her baby son Thomas near the home of her step-father, Sir John Leveson of Halling, in the parish church of Saint Michael, Cuxton, in Kent. Inside the church, partially obscured by the late-nineteenth-century organ, a wall tablet commemorating Lady Ann's death can still be seen and records that her 'sorrowing husband hath caused this monument to be erected as the last office of his love'. This is the only clue that we have to Sir Robert's personal feelings at this loss, although the death of his wife and new-born baby would not have been totally unexpected. The mortality rates attendant on child-

---

[7] Foster, *Alumni*, 651; Lewis, *Letters of the Lady Brilliana Harley*, vi; Andrew Clark, *Register of the University of Oxford*, II, part 2 (Oxford, 1887), 219; part 3 (Oxford, 1888), 216; Sturgess, *Register of Admissions to the Honourable Society of the Middle Temple*, I, 75; Marriage Settlement 12 February 1602/3, Brampton Bryan, Harley Mss., Bundle 30a.

[8] BL Harl. Mss., 1951 f.5r; Stone, *Crisis of the Aristocracy*, 82–3; *Return of the Names of Every Member*, I, 448; PRO C66/1662.

birth were high for both the mother and the infant and many women expressed their fears of dying at this time. Some women even went so far as to prepare themselves for death in advance of their labour.[9]

The survival of the couple's marriage contract does, however, illustrate the more practical side of marriage in the early modern period. The terms of the contract were agreed upon by Thomas Harley and by Sir John Leveson, and Ann brought with her a dowry of £2,300, regarded as a 'fair portion' by one contemporary.[10] Amongst the propertied classes the arrangement of a marriage was regarded primarily as a legal and economic undertaking and the final choice of a marriage partner was usually the prerogative of the parents. Before the marriage ceremony could take place there would be an exchange of contracts between the fathers of the couple, or their representatives. This provided for the payment of a marriage portion (more commonly known as the dowry today), and arranged an income known as the 'jointure' for the bride should she be widowed. Matches were made with an eye to the financial advantage provided by a fair dowry and to the social benefits of allying with a wealthy and influential family.

It was widely accepted by the early seventeenth century, however, that children should not be forced to marry against their will. Marriage purely for money or for status was increasingly frowned upon and many writers urged that there should be mutual sympathy between bride and groom. Thomas Gataker summed up this sentiment in his sermon at the marriage of Sir Robert and Brilliana Conway, when he said that 'marriage requireth a conjunction of minds, of affections, of wills'. Many people also believed that it was essential that there should be a religious affinity within marriage and by this criterion the choice of Ann Barrett could not have been bettered. She came of impeccable puritan stock, her maternal grandfather being the famous puritan, Sir Walter Mildmay, the founder of Emmanuel College, Cambridge.[11]

Within months of Lady Ann's death Sir Robert was looking for a second wife, but this certainly does not indicate a lack of affection for his first wife. A letter to Sir Robert from Sir Henry Peyton simultaneously offered condolences for his losses and conjectured that Sir Robert would now be persuaded to marry again. To the modern eye this might appear to be gross

---

[9] A. Collins, *Historical Collection of the Noble Families of Cavendish, Holles, Vere, Harley and Ogle* (1752), 197; Marriage Settlement, 12 February 1602/3, Brampton Bryan, Harley Mss., Bundle 30a; Houlbrooke, *English Family*, 129; A. Fraser, *The Weaker Vessel: Woman's Lot in Seventeenth-Century England* (1984), 76–8.

[10] Marriage Settlement, 12 February 1602/3, Brampton Bryan, Harley Mss., Bundle 30a; BL Egerton Mss., 2714 f.363r.

[11] Houlbrooke, *English Family*, 68–70, 73–4; Stone, *Crisis of the Aristocracy*, 632, 617; Gataker, *Wife In Deed*, 60; J. T. Cliffe, *The Puritan Gentry: The Great Puritan Families of Early Stuart England* (1984), 63–4; *DNB*, XIII, 376.

insensitivity, but such was the rate of rapid remarriages amongst the bereaved that it was to state nothing more than the obvious, indeed the correct, behaviour for Harley to follow. Even Ann's own mother, Lady Leveson, gave her approval to Sir Robert's next choice, saying that she had 'always wished him to take such a gentlewoman'. In the event Sir Robert's initial attempts at finding a suitable wife were unsuccessful. In February 1604 he approached the Knyvet family of Ashwellthorpe in Norfolk for the hand of Sir Thomas Knyvet's sister. These plans came to nothing and by September Sir Robert was involved in lengthy and ultimately fruitless discussions with the Here-fordshire gentleman, Sir Thomas Coningsby, for marriage to his daughter, Ann. The match was finally abandoned in January 1605, because the two families could not agree about the dowry. Ann's father was offering a handsome portion of £2,000 and he reminded Sir Robert, doubtless with some exaggeration, that it was 'a portion unusual in these countries . . . in our age there are not three examples of the like in the three adjoining countries'. The sum offered was certainly adequate by contemporary standards, but the sticking point lay in Coningsby's unwillingness to pay the money in a lump sum: he hoped to be able to pay 'from day to day to the uttermost best of my poor fortunes, to my life's end'. Staggered payment of the marriage portion was not unheard of, and some fathers took a year or two to pay off the full amount, but Coningsby's offer was open-ended, with the prospect of pay-ment dragging on indefinitely. Under such circumstances Sir Robert broke off the negotiations and informed his father that 'I will not deal with him that hath offered me so scornful usage'.[12]

Sir Robert's final choice was Mary, daughter of Sir Francis Newport, of High Ercall, Shropshire. Again we know very little about the relationship between Harley and his new wife and the details of their life together are very sparse. By the end of 1614 Sir Robert had two children, but they did not survive infancy and were probably both dead by the time that their mother died in 1622. As before, Sir Robert was looking for another wife within a matter of months and in 1623 he remarried. His third wife, Brilliana Conway, was then aged about 25, which was a late age for a gentlewoman to contract her first marriage, but it can be explained by the fact that she had three sisters and her father had to find cash dowries for each of them. This was not always an easy prospect and some women were forced to wait for marriage while their fathers accumulated the necessary cash. Brilliana's father openly admit-ted during the course of the marriage negotiations that he had already refused

[12] Stone, *Crisis of the Aristocracy*, 590–1; BL. Egerton Mss., 2714, f.363r; Sir Thomas Coningsby to Harley, 14 September (1604) and *idem* to Thomas Cornwall, 26 November 1604, BL Loan 29/202 between ff.45 and 51 and f.60r (I am most grateful to Robyn Priestley for allowing me to use her transcripts of these letters); Stone, *Crisis of the Aristocracy*, 633; Harley to Thomas Harley, 19 January 1604/5, BL Loan 29/119.

two or three matches because he had been unable to offer an adequate dowry. At the time of this marriage Sir Robert himself was in his mid-forties and, although the age difference might cause some comment today, it was not then thought remarkable. It was quite common for both widowers and widows to choose a much younger spouse when they remarried and Sir Robert of course was still looking for a wife who was young enough to give him an heir.[13]

Sir Robert was also associating himself with a family who had formidable court connections. Brilliana's father, Sir Edward Conway, had first made his career as a soldier and later served as a diplomat; in 1622 he had been admitted to the privy council and at the start of 1623 was appointed Secretary of State, through the influence of his patron, the Duke of Buckingham, who held a virtual monopoly over court patronage at this time. In the mid-1620s Conway was privy to the innermost counsels of the Duke and his royal masters and these outstanding political connections meant that Brilliana was undoubtedly a good 'catch' for Sir Robert. This is reflected in the fact that her dowry was only £1,600, a much lower sum than Ann Barrett's dowry and well below the dowries offered by the richer gentry, lawyers and merchants during the reign of James I, who were giving portions in the range of £2,500 to £3,000. As part of the marriage settlement Thomas Harley turned over the rest of his estate, including his main seat at Brampton Bryan, to the use of Sir Robert and Brilliana for life. Thomas reserved board and lodging for himself at Brampton castle, but in essence Sir Robert had taken control of his patrimony before his father's death. It was common for the groom's father to settle some land on the married couple in order to provide them with means of support, but few fathers were as generous as Thomas Harley had been and his actions bear witness to the importance which the Harleys placed on securing an alliance with the Conways.[14]

Sir Robert's choice of Brilliana was not, however, solely based on such practical considerations. There was a strong religious affinity between the two and Brilliana's puritanism had its origins in her own family background. She had spent her earliest years in the Netherlands and the Earl of Clarendon certainly believed that the religious milieu in the Low Countries had influenced Brilliana's cousin, Anne Vere, whose father, Sir Horace, succeeded his brother, Sir Francis, as governor of the Brill between 1609 and 1616. In 1637 Anne married Sir Thomas Fairfax, the Commander-in-Chief of the parliamentarian army from 1645 to 1650; and in his *History of the Rebellion and Civil Wars in England* Clarendon concluded that since Lady Fairfax had

---

[13] Lewis, *Letters of the Lady Brilliana Harley*, xii; PRO 30/53/7 no. 6; Marriage Settlement, 19 July 1623, Brampton Bryan, Harley Mss., Bundle 83; PRO SP9/95 f.188a, v; BL Add. Mss., 61989 f.81r; Houlbrooke, *English Family*, 84, 212.

[14] *DNB*, IV, 975–6; Lockyer, *Buckingham*, 275–6; Marriage Settlement, 19 July 1623, Brampton Bryan, Harley Mss., Bundle 83; Stone, *Crisis of the Aristocracy*, 639, 632.

'been bred in Holland [she] had not that reverence for the Church of England as she ought to have had, and so unhappily concurred in her husband's entering into rebellion'.[15] Holland was the traditional refuge for English protestant exiles no longer able to tolerate the established Church in England, but if this was an element in forming Brilliana's religious outlook, it was not long-lived for by 1606 she was probably living permanently in England; in that year she, her two sisters Hellweigh and Mary, and her brother Ralph, were all naturalised by private Act of Parliament. Brilliana's religious beliefs were probably more strongly influenced by those of her mother, Dorothy, who was a member of the Tracy family of Toddington in Gloucestershire. The Protestant connections of the Tracys were firmly rooted in the earliest days of the English reformation and in 1532 the will of William Tracy had been declared heretical by Archbishop Warham for its insistence on justification by faith and its rejection of the role of the clergy as mediators between man and God. At the instigation of the archbishop, Tracy's remains were exhumed and burnt at the stake and this outrage against their forebear was adopted by subsequent generations of the family as a badge of their commitment to protestantism. Samuel Clarke later recorded that Brilliana's aunt, Lady Mary Vere, a Tracy by birth, 'took much delight in speaking of one of her ancestors, as one of the greatest honours to her family (William Tracy of Toddington esquire) mentioned by Mr Foxe in his *Martyrologie*'.[16]

There was also a strong tie of affection between Sir Robert and Brilliana. While it was accepted that the choice of a first spouse was largely dictated by the parents, when a widower or a widow remarried they were normally freer to make their own choice. In 1604, when Sir Robert was looking for a second wife, he was described as 'having the power in his own hands now, considering his father had a fair portion before'. The suggestion that Harley might be in love with Brilliana was made by one of his relatives, who told him just before the marriage that she wished to know Brilliana better, 'for men in love are always held not to be their own men, and if you be not your own than I would I knew whose you are that I might let them know how much I am theirs'. Brilliana herself wrote to Sir Robert at about the same time and told

---

[15] *DNB*, XX, 236; J. Wilson, *Fairfax: A Life of Thomas, Lord Fairfax, Captain-General of all the Parliament's Forces in the English Civil War, Creator and Commander of the New Model Army* (New York, 1985), 12; W. Dunn Macray, ed., *The History of the Rebellion and Civil Wars in England Begun in 1641, by Edward, Earl of Clarendon*, IV (Oxford, 1888), 486–7.

[16] House of Lords Record Office, Bill for Naturalising the Children of Sir Edward Conway, 3. Jac. 1, no. 50; Lewis, *Letters of the Lady Brilliana Harley*, xii; *DNB*, XIX, 1067–9; J. Foxe, *Acts and Monuments of the Christian Religion*, II (1570), 317–18; S. Clarke, *The Lives of Sundry Eminent Persons in this Later Age*, II (1683), 144–9. I am grateful to Richard Eales for drawing the history of William Tracy's will to my attention.

him that 'none honours, loves and respects you more than your most affectionate cousin, Brilliana Conway'.[17]

The word 'love', of course, has many shades of meaning and Brilliana was probably not alluding to the passionate love that is thought to be essential in any western marriage today, but which was widely condemned as a poor basis for marriage in the seventeenth century. Writing in 1642, the puritan divine Daniel Rogers described those who married purely for love as 'poor greenheads' and argued that their marriages would produce 'a cursed posterity'. Nevertheless, the conventions of the arranged marriage did not prevent the growth of love between spouses after they had married. By no means all families conformed to the pattern set out by Lawrence Stone in his monumental work *The Family, Sex and Marriage in England 1500–1800*, where relationships between husbands and wives and between parents and children are largely described as remote in this period.[18]

Because none of Sir Robert's letters to Brilliana have survived it is very difficult to reconstruct his feelings towards her. In his letters to other family members he called her 'my dear Brill' or 'my dear heart' and he refers to 'my dear affection to her'. These fragments of information suggest that Harley was loving in his relationship with Brilliana and it is clear from Lady Harley's letters to Sir Robert, written throughout the twenty years of their marriage, that this feeling was reciprocal. Lady Harley clearly valued her husband's company and the times when he was absent from her were keenly felt. The many endearments of her letters also testify to the depth of her emotions for her husband. A series of letters which Lady Brilliana wrote in 1626, when Sir Robert was attending Parliament, are particularly revealing. It was a difficult time for Lady Harley as she neared the end of her second pregnancy, and her words to Harley painfully reveal her sadness at his absence and the obvious belief that his love was not as strong as her own. She begged him to 'grant me my request, which is that you answer my love with yours, and where yours comes short mine shall supply in excusing the failings'. In his reply, which is now lost, Harley clearly challenged Brilliana's belief that his love was unequal to hers and later he advised her that 'to love much was a trouble'. Her reply was typically candid: 'I know I love you much, but I find it no trouble, nor cannot think that with all your arguments you can persuade me that to love is a trouble. I desire much to see you, which I think you believe.'[19]

---

[17] Stone, *Crisis of the Aristocracy*, 619; BL Egerton Mss., 2714 f.363r; Mary Fane to Harley, 9 July 1623, Brilliana Conway to Harley, 25 July [1623?], BL Loan 29/202 ff.101r and between ff.100 and 104.

[18] Houlbrooke, *English Family*, 77; Rogers is quoted in Fraser, *Weaker Vessel*, 27; Stone, *Family, Sex and Marriage*, 651–2.

[19] PRO SP16/41/25, 70/22, 320/13, 334/41; Lady Brilliana to Harley, 25 March, 1625/6, 23 May 1626, and 17 June 1626, BL Loan 29/72.

Lady Brilliana's letters also show us intimate details about the successful growth of their young family. In October 1624 came the birth of their first child, a son named Edward after Lady Harley's father. The desire for a son was paramount amongst the wealthy, who had possessions to hand on and who would also have to part with a dowry in order to marry off any daughters. On hearing of the birth of young Ned, Secretary Conway wrote at once to express his joy 'in my Brill's safe delivery, and with advantage of the sex'. In April 1626 a second son was born and Brilliana named him Robert – 'that name I love the best it being yours' as she wrote to her husband. In 1628 there followed the birth of a third son, Thomas, and in the following year their first daughter, Brilliana, was born. The births of Dorothy and Margaret followed in 1630 and 1631 respectively. Finally a fourth daughter, Elizabeth, was born in 1634 and alone of all the children she appears to have died in early childhood. Lady Brilliana was also responsible for the upbringing of her nephew Edward Smith, whose wardship had been granted to her brother, the second Viscount Conway. Edward joined the household at Brampton in 1632 and was raised with the Harley's own children.[20]

Despite having help from both a wet nurse and her maids Lady Harley was deeply concerned with the development and welfare of her children. Women of her status frequently sent their infants to be raised in the home of a wet nurse during the first year or so of life, but Lady Brilliana employed a wet nurse at Brampton and could thus supervise the care of her own children. It is interesting that Lady Brilliana did not undertake the task of breastfeeding, since some of the most influential puritan writers of the age, such as Perkins, Dod and Gouge, were already urging mothers to suckle their own babies, arguing that the mother could pass on her own godly character traits to her infants. Despite an upsurge in such advice, including a tract written by the Countess of Lincoln in 1622, the number of mothers who did breastfeed in the higher levels of society was probably still quite low. The employment of a wet nurse cannot be cited as evidence that a mother was unnaturally cold in her relationships with her children. It merely indicates that wealthy women could hire someone to perform a domestic task which could be both tiring and time-consuming.

As parents the Harleys clearly delighted in the doings of their growing brood of children and there is a strong sense of warmth and affection in the descriptions of them penned by their mother. Her letters to Harley describe the milestones in the youngsters' lives, such as Ned's first steps and the trouble he experienced in 'breeding of teeth'; Robin growing 'fat and big'; Brill's first

---

[20] Sir Edward Conway to Harley, 27 October 1624, Lady Brilliana to Harley, 21 April 1626, BL Loan 29/202 ff.144r, 204r; Lewis, *Letters of the Lady Brilliana Harley*, xx; PRO SP16/220/47; Lewis, *Letters of the Lady Brilliana Harley*, 7, 18, 22, 28. Smith later joined the royalists during the First Civil War, CCAM, 1395.

two teeth; the colds and other illnesses which afflicted them and the good news when all the children were well. The letters also contain touching glimpses of the joy which the young family brought to their ageing grandfather, who was living at Brampton in his own quarters and was not always in the best of health. Relationships between children and elderly parents who had been forced to relinquish control over their estate through age or ill-health were not always harmonious, but Lady Brilliana described Thomas as being 'very kind to me, I think he is the best father-in-law in the world'. Young Ned was clearly a delight to his grandfather, who 'will not yield that any should be loved like him, he must be the finest boy in his eyes'.[21]

Lady Harley was also responsible for the initial education of her children. In 1629 when Ned had just turned five she asked Harley to send a bible for him: 'he begins now to delight in reading and that is the book I would have him place his delight in', she wrote. The early religious instruction of children was commonly placed in the hands of their mother, and in order to undertake this duty most women of upper-gentry status would have had to attain a competent level of literacy themselves. Lady Brilliana was obviously well-educated and her commonplace book reveals that she was widely read in theological works. She also professed to being able to read in French with greater ease than in English, an educational bias that was shared by other women of her rank.

Mothers would often start their children in the habits of reading and writing, but it was expected that the boys would later be handed over to the care of a tutor, or perhaps sent out to boarding school, before being sent on to university. There was no set age for these transitions and it was common for two or more brothers to start on the different stages of study together. The education of daughters followed a different pattern. It was probably exceptional for them to benefit from the attention of a tutor or governess except at the very highest reaches of society. Although there were schools which admitted girls, they did not receive the intensely academic education reserved for their brothers and, of course, they could not attend the universities or inns of court. Lady Harley's letters record very little about the upbringing of her daughters, but we do know that the eldest, Brilliana, was sent to stay with her great aunt, Lady Mary Vere, in London in May 1642. It was quite common for girls to be sent to the homes of relatives to finish their education and in

[21] D. McLaren, 'Marital Fertility and Lactation', in M. Prior, ed., *Women in English Society, 1500–1800* (1985), 28–32; Lady Brilliana to Harley, 14 March 1625/6 and 8 April 1626, BL Loan 29/72, *idem* to Harley, 21 April 1626, Loan 29/202 f.204r; Stone, *Family, Sex and Marriage*, 428–9; Lady Brilliana to Harley, 3 June, 1 April, and 10 June 1626, BL Loan 29/72; Lewis, *Letters of the Lady Brilliana Harley*, 5, 7; Lady Brilliana to Harley, 19 May 1626, BL Loan 29/72, *idem* to Harley, 21 April 1626, Loan 29/202 f.204v.

London Brilliana would have had a greater chance of finding herself a suitable husband, the ultimate aim for most parents with daughters.[22] Evidence about the boys' education is more plentiful. In 1631 Sir Robert was looking for a tutor for the boys, but we do not know whether he found a suitable man. The boys were subsequently sent away to school; first they went briefly to Gloucester and then on to Shrewsbury. In October 1638, just before his fourteenth birthday, Ned Harley went to study at Oxford.

Amongst puritans, however, the universities were acquiring poor reputations as places of lax moral discipline. Parents frequently admonished their sons to avoid the lure of sinful living at both Oxford and Cambridge, and some of the more high-minded students later complained of the conditions that they had encountered as undergraduates. Lady Brilliana feared that Ned would fall victim to these temptations and warned him that 'now I fear you will both see and hear men of nobility and of excellent parts of nature abandon themselves to swearing and that odious sin of drunkenness, and to scorn all religion'. Sir Robert reinforced his wife's advice in a letter to Ned, which complained of the 'base ways wherein many young men wallow' and continued 'I fear the universities do too much abound with such pigs, from which the preservative must be daily prayer for God's blessing on your own and the endeavours of your loving and gracious tutor'.[23] In the eyes of the puritans the problems had worsened in the later 1620s and 1630s because many colleges had come under the influence of Arminian heads and tutors. The Harleys avoided this pitfall by sending Ned to Magdalen Hall, where the principal, John Wilkinson, was a solid Calvinist. For many parents the choice of a tutor was more important than the choice of a college and the man chosen by the Harleys, Edward Perkins, held similarly staunch Calvinist views. The tutor was expected to act *in loco parentis* and the Harleys took this to the extreme view that Ned should not travel anywhere in the vacations unless accompanied by Perkins. Lady Brilliana was alarmed in May 1639 when she heard that the celebrated puritan vicar of Banbury, William Whately, was on his death-bed, for she feared that 'Banbury men would desire to have Mr Perkins' in his place. 'I fear me,' she wrote to Ned, 'that that has been the spoiling of the universities and the corrupting of the gentry there bred, because that as soon as any man is come to any ripeness of judgement and

---

22 Lewis, *Letters of the Lady Brilliana Harley*, 5; Houlbrooke, *English Family*, 148; *Crisis of the Aristocracy*, 681; Stone, *Family, Sex and Marriage*, 204; Houlbrooke, *English Family*, 150; Lewis, *Letters of the Lady Brilliana Harley*, 160, 161, 168, 172; Fletcher, *A County Community in Peace and War*, 38.

23 Harley to Dr Thomas Hill, 25 Nov. 1631, BL Loan 29/123/39d; Lewis, *Letters of Lady Brilliana Harley*, xx, 15; Cliffe, *Puritan Gentry*, 83; paper of advice from Lady Brilliana to Edward Harley, undated, BL Loan 29/78; Lewis, *Letters of the Lady Brilliana Harley*, xlix–1.

holiness he is taken away, and so they still glean the garden of the ripe grapes and leave sour ones behind.'[24]

Lady Brilliana's letters to Edward show that she missed him greatly and wanted to know as much as possible about his life at Oxford. She frequently exhorted him to write to her, reminding him that 'nothing can more please me than to have a sympathy with you, therefore not to know how it is with you would be a torture to me'. Her letters contained constant advice about both spiritual and physical matters. She reminded him of her concern for 'the well-being of your soul', which 'is most dear to me, next to my own' and she pleaded with him to observe the 'means to preserve' physical health, which consisted of 'good diet and exercise'. With her letters she sent a variety of medicines to ensure Ned's health, including liquorice for colds, 'eye water' for sore eyes and to preserve the sight, and *aurum potabile*, literally 'drinkable gold', tiny slivers of gold to be drunk in water and believed to be a powerful restorative. Lady Brilliana also sent presents of food, clearly worried that if she did not, then Ned would fail to eat well. At first she resolved not to send any food, since Sir Robert told her that Ned cared 'not for it'. Eventually Lady Brilliana's maternal feelings overruled Sir Robert's prudence and pies made from turkey, pigeon and kid, presents of bacon and sweetmeats for Lent, a loin of veal, apples and violet cakes all found their way by messenger or carrier from Brampton to Oxford.[25]

Ned's only indulgence at university seems to have been a desire to wear fashionable clothes. Attitudes towards dress were somewhat ambivalent amongst the puritan gentry, some of whom were happy to wear plain clothing at times of worship, but also wished to dress as befitted their rank on other occasions. A miniature portrait of Sir Robert painted by Peter Oliver in the early 1620s shows him to have dressed fashionably, but not flamboyantly, with his hair worn fairly short. At Brampton Lady Brilliana would have had little opportunity or reason to dress in the high fashions of the age, as she herself noted when inquiring after a distant relative, Lady Cope: 'I believe she keeps her state, as all noblemen's daughters do; though I do not.' Sir Robert decreed that Ned should wear sober clothing at university and at first Ned followed this precept. His mother commended his actions: 'it is very well done that you submit to your father's desire in your clothes; and that is a happy temper both to be contented with plain clothes, and in the wearing of better clothes, not to think oneself the better for them, nor to be troubled if you be in plain clothes and see others of your rank in better'.[26]

---

[24] Cliffe, *Puritan Gentry*, 84–9; Lewis, *Letters of the Lady Brilliana Harley*, 22, 54–5.
[25] Lewis, *Letters of the Lady Brilliana Harley*, 47, 17, 14, 16, 24, 83, 9, 36, 46, 13, 30, 44, 53, 82, 70, 64, 88.
[26] Cliffe, *Puritan Gentry*, 54–7; Lewis, *Letters of the Lady Brilliana Harley*, 25, 16.

Gradually, however, Ned seems to have acquired a wardrobe more suited
to his wants, somehow bringing his mother around to his point of view. Later
Lady Brilliana admitted that 'I like it well that your tutor has made you
handsome clothes and I desire that you should go handsomely.' She arranged
for Ned to have a silk suit, silk stockings and Spanish-leather shoes. The outfit
was to be completed by a hat which arrived from London with 'a gold and
silver hatband . . . sent by the commands of your lady mother'. The factor
assured Ned that 'the hat and band is of the newest fashion and I suppose very
good'. A year later Ned sent to London for another hat giving precise
directions about the height and the width of the brim. On this occasion the
factor failed to find such a hat and wrote back: 'we could not find any so high
as yet in the fashion, it is the newest fashion in *altissimus*'. Ten years later Ned
looked back on his time at Oxford and commented that 'I was not given up to
the evils of that place'. The advice in his parents' letters had in general been
well observed.[27]

Ned did not stay at Magdalen long enough to take a degree. In November
1640 he left Oxford and went to London to witness the opening of the Long
Parliament. At first his visit was prolonged because an outbreak of the plague
prevented him from returning to his college. Lady Brilliana told Ned that he
could not go back for several weeks, 'for the infection of such a disease is not
gone in four weeks at the least, but I think it will stay longer in the beds'. She
also believed that Ned would gain greater advantage from staying in London
than he would at Oxford and her opinion was endorsed by Lady Vere. Lady
Brilliana was undoubtedly thinking of the benefits that Ned would gain from
being in London during a Parliament, particularly such a momentous
Parliament as this was proving to be. Gradually all thoughts of Ned returning
to college were abandoned and he remained in London, making brief return
visits to Brampton at the first recess of the Long Parliament in 1641 and again
in the autumn of 1642.[28]

When Ned had left for Oxford in 1639 the education of his brothers and
Edward Smith had been left in the care of a succession of schoolmasters who
were to prove unsuitable for a variety of reasons. Richard Symonds fell in
with a group of separatists and in 1639 he and his wife hastily packed up and
left Brampton. Mr Ballam was sick a good deal, which meant that the boys
were left to their own devices and 'lose their time very much'. The youngest,
Tom, made good use of his enforced leisure, and at the start of 1641 was 'as
busy as can be about the Parliament and holds intelligence with all that will
give him true notice of things'. Lady Brilliana confided to Ned that Tom 'is the

[27] Lewis, *Letters of the Lady Brilliana Harley*, 22, 50; Thomas Burgh to Edward Harley, 28 June
    1639, BL Loan 29/73, Thomas Smith to Edward Harley, 26 June 1640, Loan 29/83;
    catalogue of 'mercies' drawn up by Edward Harley, 1650, BL Loan 29/176 f.201r–v.
[28] Lewis, *Letters of the Lady Brilliana Harley*, 100–1, 113, 114, 116.

likest you, and loves you dearly'. Robin, on the other hand, was at a loss without the discipline provided by school work. He quarrelled with Tom and 'cares not to know how it goes in the Parliament'. His mother had no sympathy for such an attitude and she took him to task for his lack of interest. This had little effect and Robin preferred to spend his time with the servants rather than trying to conform to his family's expectations. Part of Robin's problems lay in the fact that he was subject to frequent fits, which may have been connected with epilepsy. His ill-health and self-neglect combined to make Robin a pathetic figure and Lady Brilliana did her best to persuade him to take 'physic'. She also attempted to supervise the boys' study herself and made them 'translate something out of Latin into English', but admitted that 'it is but a little which they do'. A brief experiment was tried in the summer of 1641 when the boys were sent to school at nearby Llanfairwaterdine, where they were to be taught by the curate William Voyle. This proved to be another failure and within less than a month they were home again because 'the diet was so bad . . . they ate nothing but salt meat'. Lady Brilliana lamented that 'I am in great trouble to get one to teach them'.[29]

In strange contrast to the wealth of detail about the period from 1639 to 1641, during the next two years we see very little mention in Lady Brilliana's letters to the boys' education. Perhaps because a satisfactory teacher was found, or possibly because Lady Brilliana was more concerned by the gathering pace of events leading to the Civil War, which became the central theme in her letters. In May 1642, when she knew that a war could not be far off, she asked Sir Robert to consider sending Robin and Tom to Oxford. Harley refused this suggestion, a prescient move since Oxford was to become the royalist headquarters after the battle of Edgehill in 1642, although Harley could not have known this in advance. In June 1643 Robin joined the parliamentarian forces of Sir William Waller and missed out on a university education altogether. Ned had enlisted with Waller a few weeks earlier and it was he who had persuaded Lady Brilliana to let Robin leave Brampton to fight. The younger children, Tom, Dorothy and Margaret, and their cousin Edward Smith remained at Brampton with Lady Brilliana and were present during the two royalist sieges of Brampton Bryan castle. They were taken prisoner at the capitulation of the castle in 1644, but were soon released and were allowed to join their father in London that same year.[30]

THE HISTORICAL FAMILY AND MANAGEMENT OF THE ESTATE

The Harleys had first settled in Herefordshire in the early fourteenth century and in 1309 Brampton Bryan had become the property of Sir Robert de

[29] *Ibid.*, 77–8, 135, 112, 119–20, 121, 122, 128, 137, 140, 141, 144.
[30] Lady Brilliana to Harley, 17 May 1642, BL Loan 29/72; Lewis, *Letters of the Lady Brilliana Harley*, 204, 205; HMC, *Manuscripts of the Marquess of Bath*, I, 33.

Harley of Harley, Shropshire, through his marriage to the heiress Margaret Brampton. Three centuries later, at the start of the seventeenth century, the Harleys had become established as one of the leading gentry families in Herefordshire. By 1600 Thomas Harley owned not only Brampton Bryan but also the smaller manors of Buckton and Aylton. Within the county administration he had served as both a justice of the peace and a deputy lieutenant and had been sheriff of Herefordshire in 1596, acting in that capacity again in 1603. Strangely, Thomas never sat in Parliament and no member of the Harley family had done so since the mid-fourteenth century. This is surprising, for in the sixteenth century the county gentry had increasingly turned to a seat in Parliament as a means of increasing their own local power and prestige.[31]

We can only guess why the Harleys did not serve in Parliament during this very long period. Perhaps it was a result of the fact that the Harleys were not yet at the very pinnacle of gentry society in Herefordshire. In the second half of the sixteenth century that place was occupied by the Croft, Scudamore and Coningsby families, who dominated county politics and monopolised the county seats in Parliament throughout the fifty years from 1571 to 1621. The Harleys may well have felt that if they could not have one of the county seats then they would not bother with the less prestigious borough seats available. Sir Robert's return to Parliament as burgess for Radnor in 1604 suggests, however, that he was ambitious for a more public career than his father. In 1624 Sir Robert Harley was finally able to break the hegemony of the county magnates when he was returned to Parliament as junior knight for Herefordshire. This was a notable achievement since he had served only once previously in 1604.[32] It was also a clear demonstration that the Harleys had finally reached the highest levels of local society. This success was the direct result of a series of marriages and land transactions between 1603 and 1623, which had been designed to increase Sir Robert's wealth and status in the county and which had culminated in his marriage to Brilliana Conway.

In 1603 Thomas Harley had been able to improve the family fortunes by the purchase of the manor and borough of Wigmore from Sir Henry Lyndley, a former steward of the Earl of Essex. Wigmore was former monastic property and was part of the great influx of land onto the market which had

[31] G. Grazebrook and J. P. Rylands, eds., *The Visitation of Shropshire Taken in the Year 1623*, Harleian Society, XXVIII (1889), 213–15; Royal Commission on Historical Monuments, *Herefordshire*, III (1934), 20; marriage settlement, 12 February 1602/3, Brampton Bryan, Harley Mss., Bundle 30a; PRO C66/1594; Folger Library Mss., Xd. 140; PRO Lists and Indexes, *List of Sheriffs for England and Wales*, IX (1898), 61; *Return of the Names of Every Member*, I, 120, 122, 127, 135, 151, 178, 183; J. E. Neale, *The Elizabethan House of Commons* (1949), 148–50.

[32] Williams, *Parliamentary History of the County of Hereford*, 41–4; *Return of the Names of Every Member*, I, 448, 458.

followed the dissolution of the monasteries. Between the period of the dissolution and the Civil War the land market was very active as many gentry families tried to build up their estates, by buying the new land that was suddenly available. Some families were lucky enough to be able to purchase properties adjacent to their own. In other cases they would buy a more distant holding in the hope of later exchanging it for property nearer their main estate, a practice which helped to keep the market in land buoyant. The acquisition of Wigmore was of particular value to the Harleys, not only because it was a substantial manor, but also because it lay so close to Brampton Bryan (fig. 1).[33]

The asking price for Wigmore was £2,600, a sum which Thomas Harley might have had difficulty raising under normal circumstances, but he was able to draw upon the dowry provided by Ann Barrett's marriage to his son, which took place almost simultaneously with the purchase of Wigmore. As part of the marriage settlement Thomas immediately conveyed the entire estate of Wigmore, including the advowsons of Brampton Bryan and Wigmore, to the use of Robert Harley for life. This was the first in a series of carefully planned conveyances between Thomas and his elder son, which were designed to secure an income for Robert and simultaneously to enhance his social standing. This policy proved to be very successful and during the later marriage negotiations between the Harleys and the Coningsbys, Sir Thomas Coningsby referred to the 'great and goodly estate' that Sir Robert's father had 'laid together for him'. Sir Robert's improved financial status was also recognised by a series of royal grants and local appointments, including the knighthood and his appointment as a JP in 1604. In that year Sir Robert also received a grant from the crown of the keepership of the forests of Bringwood and Prestwood. Two years later he was appointed itinerant justiciar in the royal forests, chases, parks and warrens in Herefordshire, as the deputy of Charles, Earl of Nottingham, who may have been Sir Robert's patron in these early years. In 1606 Sir Robert was also chosen as sheriff of Radnorshire.[34]

Sir Robert's income was thus derived from a variety of sources. In 1623, before he married Brilliana Conway, he estimated that his annual income from Wigmore was £300; added to this was an income of £140 annually from the manor of Eyton, which the Harleys had purchased from the Coningsbys in 1611, and £100 annually from the rectory of Presteigne, which Sir Robert

[33] Indentures, 22 January 1602/3, Brampton Bryan, Harley Mss., Bundle 77; G. E. Mingay, *The Gentry: The Rise and Fall of a Ruling Class* (1976), 10, 44–5.
[34] Indentures, 22 January 1602/3, Brampton Bryan, Harley Mss., Bundle 77; marriage settlement, 12 February 1603, Brampton Bryan, Harley Mss., Bundle 30a; Thomas Coningsby to Thomas Harley, 28 December [1604], BL Loan 29/202 f.75r; *DNB*, VIII, 1282; PRO C66/1662; letters of appointment, 9 May 1606, Brampton Bryan, Harley Mss., Bundle 28; *List of Sheriffs for England and Wales*, IX (1898), 269.

had bought in 1619. The annual income paid out of chancery for the keepership of Bringwood and Prestwood was purely nominal, although Harley was probably able to make some money from fines and other perquisites attached to these offices.[35]

In 1623 Sir Robert's finances were greatly enhanced by his father's decision to lease him the estate of Brampton Bryan and the demesne lands of Buckton. Thomas Harley took this generous course in the hope of achieving two objectives: first to speed up the payment of Brilliana's dowry, and secondly to give his son sufficient financial status to make him an attractive husband for Brilliana, the daughter of a leading courtier. Sir Robert's acquisition of the main Harley estates and his marriage alliance with Conway also resulted in a distinct increase in his social status, which was reflected in his return to Parliament for the county in 1624. Conway was also responsible for Harley's appointment as Master of the Mint, undoubtedly using his influence at court to secure this post for his son-in-law.[36]

These were years in which Sir Robert seemed to be well off financially. The Mastership of the Mint brought him an annual income of just under £500, amounting to a total of £3,388 4s 3d between November 1626 and September 1633. In 1627 Harley was granted the monopoly for discovering abuses in the manufacture of gold and silver thread, which would have brought in some extra revenue from fines. In that year Sir Robert also sold the tithes and advowson of Presteigne for a profit and in the same year purchased a lease of crown land in Kingsland, the rents of which were used to provide Thomas Harley with an independent income until his death in 1631. Sir Robert was then able to enjoy the income from Kingsland, which by 1640 amounted to just over £460 per annum. In 1638 Harley leased the manor of Burrington from the Earl of Lindsay. This brought in a very small rent, only £18 8s 4d in 1640, but it was valuable because of its timber.[37]

Alongside the information about Sir Robert's land purchases there is parallel evidence which suggests that he also experienced periods of debt from as early as 1611 onwards. In 1615 Thomas Harley sold off his life interest in the rectory of Clun, which included the tithes and the advowson and was worth £300 per annum, in order to pay off his son's debts. Yet two years later Sir Robert was still in debt for the sum of £2,217 and again

---

[35] PRO SP14/146/82; Hereford and Worcester County RO, Miscellaneous Deeds, f.49/1; letters close, 16 July 1604, Brampton Bryan, Harley Mss., Bundle 88.

[36] Lease, 6 May 1623, Brampton Bryan, Harley Mss., Bundle 83; *Return of the Name of Every Member*, I, 458.

[37] PRO SP16/246/102; Birmingham Reference Library, Coventry Mss., Grants and Patents No. 23 (I am grateful to Professor Conrad Russell and Dr Richard Cust for help with this reference); W. H. Howse, 'Contest for a Radnorshire Rectory in the Seventeenth Century', *Journal of the Historical Society of the Church in Wales*, VII (1957), 70; Indentures, 19 June 1627, Brampton Bryan, Harley Mss., Bundle 73, list of rents 1640, Bundle 22, acquittance dated 13 June 1638, Bundle 26.

Thomas Harley undertook to pay off the debts. Just prior to the marriage with Brilliana it was disclosed that Sir Robert Harley's estates were encumbered for the sum of £1,000. Even the handover of Brampton did not totally remove the burden and in the mid-1620s and again in the mid-1630s Harley included the plea for 'delivery from debt' in his prayers.[38]

These stray details of indebtedness do not square easily with Sir Robert's ability to make substantial property purchases and his obvious accumulation of social prestige from 1603 onwards. The answer to this apparent conundrum lies in the simple fact that evidence of debt was not necessarily an indication of severe financial strain. In an age when there was no formal banking system it was quite common for friends, relatives, and associates to lend money on bond, and a certain amount of borrowing was a normal state of affairs for most gentlemen. Sir Robert certainly did not seem to have been unduly pressured by these debts, and the fact that he chose to pray for delivery from debt does not constitute proof that his debts were overly severe. There is a possible parallel in Harley's recourse to prayer in this matter and the practice of Robert Woodford, the puritan steward of Northampton, who listed his debts in his diary in order, as his biographer explains, to acknowledge God's providence in that area.[39]

By the late 1630s Harley had achieved an undoubted position as one of the wealthiest and most powerful gentlemen in Herefordshire. In 1640 his receipts from rent alone amounted to £1,500 and this figure probably represented just under a half of his total yearly income. This would certainly have placed him amongst the highest earning English gentry, since it has been estimated that average incomes for the greater gentry in 1640 were between £1,000 and £1,500. Sir Robert's rents would have been supplemented by a variety of other sources which were too irregular to be reconstructed accurately, but they would have included the sale of livestock, wool, timber and grain. Between 1623 and 1629, for example, Sir Robert made nearly £1,000 from the sale of wood. He also received an income from renting out tithes: in 1640 he was leasing out the tithes of no fewer than six different livings, which brought in £69 12s in that year. Incidental income also accrued from heriots payable on the death of a tenant and from entry fines which were levied when a new lease was granted. The heriot normally took the form of the tenant's best beast, but at some time was commuted to a money payment. After Ned Harley had inherited his father's estate in 1656 money payments of between 5s and 10s were acceptable in lieu of handing over livestock and this

---

[38] PRO LC4/197 f.220r; HMC, *10th Report, Appendix*, part IV (1885), 379; lease, 8 July 1615, lease, 1 March 1617, Brampton Bryan, Harley Mss., Bundle 83; PRO LC4/199, part II, f.449r; lists of prayers, 17 December 1624, 8 June 1625, BL Loan 29/52/93, and 22 February 1632/3, 12 April 1633, 24 January 1633/4, Loan 29/27 part 1.

[39] Stone, *Crisis of the Aristocracy*, 517–36; Fielding, 'Opposition to the Personal Rule of Charles I: The Diary of Robert Woodford, 1637–1641', 772.

change may well have been under way during Sir Robert's lifetime. Entry fines brought in much larger sums than did heriots, but they could vary enormously according to the size and value of the land leased. In 1629 Edward Pinner paid an entry fine of £90 to Sir Robert for a lease of land in Brampton, while in 1639 William Bagley paid an entry fine of £240 for a Brampton tenancy.[40] As other leases were renewed they would bring in similarly disparate amounts.

There is some evidence that the Harleys were introducing improvements in order to increase the income from their estates. By 1626 Sir Robert had started an irrigation scheme in one meadow on the Brampton estate, but we do not know if he extended this. Some historians have traced links between puritanism and 'progressive' estate management, but in the case of the Harleys there was no ruthless exploitation of their estates and tenants. The improvements they did introduce were on a fairly small scale and there is insufficient evidence to suggest that their puritanism was the ideological basis for any changes that were made. There had also been 'a marked revival of demesne farming' in the late sixteenth century, as rising agricultural prices and an increase in population had made it more profitable than renting out the demesne lands, but it appears that the Harleys were not extensively involved in farming by 1640. Some of the Brampton and Wigmore demesnes were probably rented out and those of Kingsland were certainly rented out. The Harleys kept a small stock of cattle and pigs, which were used primarily to feed the household at Brampton, and the only large-scale farming in which they were involved was the flock of 1,000 sheep kept at Clun, just over the border in Shropshire.[41]

Another profitable new practice was the granting of leases for specified terms of years, which was beginning to replace the traditional term of the lives of three named persons. Leases for lives had the disadvantage that landlords could never predict when they would expire and some tenants might live to extreme old age, thus robbing the landlord of income from new entry fines.[42] On the Harley estates, however, the new practice was not widely adopted and the bulk of Sir Robert's leases were made for the traditional terms of lives.

---

[40] List of rents, 1640, Brampton Bryan, Harley Mss., Bundle 22; Mingay, *The Gentry*, 11–13; assignment of lease, 10 October 1608, Brampton Bryan, Harley Mss., Bundle 101; will of Thomas Harley, Hereford and Worcester County RO, Wills, no. 115; Sir Edward Harley's valuation of his lands, Brampton Bryan, Harley Mss., Bundle 22, Leases, 20 August 1629 and 2 January 1638/9, Bundle 70. Details of rents and other income are scattered throughout the Harley papers and I have endeavoured to give the major references here in this chapter.

[41] Lady Brilliana to Harley, 3 March 1625/6, BL Loan 29/72; Lewis, *Letters of the Lady Brilliana Harley*, 62; Stone, *Crisis of the Aristocracy*, 330; Mingay, *The Gentry*, 43; list of rents 1640, Brampton Bryan, Harley Mss., Bundle 22, schedule of the goods and chattels of Thomas Harley, annexed to lease, 6 May 1623, Bundle 83.

[42] Stone, *Crisis of the Aristocracy*, 312–13.

Overall the evidence suggests that the Harleys were not systematically exploiting their estates, but they were able to accumulate and consolidate land in the early seventeenth century, which gave them both a comfortably high income and a secure stake in the social hierarchy of the county.

THE EXTENDED FAMILY

Through ties of blood and of marriage the Harleys were related to a bewildering network of families scattered throughout the Midlands and parts of southern England. Within Herefordshire it is possible to trace links between the Harleys and many of the other major gentry families, including the Crofts of Croft Castle, the Scudamores of Holme Lacy, the Pyes of Mynde Park, the Kyrles of Walford and the Rudhalls of Rudhall. The most notable exceptions in this extended family circle were the Coningsbys of Hampton Court. The importance of such ties in county affairs has been emphasised in numerous local studies; thus kinship has been described as 'the dominant principle of Sussex society' and in Kent family 'connexions spread far and wide and united the whole body of the gentry'.[43]

Family connections amongst the gentry were obviously not confined to one single county, and indeed the upper gentry were the social grouping most likely to contract marriages outside their home county. Between them Sir Robert and his father married five times, but none of their wives was from Herefordshire (fig. 2). Sir Robert's mother and his second wife were both from Shropshire and the Harleys thus had very strong links with families in that county, including the Corbets, the Newports, the Levesons, and the Cornwalls. Sir Robert also had contact with kin in more distant counties, such as Sir Henry Wallop in Hampshire, the Levesons in Kent and the Fane Earls of Westmorland in Nottinghamshire. Lady Brilliana had a similarly widespread network of kindred outside Herefordshire (fig. 3). After her marriage she remained on good terms with her brothers and sisters, particularly her sister Frances, who married Sir William Pelham of Brocklesby in Lincolnshire. Letters frequently passed between Brampton and Brocklesby, and the news which Lady Brilliana received ranged from the education of young Edward Pelham, who was a contemporary of Ned Harley at Magdalen, to the choice of a new minister for Brocklesby and Sir William's refusal to stand for election to the Short Parliament. Lady Brilliana was also in contact with her half-brother, Sir Giles Bray of Barrington, Oxfordshire, who acted as a trustee to the Harleys' marriage settlement in 1623. Ned visited Barrington on several occasions when he was at Oxford and Bray remained a friend of the Harleys until his death in 1641.[44]

[43] Fletcher, *A County Community in Peace and War*, 48; Everitt, *Community of Kent*, 35.
[44] Levy, 'Thesis', 46–61.

The Harleys were careful to cultivate their many relatives, because the extended family was regarded as an important source of mutual aid in Tudor and early Stuart times, an idea expressed by Secretary Conway in florid terms when he addressed Sir Robert Harley as 'my good son', adding, 'for so methinks it is your good pleasure that the style run and methinks it is as rich an embroidery to me as it can be silk lace to you'. The aid that kinsfolk could dispense was various; it might range from the simple gift of turkeys, capons and brawn that Lady Brilliana sent to her aunt Lady Vere in 1626, to more complex matters such as giving advice in the negotiation of a marriage or standing as a trustee to a settlement. Finally there were the more concrete uses of patronage such as Secretary Conway's help in getting Harley the position of Master of the Mint or the second Viscount Conway's efforts in 1639, when he used his personal influence with the Earl of Strafford to ensure that Harley was not chosen as sheriff of Herefordshire. This was an office which had become particularly unpleasant in the 1630s, when the collection of ship money was added to the numerous unpaid burdens that the sheriff had traditionally undertaken. Sir Simonds D'Ewes, who was picked as sheriff of Suffolk in 1639, lamented that 'it hath pleased God to send an unwelcome preferment upon me this year of the shrievalty of Suffolk'. Lady Brilliana revealed a similar attitude towards the post. In a letter to Ned Harley she explained that 'my brother got your father off from being sheriff, for which I thank God'.[45]

The exercise of this sort of influence was expected of one's relatives, because kinship carried with it a certain obligation to one's kin. Sir Herbert Croft alluded openly to this in a letter directed to Sir Robert, which ended, 'in the due of a kinsman, so by the tie of so frank a courtesy, I profess myself bound to remain ever your faithful friend and cousin'. Croft was related to Harley through a complicated series of marriages which had taken place in the first half of the sixteenth century. The subsequent contacts between the two families serve as a perfect illustration of the ways in which the extended family could be a practical support to its members. In 1520 John Harley the elder had married Ann Croft, an aunt of the Sir James Croft who would later become Comptroller of the Household and a Privy Councillor during the reign of Elizabeth. These family links were reinforced when John Harley the younger and Sir James Croft married two sisters, the heiresses Maud and Alice Warncombe of Hereford (fig. 2). In 1582 Thomas Harley was able to exploit his connections with the Crofts in unusual circumstances. In that year his father, John Harley, had died excommunicate and thus could not be buried in consecrated ground. Thomas enlisted the help of Sir James Croft,

---

[45] Sir Edward Conway to Harley, 25 July 1623, BL Loan 29/202 f.104r; Lady Brilliana Harley to Harley, 24 February 1625/6, BL Loan 29/72; Lewis, *Letters of the Lady Brilliana Harley*, 73; Cliffe, *Puritan Gentry*, 212.

who procured a letter from the privy council to the Bishop of Hereford directing that John Harley be given a christian burial.[46]

During the seventeenth century relations between the families were more routine. Sir Herbert Croft, grandson of Sir James, acted as a trustee in a number of Harley family estate settlements and in 1610 he sold land to the Harleys in order to raise cash to pay for his daughter's marriage portions. In 1616 when Sir Herbert was selling off more land he asked Sir Robert for details of an entail described in Maud Harley's will.[47] Amongst landed society there was an obvious need to be able to trace the descent of land, both to prove who had the right to inherit it and also by what tenure it was held. This made a knowledge of one's ancestry and an acquaintance with the extended family a matter of practical necessity for the gentry and other landed classes. In 1617 it became publicly known that Sir Herbert Croft had embraced catholicism, and he suddenly left England for the Continent. His son, Sir William Croft, maintained the friendship between the two families and in 1640 campaigned for Sir Robert Harley's election to the Short Parliament. Although Sir William supported the initial reforms made by the Long Parliament, by 1642 he had become a staunch royalist and he vainly tried to persuade the Harleys to abandon their parliamentarianism, using their friendship and their blood ties as reasons for avoiding enmity between the families.[48]

The relationship between the Harleys and the Crofts demonstrates that family links could be of practical benefit through the course of several generations, but not all family ties were so harmonious. In 1626 Sir Robert Harley was involved in an argument over precedence with 'his much respected cousin' Sir Walter Pye, which was resolved when Pye agreed to accept the junior county seat in the coming Parliament and to allow Harley the senior seat. At the same time that this dispute took place Sir Robert was also involved in a disagreement with another of his kinsmen, Sir John Scudamore. Evidence about this quarrel is to be found in two letters amongst the Scudamore papers, but the exact nature of the rift is not set out in any

---

[46] Sir Herbert Croft to Harley, 27 October 1616, BL Loan 29/202 between ff.151 and 155; C. J. Robinson, *A History of the Castles of Herefordshire and Their Lords* (1869), 82; settlement, 26 August 1545, Brampton Bryan, Harley Mss., Bundle 83; Grazebrooke and Rylands, *Visitation of Shropshire*, XVIII, 214; Sir James Croft to Thomas Harley, 9 April 1582, BL Loan 29/202 before f.38.

[47] Marriage settlement, 12 February 1602/3, settlement, 24 August 1613, Covenant, 10 November 1615, Brampton Bryan, Harley Mss., Bundle 83, Bargain and sale, 3 February 1610, Bundle 88; Sir Herbert Croft to Harley, 27 October 1616, BL Loan 29/202 between ff.151 and 155.

[48] PRO SP14/93/129; Hereford and Worcester County RO, Croft Mss., S33/8; Sir Walter Pye to Harley, 10 February 1639/40, BL Loan 29/172 f.254r, Sir William Croft to Harley, 1 January 1640/1, Loan 29/173 f.7r–v, Sir William Croft to Harley, 20 August 1642, Loan 29/174 ff.33r–34r.

detail. In a letter to Scudamore Harley referred to their quarrel and signed himself 'your kinsman that desires to rejoice in the assurance of your friendship'. In his reply Scudamore also drew on their kinship as a reason for trying to settle the problem amicably, declaring 'I know Sir Robert Harley is my kinsman. I believe he is my friend; between such and myself I shall be sorry if any misunderstanding happen, wheresoever the fault be'. Scudamore signed the letter with the words 'your kinsman that will ever hold himself happy in your love to the end'.[49]

In both this instance, and in the earlier episode concerning Sir Walter Pye, bonds of kinship were evoked as a means of ameliorating the tensions which had developed between Harley and his kin. Sir Walter Pye was apparently content to give in to Sir Robert, although it is possible that he privately felt aggrieved at what had happened. We do not know the outcome of the quarrel with Scudamore, but by 1627 he acted as a trustee in a land settlement on behalf of Sir Robert, so it seems likely that their difference had been ended or was not serious enough to cause a permanent rift. Four years earlier, in 1623, the Harleys had chosen Scudamore to act as a trustee to the marriage settlement between Sir Robert and Brilliana.[50] The choice of Scudamore as a trustee in these two instances is strong evidence that Sir Robert could co-operate with the other Herefordshire gentry who were not puritans in the years before the Civil War. These links between Harley and Scudamore are all the more important in this respect because the two men were of very different religious temperaments.

Scudamore was a life-long friend of William Laud, who visited Holme Lacy on at least two occasions, in 1621 and again in 1625. In the 1630s Scudamore enthusiastically supported the policy of introducing more ornamentation into churches, and he was responsible for the refurbishment of the church of Abbey Dore in Herefordshire, where he was the patron. The new embellish-ments included stained glass, a railed altar, and a screen described by Pevsner as 'the most ambitious piece of church furnishing of the Laudian years in Herefordshire'.[51] These were exactly the sort of church decorations that were denounced by the puritans in the 1630s and which were destroyed *en masse* by the parliamentarians in the 1640s. Harley himself was in the vanguard of this iconoclasm both privately and in his public role as chairman of the parliamentary committee for demolishing superstitious monuments in London churches, set up in 1643. In his *History of the Rebellion*, Clarendon later related how Scudamore, as English ambassador to France in the late

---

[49] Harley to Sir Walter Pye, 6 January 1625/6, Pye to Harley, 14 January 1625/6, BL Loan 29/ 123/39i; BL Add Mss., 11044 ff.5r, 7r.

[50] Assignment, 19 June 1627, Brampton Bryan, Harley Mss., Bundle 73, marriage settlement, 19 July 1623, Bundle 83.

[51] H. R. Trevor-Roper, *Archbishop Laud, 1573–1643* (1940), 62–3, 76, 437–56; N. Pevsner, *The Buildings of England: Herefordshire* (1963), 46, 57–62.

1630s, had 'furnished his own chapel in his house with such ornaments (as candles upon the communion table and the like) as gave great offence and umbrage to those of the Reformation'. The religious differences between Harley and Scudamore were quite sufficient to keep their friendship at a very formal and polite level and there is no surviving evidence amongst the Harley papers to show that the two families exchanged social visits, for example, which would almost certainly have been recorded by Lady Brilliana in her letters. The distance between Brampton and Holme Lacy may have precluded casual social visiting, for the two houses lay over thirty miles apart by road, but religious differences also clearly helped to restrict the meetings of Harley and the Viscount to occasions of personal or official business.[52]

Religious differences were quite definitely the root cause of an estrangement between Sir Robert and another relative, Sir Edward Herbert (later Lord Herbert of Cherbury), who was a first cousin of Harley's second wife, Mary Newport. At one time the two men had a very close friendship, which was reflected in Herbert's nomination of Harley in 1610 as guardian of his children in the event of his own death. Their amity was still strong in 1617, when Herbert challenged a man named Emerson to a duel for speaking 'very disgraceful words of Sir Robert Harley . . . my dear friend'.[53] From that year onwards, however, there was a decline in their relationship, which hinged on Harley's inability to accept Herbert's rationalist religious beliefs, which were well in advance of the age. Between 1617 and 1619 they conducted a lengthy correspondence in which each man tried to persuade the other he was wrong. Herbert was clearly in the midst of working out his ideas and much of what he wrote appears to be ambiguous or contradictory. Harley challenged Herbert to give a clear explanation of his views and he remained dissatisfied with Herbert's replies. Herbert had adopted an anti-Calvinist stance and argued that 'God's Church is all mankind, though some are his more beloved, neither doth he make any, whom he denies the means to come to him'. Such a notion of salvation available to all ran clean counter to the doctrine of predestination, which formed the core of the Harley's religious beliefs. Not only did Harley find this untenable, but he also believed that Herbert was suggesting that 'all religions are capable of salvation', which he sharply refuted by insisting that 'if other religions can save, the christian religion cannot, it teaching salvation only by faith in Christ Jesus according to the written word'. Herbert denied this construction of his words, but then went on to make another highly ambiguous statement by concluding 'I think there is in

---

[52] *CJ*, III, 57; Macray, *History of the Rebellion and Civil Wars in England*, II, 418; Ogilby, *Britannia, Volume the First*, plate 71.

[53] Grazebrook and Rylands, *Visitation of Shropshire*, XIX, 374; HMC, *Calendar of the Manuscripts of the most Honourable the Marquess of Salisbury, preserved at Hatfield House, Hertfordshire*, XXI (1970), 192; J. M. Shuttleworth, ed., *The Life of Edward, First Lord Herbert of Cherbury* (Oxford, 1976), 88.

every religion . . . enough taught to bring a man to happiness eternal, if he follow it.' Such ideas were well in advance of their age, for this was a time when most Europeans saw religion in terms of a massive international struggle between protestants and catholics to establish the one true religion. The notion that all religions were equally valid would have seemed totally preposterous to most people. Herbert knew that his thoughts were highly unorthodox and warned Harley to 'keep these things to yourself, until the world be better prepared to hear them'.[54]

Harley was a man of such fixed religious principles that he was hardly the right choice for Herbert's confidence. In 1619 Harley felt that they were moving towards 'the ruin of our friendship'. At this point the letters between the two men stop, but they did meet at Whitehall in 1624, when Harley confessed that his love for Herbert had nearly been swallowed in grief, 'for you, that did then magnify the goodness of God the creator, denied his wisdom and love in the redemption of mankind only by Christ Jesus'. This is the last surviving evidence of contact between the two amongst Sir Robert's papers until 1631, when Harley recommended a puritan cleric to Herbert for the living of Montgomery. Herbert ignored this advice and chose a Dr Coote, who later displayed possible Arminian leanings, when he turned the communion table at Montgomery 'altar-wise' and introduced rails in opposition to the wishes of the local godly elite.[55]

Religious factors were undoubtedly the underlying principle governing the Harleys' relationships with most of the members of their extended family circle. It is quite noticeable, for example, that the Harleys completely ignored the catholic branches of their family in Herefordshire. Surviving Harley correspondence from the early seventeenth century makes no reference to Sir Robert's uncle and aunt, William Harley and Jane Mynors, who were both catholic recusants.[56] If there was any contact between the Harleys and these relatives there would almost certainly be some recorded evidence in their personal letters. In particular we might expect Lady Brilliana to have mentioned something in her many letters, for she wrote frequent accounts of the visits and messages which the Harleys received at Brampton from other kinsfolk.

Her letters abound with details concerning Sir Robert's mother's family, the Corbets, which show that well over fifty years after the death of his mother the connections between the families were still very strong. In 1626

---

[54] Sir Edward Herbert to Harley, 17 July 1617, BL Loan 29/202 f.162r, Harley to Herbert, 6 April 1618, Loan 29/119, Herbert to Harley, 8 June 1618, Loan 29/202 between ff.164 and 165.

[55] Harley to Herbert, 26 March 1619, BL Loan 29/119, *idem* to Herbert, 27 December 1624, Loan 29/27 part I, Harley to John Brinsley, 8 December 1631, Loan 29/172 f.42r–v; PRO 30/53/7; statement by Nathaniel Harrison, 9 April 1637, BL Loan 29/172 f.138r.

[56] For the catholicism of William Harley and Jane Mynors see above, n.6.

Sir Andrew Corbet and his mother stood as godparents to the Harleys' second son, Robert. Later letters record the death of Harley's 'aunt Corbet' and the news that Sir Andrew was standing for election to the Short Parliament in Shropshire.[57] Similarly Lady Brilliana recorded the comings and goings of the Hackluit family of Eyton in Herefordshire, who were connected to the Harleys by a marriage which had been contracted in the late fifteenth century. In the late 1630s one of the Hackluits lived at Brampton and served as a companion or maid for the Harley children. The Harleys were also on very friendly terms with the descendants of Edward Harley, Sir Robert's great uncle. Edward had died in 1586, but his relatives, the Davies families of Coxhall and Wigmore, were welcome visitors to Brampton in the 1630s.[58]

In a society in which family relationships were remembered through four or more generations the lack of reference to the catholic lines of the Harley family is a notable and pointed exclusion. Further evidence that the Harleys were not friendly with their catholic kin is provided by the land settlements made by Sir Robert and his father between 1603 and 1623. The catholic members of the family were not called upon to act as trustees to these transactions, whereas the names Corbet, Newport, Cornwall, Croft and Herbert appear repeatedly. In choosing men to act as trustees the Harleys would have selected their most trusted friends and relatives, and once again the absence of the families of William Harley and Jane Mynors strongly suggests that they were estranged from the Harleys.

Although religious differences did cause rifts within the Harley family, religious sympathy could also serve to cement familial relationships. The Harleys were particularly close to Lady Brilliana's uncle and aunt, Lord and Lady Vere, who were both puritans. Sir Horace Vere was a professional soldier and had employed a number of puritan ministers as army chaplains. In 1620 he commanded the English volunteer force which fought for the return of the Palatinate. There was a clear religious affinity between Vere and Sir Robert and in a letter written to Vere in 1621 Harley emphasised the religious nature of the battle for the Palatinate: 'your enemy is God's also and so you may with more assurance wait in faithful prayer for the victory'. Enclosed with this letter Harley sent a detailed definition of a puritan. It was the sort of document that Harley could only send to a confidant and which only someone of a similar religious outlook to his own would truly appreciate.[59]

---

[57] Lady Brilliana to Harley, 21 April 1626, BL Loan 29/72. Lewis, *Letters of the Lady Brilliana Harley*, 34, 35, 55, 86.

[58] Levy, 'Thesis', 109–10.

[59] A representative sample of Harley family deeds can be found in Bundle 83 of the Harley Mss. at Brampton Bryan; *DNB*, XX, 235–9; Harley to Sir Horace Vere, 14 February 1620/ 1, BL Loan 29/202 ff.47r–48v, Sir Robert Harley's holograph notes, endorsed 'P', Loan 29/ 27, part I.

The sympathy between Vere and Harley was reinforced by the marriage to Brilliana in 1623, for it was Lady Vere who acted as the matchmaker, giving a most favourable account of Harley to her brother-in-law, Conway. In a subsequent letter to Thomas Harley, Sir Edward Conway recorded that it was Lady Vere who 'acquainted me with the affection of your son to my daughter Brilliana; laid before me his parentage; the abilities of his mind, his ripe discretion; his well-grounded religion; the value of your estate; all of which, part by knowledge, part by report, I had like opinion'. Many years later, when the Harleys decided to send their eldest daughter to London, she was sent to stay with Lady Vere, who was a woman of strongly puritan views. She corresponded with a wide circle of puritan ministers, including William Ames, who was in self-imposed exile in the Netherlands, and John Dod the vicar of Fawsley. Shortly after her daughter had arrived in London Lady Brilliana wrote to her and reminded her of the respect that the Harleys had for Lady Vere: 'believe it there is not a wiser and better woman'.[60]

Their religious sympathies clearly helped to define the intensity of the Harleys' relationships with other members of their extended family. Their religious affinities also drew the Harleys into contact with a wide circle of puritan clergy and laity in Herefordshire and elsewhere. These puritan contacts provided yet another social network which transcended the geographical boundaries of the county and which gave the Harleys a system of loyalties which, as with the family, were not founded on the restricted principles of localism.

[60] BL Add. Mss., 61989, f.81r; Lady Brilliana to Brilliana Harley, 25 June 1642, BL Loan 29/ 173 f.260r. Lady Vere's correspondence is preserved in the British Library, see BL Add. Mss., 4275; I am once again indebted to Robyn Priestley for allowing me to use her transcripts of these letters.

The Harleys and the godly community

The religious preferences displayed by the Harleys in relation to their kin also governed their dealings with people outside the family, and in her commonplace book Lady Brilliana noted: 'we must be careful of our families, of our parents, of our kindred, if they be of the household of faith; strangers is they righteous [sic]; but our delightest love must only be to the saints on the Earth'. The Harleys were therefore drawn to those who shared their religious assumptions and they believed themselves to be part of a godly community that was not grounded in a particular time or place. Other religious groups, such as catholics, obviously felt similar strong sympathies for their co-religionists, but for Calvinists, such as the Harleys, their belief in the godly community was constantly validated and reinforced by their belief in predestination. This doctrine held, in Lady Brilliana's own paraphrase of Calvin's *Institutes*, that 'God, by his eternal and unchangeable counsel has once appointed whom in time to come he will take to salvation, and on the other side whom he would condemn to destruction. This cause touching the elect was grounded upon his free mercy, without respect of the worthiness of Man.' It was axiomatic that the godly should avoid the company of the reprobate who would try to tempt them to transgress, since, as Lady Brilliana recorded in her commonplace book, 'we must abstain from such company as will drive us to sin and from such sports as make us sin'.[1]

The great value which the Harleys placed on keeping company with the godly was reflected in their wide circle of puritan relatives and friends. These were people whose desire for further Church reforms linked them with like-minded people in London and the localities and they believed they had more in common with the protestant Scots, the French Huguenots and the members of the Dutch reformed Church than they did with many of their fellow countrymen.[2] This group felt increasingly isolated and threatened in

---

[1] Commonplace Book ff.62r, 65r, 203r.
[2] For a thorough discussion of the cause of international protestantism in England see S. L. Adams, 'The Protestant Cause: Religious Alliance with the Western European Calvinist Communities as a Political Issue in England, 1585–1630' (D. Phil. Thesis, Oxford University, 1973).

the 1620s as Arminian theologians began to challenge the doctrine of predestination. Arminians argued that salvation depended on the behaviour of the individual during his or her lifetime on earth, a contention that struck at the very basis of Calvinist predestinarian teaching. Many puritans were further alarmed by the introduction under Laud of church ceremonies such as bowing to the altar, and ornamentation such as the railed altar, which they saw as redolent of catholic practices. They thus regarded the Arminians as dangerous innovators who wished to re-establish links with Rome.[3]

The 1620s and 1630s were decades in which a close-knit group of Arminians were gaining the highest preferment within the English Church. The Remonstrance drawn up by the House of Commons in 1628 advised the King that the Arminians

are much favoured and advanced, not wanting friends even of the clergy near to your Majesty, namely Dr Neile, Bishop of Winchester, and Dr Laud, Bishop of Bath and Wells, who are justly suspected to be unsound in their opinions that way. And it being now generally held to be the way to preferment and promotion in the Church, many scholars do bend the course of their studies to maintain those errors.[4]

In response to these complaints Charles I openly employed Arminians as royal chaplains and sanctioned their promotion in the Church. Richard Montagu had been made a royal chaplain in 1626 and in 1628 was elevated to the see of Chichester. Richard Neile was elected to the archbishopric of York in 1631 and was himself the patron of William Laud, who had become his chaplain in 1608. Laud was installed as Bishop of St David's in 1621 and translated first to the see of Bath and Wells in 1626 and then to the see of London in 1628. In 1633 he was appointed Archbishop of Canterbury. By the mid-1630s the Arminians had captured the major seats of power within the English Church and both Neile and Laud were able to promote the careers of Arminian clerics such as Matthew Wren, who was elected Bishop of Hereford in 1634 and translated to Norwich the next year.[5]

One of the earliest Arminian authors to draw the wrath of the godly was Richard Montagu, whose book *A Gag For The New Gospel?* was published in 1624. Montagu set out the Calvinist doctrine of predestination in the following terms:

that God, by his sole will and absolute decree, hath irrespectively resolved, and inevitably decreed, some to be saved, some to be damned, from all eternity.

He denied that this was part of the teaching of the English Church:

the Church of England hath not taught it, doth not believe it, hath opposed it, wisely contenting herself with this *Quosq*; and limitation, Ar[ticle] 17. We must receive

[3] Tyacke, *Anti-Calvinists, passim.*
[4] *1628 Debates,* IV, 313.
[5] *DNB*, XIII, 714, 715; XIV, 172; XI, 626–30; XXI, 1010.

God's promises in such wise as they be generally set forth to us in holy scripture; and not presuming to determine of when, how, wherefore, or whom; secrets reserved to God alone.[6]

On the complaint of two Ipswich ministers, John Yates and Samuel Ward, the House of Commons investigated Montagu's writings in 1624. The attack in Parliament was led by John Pym, who was one of the first members of the Commons to argue the danger of Arminianism. Members were to become increasingly outspoken in subsequent Parliaments about what they perceived as the attempt to reintroduce catholic doctrines and practices into England. By 1628 some of the most heated debates in the Commons chamber concerned religion and Sir Robert was amongst those MPs who linked Arminianism with Rome.[7] Ardent predestinarians, such as Harley, saw no distinction between the Arminian theory of salvation as set out by Montagu and other writers, and the teaching of the catholic Church on the subject. Thomas Pierson, the rector of Brampton Bryan from 1612 until his death in 1633, wrote of the 'uncomfortable doctrine of the papists and Arminians, that teach the true saints of God may fall from grace'. In the 1620s and 1630s the Arminians gradually gained control of the censorship of the presses in London, Oxford and Cambridge, and during the 1630s the vast majority of books licensed for publication were Arminian in tone. In 1641 Stanley Gower, Pierson's successor at Brampton, thus railed against the bishops' 'impositions upon lectures and lecturers, restraining them from preaching many edifying points, or against Arminianism, of predestination, faith, effectual vocation, regeneration etc., whilst they license sermons and treatises to be preached and printed, and otherwise vented and countenanced, which tend to gross popery'.[8]

It was not solely the identification of Arminianism with popery which caused such alarm to Calvinists. As Dr Tyacke has pointed out, 'the English Arminians redefined puritanism so as to include doctrinal Calvinism'. In establishing the orthodoxy of their own beliefs Arminian apologists developed a new rhetoric, which linked predestinarian beliefs not only with religious dissent, but also with political subversion. This polemic is exemplified in a letter written in 1630 to Laud by Samuel Brooke, the master of Trinity College, Cambridge, who asserted that 'predestination is the root of puritanism, and puritanism is the root of all rebellious and disobedient intractableness in Parliaments etc. and all schism and sauciness in the

---

[6] R. Montagu, *A Gag for the New Gospel? No: A New Gag for an Old Goose* (1624), 178, 179.

[7] K. W. Shipps, 'Lay Patronage of East Anglian Clerics in Pre-Revolutionary England' (Ph. D. Thesis, University of Yale, 1971), 246, 277; Russell, *Parliaments and English Politics*, 29–32; *1628 Debates*, II, 86.

[8] T. Pierson, *Excellent Encouragements Against Afflictions*, part IV (1647), 125; Cliffe, *Puritan Gentry*, 156–8; Corpus Christi Mss., 206 f.10v.

country, nay in the Church itself'.[9] The relationship between belief in predestination and puritanism has been disputed by modern historians. William Haller described predestination as 'the central dogma of puritanism', but this has been challenged by Dr Tyacke, who argues that 'Calvinist predestinarian teaching was . . . a crucial common assumption, shared by a majority of the hierarchy and virtually all of its non-conformist opponents, during the Elizabethan and Jacobean periods'.[10] At first sight these two schools of thought appear to be irreconcilable. Yet in accepting that there was some shared ground before the mid-1620s, it is necessary to understand that there were also differing shades of opinion and resulting differences in practical piety.

These variations have been explored in the research of Dr Kendall, who rejects the use of the word 'puritan' altogether, replacing it with the highly descriptive 'experimental predestinarians', who 'not only believed but vigorously stressed that one's election may be known by experimental knowledge; indeed it must be known lest one deceive himself and in the end, be damned'. Dr Kendall uses 'experimental' in the way in which seventeenth-century contemporaries used the word, denoting experience of, our modern equivalent being the word 'experiential', and his work illustrates the need to recognise a specifically puritan assimilation of the doctrine of predestination, despite his own rejection of the term 'puritan'. This is not to suggest that puritanism and belief in predestination were simply one and the same thing. As Dr Lake has argued, 'puritanism is not best regarded as a distinctive or novel body of ideas or doctrines, held only by puritans, but as a style of piety, a mode of behaviour, a set of priorities, which contemporaries . . . were quite capable of recognising when they saw them'.[11]

The survival of an exceptional manuscript amongst Sir Robert Harley's papers allows us to discover exactly which religious issues he saw as priorities. In 1621 Harley drew up his own definition of a puritan, which he intended to send to Sir Horace Vere. This document is not only a sympathetic account, written at a time when most examples of the word puritan are to be found in a hostile context, but it is also an accurate synopsis of Harley's own religious attitudes. Perhaps rather obviously he emphasised the characteristic stress by puritans on a scrupulous conscience. Using the abbreviation 'p' for puritan, Sir Robert noted that 'a p. is he that desires to practice what others profess, is one that dares do nothing in the worship of God or course of his

---

[9] Tyacke, 'Puritanism, Arminianism and Counter-Revolution', in Russell, *Origins of the English Civil War*, 139; PRO SP16/177/8.

[10] W. Haller, *The Rise of Puritanism* (Philadelphia, 1972), 83; Tyacke, 'Puritanism, Arminianism and Counter-Revolution', in Russell, *Origins of the English Civil War*, 128.

[11] R. T. Kendall, *Calvin and English Calvinism to 1649* (Oxford, 1979), 5–9, 80; P. G. Lake, 'Serving God and the Times: The Calvinist Conformity of Robert Sanderson', *JBS*, XXVII (1988), 115.

life, but what God's word warrants him . . . his sins are more than other men's, because he sees them, and greater because he feels them'. Sir Robert also touched on the subject of symbolism in church worship, which puritans regarded as superstitious: 'to things indifferent he thinks himself not born a bond man and wonders why he is styled a man of disorder when he is so willing to obey all law commands . . . He thinks the making of the cross between the holy sacrament of baptism and the humble thanksgiving of the congregation is like the placing of the Apocrypha between the Old and the New Testaments, which being a stream without a fountain is unworthy to be joined with the living water of life.'

Much of the non-conformity in the English Church between 1559 and 1640 hinged on the argument that the surplice, the sign of the cross, kneeling during divine service, and other symbolic practices or images, had no warrant in scripture and were inherently superstitious. Harley was keen to remove what he and other puritans regarded as remnants of catholic symbolism from the English Church. In the Parliaments of 1626 and 1628 he spoke out against idolatry in England and he was prepared to destroy offending images with his own hands. In 1639 young Brilliana Harley wrote to her brother Edward at Oxford and told him that their father had broken up a painting of 'the great God of Heaven and Earth' found in a stable on his estate of Buckton. Brilliana herself had then thrown 'the dust of it upon the water'.[12]

Sir Robert's definition of a puritan also dwells on the role of the ministry: 'he says a dumb minister is a man not sent by God, for He gives his messenger the tongue of the learned, neither can he be that witness of His truth when he cannot speak it . . . a non-resident is a profane wretch'. This passage reveals the importance which puritans placed on the preaching function of the ministry, in sharp contrast to the priestly function of ministers stressed by both catholics and Arminians. Sir Robert's notes also dwelt briefly on the role of the bishops: 'a L[ord] B[ishop] is a fallacy, a *bene divisis ad male coniuncta* B.'. This is a powerful indication that Harley was already dissatisfied with the powers of the English bishops. His disapproval of the bishops is also evident in his suggestion that a puritan was someone who desired 'discipline in the Church according to God's word'. Discipline could mean the correction of faults, but for puritans it also had a wider meaning signifying the active regulation, in every congregation, of the behaviour of the individual, using

---

[12] Sir Robert Harley's holograph notes, endorsed 'P', BL Loan 29/27 part 1, Harley to Sir Horace Vere, 14 February 1620/1, Loan 29/202 ff.47r–48r; Collinson, *Puritan Movement*, 66–79; R. C. Richardson, *Puritanism in North-West England: A Regional Study of the Diocese of Chester to 1642* (Manchester, 1972), 23–40; Grosvenor Diary, 9 May 1626; *1628 Debates*, IV, 338, 342; for Harley's iconoclasm see Brilliana Harley to Edward Harley, 14 January, and 8 February 1638/9, BL Loan 29/172 ff.207r, 213r. For a fuller discussion of Sir Robert Harley's notes on a puritan, see J. S. Eales, 'Sir Robert Harley KB (1579–1656) and the "Character" of a Puritan', *British Library Journal*, XV (1989).

both spiritual and moral sanctions ranging from private admonition to excommunication, in order to enforce godly standards of behaviour on all church members. There was also the implication that in the apostolic Church discipline had been rooted in the congregations, only to be usurped later by the bishops and other church officials. The idea that the congregations had lost a great deal of power is also implicit in a list of prayers drawn up by Harley in 1627 and 1628, which include the plea 'that God would in great mercy establish his gospel and restore our liberty unto us'.[13]

Although Sir Robert made no mention of the doctrine of predestination in these notes, the Harleys certainly regarded themselves as part of a group distinguished from the rest of society primarily by the dynamics of predestination and it was this doctrine which underpinned their religious beliefs. In her commonplace book Lady Brilliana wrote: 'God has his privy seal to distinguish us from the world and that is his secret knowledge, by which he knows whom are his'. The Harleys believed that those whom God had chosen for salvation were part of a definable and recognisable community on earth. They did not use the term 'puritan' to refer to the members of this group, instead they used 'the elect', 'God's saints', 'the godly' or 'God's children', all of which stemmed from their steadfast belief in the doctrine of predestination. The existence of what might be termed a 'godly community' was thus tangible reality to the Harleys, and the correct religious behaviour displayed by the elect was a constant guiding principle in their lives. The chief sign of election was complete faith in God, which was revealed by a religious and sober life. In her commonplace book Lady Brilliana recorded: 'he that is the adopted son of God shall be saved and we are known to be his sons if we believe in Christ and this faith shows itself by obedience'.[14]

According to these precepts it was possible for the godly to recognise the signs of salvation both in themselves and in others. When Sir Robert drafted a letter to Lady Vere after an outbreak of smallpox among her children, he comforted her with the assurance that she numbered amongst the elect: 'nothing befalls God's children without his special providence, of which number you likewise know yourself one . . . because you love him, which is the reflection of his love first upon you; and all things shall work together for good to those that love him, for they are his chosen'. Similarly, the cleric Robert Horn, when writing to Sir Robert in 1626 and 1627, referred to Lady Brilliana as 'that elect lady', a compliment which was repeated by John Ley, the puritan vicar of Great Budworth, Cheshire, in 1640 in the dedication of

---

[13] Collinson, *Puritan Movement*, 39–40, 346; lists of prayers, 30 March 1627, 29 February 1627/8, BL Loan 29/202 f.238r–v; for the importance attached to preaching see Hill, *Society and Puritanism*, 30–78.

[14] Commonplace Book f.42r, 116v.

his book *A Pattern of Piety* to the 'elect ladies' Lady Brilliana Harley and Lady Alice Lucy of Warwickshire.[15]

The importance which the Harleys placed on recognising the signs of election is well illustrated by the contents of Lady Brilliana's commonplace book, which bears the date 1622 – the year before her marriage. The book contains transcripts from her reading and is primarily based on the bible, Calvin's *Institutes*, William Perkin's *Cases of Conscience*, and his *Exposition of the Lord's Prayer*. There are also notes from the sermons of Thomas Case, vicar of Arrow in Warwickshire, the Conways' home parish where Brilliana's father was patron. Lady Brilliana probably took the book with her to Brampton, but she may not have added to its contents after her marriage, since it contains no sermon notes from Brampton.[16] In all, the commonplace book runs to over two hundred folios, but it contains no reference to any Church reforms and gives no evidence of the later anti-episcopal stance which can be discerned in Lady Brilliana's letters from January 1641 onwards. The central theme of the commonplace book was the religion of the individual, which was also a dominant concern of Lady Brilliana's letters. The book is almost entirely devoted to the religious behaviour discernible in the elect, and Lady Brilliana meticulously recorded passages which would help the individual to know whether he was a member of this group. Her letters to Ned Harley reflect the same concern to maintain the correct religious behaviour, which was the hallmark of election. In the letters, however, these attitudes are revealed as part of a practical religious piety which was applied constantly to the real problems encountered in everyday life.

The pivot of Lady Brilliana's religious beliefs was quite clearly her belief in predestination, and her certainty that faith, good works, and obedience to God's laws were not, as the catholics believed, the means of salvation, but were instead the external signs of election. Believing and obedience were not the free actions of Man, who could only believe if God had chosen him for salvation. Lady Brilliana firmly believed that there was no free will in the process of acquiring faith and obeying God's laws. She wrote in her commonplace book:

Man since his fall has his will so detained with such bondage to sin that he can not once move it to goodness, for moving is the beginning of turning to God, which the scripture does wholly give to God. Man since his fall sins willingly by his own lusts and by foreign constraint. It is God that first turns our will to that which is good and we are converted by the power of God only, it is God that works all in us.

[15] Harley to Lady Vere, 14 May 1621(?), BL Loan 29/123/39L; Robert Horn to Harley, 7 November 1626, 31 March 1627, BL Loan 29/119; John Ley, *A Pattern of Piety* (1640), Epistle Dedicatory.
[16] For notes of Case's sermons see Commonplace Book ff.112r–v, 113r, 124v, 132r, 138r, 140r, 144r, 146r. For Case's institution at Arrow see PRO, Bishops' Institution Books, Ser. A, 1556–1660, IV, 150 (Round Room Press Mark 19/62).

Sir Robert Harley openly ridiculed the catholic belief in free will in one of his letters to Sir Edward Herbert, in which he observed that 'the position of the papists, that everyone has free will to good is insipid, for with what face can they beg mercy for that, which was in their power not to have committed?'[17]

Their belief in predestination led many puritans to an intense religious introspection on the subject of whether they themselves were destined for salvation. In turn this led to a characteristic view of Man, his relationship with God, and his life on earth, which the Harleys shared with other puritans.[18] The belief of the individual that he was a member of the elect was not, however, lightly achieved. Many puritans were intensely concerned with searching for assurance, or signs that they were bound to be saved. Looking for evidence of election could bring peace of mind, but it could also have the converse effect. It was an exercise which was made all the more difficult because the ungodly, those who were not elect, could show the signs of faith without having a sincere belief in God. Quoting from Calvin, Lady Brilliana wrote in her commonplace book: 'those that make a profession of religion and having of faith and fall away, they have some signs of calling, as the elect have, but they did never cleave to Christ with that assuredness of heart with which the assurance of our election is established, they depart from the Church because they are not of the Church'. Whereas 'the elect and chosen of God can never finally fall away from God'. Doubts about the sincerity of one's own faith were thus by no means uncommon amongst puritans. In 1640 one of Lady Brilliana's own maids at Brampton was plunged into 'grievous agony of conscience and despair' when she became convinced that 'she shall be damned'. Even ministers could suffer, and in 1611 the Harleys' new rector, Thomas Peacock, became mortally ill at Oxford before he could set out for Brampton. As he lay dying he fell prey to similar fears, maintaining that there was 'no stamp of grace in me'. The renowned puritan preacher John Dod was summoned to provide spiritual solace, and Sir Robert despatched a servant to Oxford bearing *aurum potabile* 'together with a book, which a doctor had made in praise thereof'.[19]

Such religious doubts could be interpreted as the signs of an imperfect faith, which made them all the more frightening to the afflicted, but they could also

---

[17] Commonplace Book f.207r; Harley to Sir Edward Herbert, 26 March 1619, BL Loan 29/119.

[18] See, for example, P. G. Lake, *Moderate Puritans in the Elizabethan Church* (Cambridge, 1982).

[19] Commonplace Book, unfoliated section and f.6r; Keith Thomas, *Religion and the Decline of Magic: Studies in Popular Beliefs in Sixteenth and Seventeenth Century England* (1971), 481–2; Lewis, *Letters of the Lady Brilliana Harley*, 94; Robert Bolton, *A Narration of the Grievous Visitation and Dreadful Desertion of Mr Peacock in his Last Sickness* (1641), 9, 47–8, 57, 84–5.

be the prelude to a reconfirmation of faith akin to a conversion experience. The test of true belief lay in an almost continuous process of self-examination in order to ensure that the individual was assured of salvation. Citing Nathanial Cole's *The Godly Man's Assurance, or a Christian's Certain Resolution of his Own Salvation*, Lady Brilliana noted in her book: 'we must examine ourselves whether we have only a general faith or the special faith, which is called a saving faith'. The times of examination set out by Cole were recorded by Lady Brilliana: '1. every night and morning. 2. in the time of judgement. 3. upon our death bed. 4. before the sacrament.' In practice this led Lady Brilliana to a constant self-examination, which she also recommended to Ned when he went to Oxford.

Her letters repeatedly advised Ned not to 'neglect that constant service you owe to your God'. One letter in particular, dated 1 November 1639, gave the most detailed instructions on the method of examination which Ned was to use:

My dear Ned, keep always a watch over your precious soul; tie yourself to a daily self-examination. Think over the company you have been in, and what your discourse was, and how you found yourself affected. How in the discourses of religion, observe what knowledge you were able to express, and with what affection to it, and where you find yourself to come short, labour to repair that want. If it be in knowledge of any point, read something that may inform you in what you find you know not. If the fault be in affections, that you find a weariness in that discourse of religion, go to God, beg of Him new affections to love those things, which by nature we cannot love. After discourse call to mind whether you have been apt to take exceptions, or whether any have provoked you, and examine yourself how you took it . . . this is the rule I take with myself and I think it is the best way to be acquainted with our own hearts.[20]

The need to examine one's faith so minutely led puritans to emphasise their own experience of discovering the signs of a 'saving faith'. Citing Calvin once again, Lady Brilliana noted that 'inward calling is a pledge of election that cannot deceive us, for we know that we are the children of God by his spirit, which he has given us'. Lady Brilliana thus valued the practical effects of faith above a mere intellectual appreciation of faith. Again in her commonplace book she noted: 'the difference between speculative knowledge and saving knowledge is that by speculative knowledge we know God, what he is in himself, but by saving knowledge we know what God is to us and to know Christ in himself the Devil did so much, but to know Christ is saviour, never any Devil did'.[21]

The desire to discover the signs of salvation in oneself thus led puritans to a highly experiential view of religion. Lady Brilliana's letters to Ned repeatedly

---

[20] Commonplace Book f.80r; N. Cole, *The Godly Man's Assurance, or a Christian's Certain Resolution of his Own Salvation* (1615), 392–3, 403; Lewis, *Letters of the Lady Brilliana Harley*, 7, 15, 28, 65, 69–70.
[21] Commonplace Book f.132v and unfoliated section.

stress the value which she placed upon her own experience: 'there is no sweetness in anything in this life to be compared to the sweetness in the service of our God, and this I thank God I can say, not only to agree with those that say so, but experimentally'. This did not lead either Lady Brilliana or Sir Robert to denigrate the value of knowledge or education, and they both firmly believed that education had primarily religious ends. When Ned first went to Oxford, Sir Robert advised him that his academic training would be the means 'to get enlargement of knowledge in the understanding chiefly of God in Christ, which is life eternal . . . which will not only enrich the mind, but set off your conversation amongst men'.[22]

Lady Brilliana also put her own education to religious use, not only in her reading, but also spending time during one of her illnesses in translating part of Calvin's *Life of Luther*, in order to assess for herself Luther's character:

he is generally branded with ambition, which caused him to do what he did, and that the papists do so generally upbraid us that we cannot tell where our religion was before Luther; and some have taxed him of an intemperate life. These reasons made me desire to read his life, to see upon what ground these opinions were built; and finding such satisfaction to myself, how falsely these were raised, I put it into English.

She translated only that part of the work which was not in Foxe's *Book of Martyrs* and sent it to Ned.

For Lady Brilliana the final result of her religious introspection, her emphasis on self-examination, prayer, reading and meditation, was the certain knowledge of her own salvation. Despite the difficulties encountered in attaining that knowledge Lady Brilliana believed that 'the children of God may know that they have true faith, notwithstanding that there are many that think they have faith when they have none'. Her own confidence is reflected in her commonplace book, where she wrote as if she was undoubtedly a member of the elect. Phrases such as 'He elected us' and 'by grace we were elected' are typical of the quotations she recorded.[23]

Although the puritanism of the Harleys revolved around their stress on the conscience of the individual and his godly behaviour, both Sir Robert and Lady Brilliana were also interested in seeing further reforms within the Church and the religious life of the nation. In Parliament Sir Robert lent energetic support to bills which would have effected reforms both of public morals and of the Church itself. In 1610 he helped prepare a bill for restraint of swearing. In 1626 he sat on a committee which considered harsher penalties for adulterers and 'fornicators'. He also supported a bill to punish 'scandalous and unworthy ministers'. Two years later he supported a bill to reform abuses of the sabbath; another bill to prevent drunkenness and

[22] Lewis, *Letters of the Lady Brilliana Harley*, 34, xlix–l.
[23] *Ibid.*, 52; Commonplace Book ff.191v, 13r, 2r.

adultery amongst the clergy similar to that of 1626; and a bill which would have increased the stipends of the parish clergy. Support for these bills was not, of course, limited to puritans, but Sir Robert's involvement in the debates and committees stemmed from his personal desire to see further reformation. In a Commons debate concerning the 1628 bill against scandalous ministers, Harley declared: 'if we go about to reform the Church it is the honour of our Church. All the scandal is that now we have drunken ministers.'[24]

In 1628 Sir Robert also worked actively on a bill designed to release the clergy from subscription to those of the 39 articles concerning Church polity, thus finally securing the application of the Act of Subscription passed in 1571. Amongst the clergy, presbyterian beliefs had clearly survived into Charles's reign, despite the drive against the opponents of episcopacy in the later Elizabethan period. Sir Robert's support for the subscription bill and his clear disapproval of the powers exercised by the bishops, which was revealed in his notes of 1621 defining a puritan, are strong indicators of his sympathy for presbyterianism, but it was only after the calling of the Long Parliament that Sir Robert and other puritans in his circle could make concrete proposals for an alternative Church government. Then a presbyterian settlement was seen as a distinct possibility for the first time in England, but there was great uncertainty in 1640 about how far reforms could be taken. At the start of 1641 Sir Robert was probably flexible enough to accept a Church settlement which included bishops with greatly reduced powers. During the course of 1641 his confidence developed to the point where he advocated the abolition of episcopacy by supporting the 'root and branch' bill, which in itself was also a tactical device aimed at retaining Scottish military support for the English Parliament.[25]

The Church reforms which the Harleys supported before the Long Parliament are best illustrated by an examination of the ways in which religious observance was organised at the Harleys' home parish at Brampton Bryan and by the contacts which they cultivated with other puritans. Sir Robert became patron at Brampton in 1603, when he received the lease of the Wigmore estate from his father on the occasion of his marriage to Ann Barrett. Following the death of Thomas Peacock in 1611, Sir Robert chose Thomas Pierson, a fellow of Emmanuel College, Cambridge, as his replacement. Pierson was born in Weaverham, Cheshire, in about 1570, and had acted as a lecturer in both Weaverham and Northwich. He was associated with a notable group of Cheshire puritans, including the minister of Bunbury,

---

[24] *CJ*, I, 434; Whitelocke Diary, 15 February 1625/6; *1628 Debates*, II, 374, 383; III, 431, 557, 586.

[25] *1628 Debates*, III, 185; J. E. Neale, 'Parliament and the Articles of Religion, 1571', *English Historical Review*, LXVII (1952), 510–21; Collinson, *Puritan Movement*, 385–467, the Harley's attitudes to episcopacy are discussed in fuller detail in chapter 5, below.

Christopher Harvey (whose widow, Helen, subsequently married Pierson), and the iconoclast, John Bruen of Stapleford, who removed the stained glass and defaced the sculptured images in Tarvin church. Bruen corresponded regularly with Sir Robert Harley in the early 1620s, before his death in 1625. Before taking up the living at Brampton, Pierson acted as chaplain to Oliver, third baron St John of Bletsho in Bedfordshire, and he was highly regarded in academic circles. The executors of William Perkins, the noted puritan divine, chose Pierson to edit some of Perkins' works for posthumous publication.[26]

Soon after arriving at Brampton, Pierson was in trouble with the Bishop of Hereford, Robert Bennet, for not 'conforming to some ceremonies'. Pierson was charged in the diocesan court with not wearing the surplice and not using the sign of the cross in baptism. At the beginning of 1614 he was summoned before the bishop and was delighted to be 'returned without suspension or censure' with the bishop's 'advice to consider seriously what will be the issue of my course, having my promise to come unto him and give him reasons of my refusal to conform when he sends for me'. Pierson was questioned again in September 1615; at this second hearing he explained his scruples against using the surplice and asked for more time, but Bennet irately reminded Pierson that he had already had three years and 'he would not lose his bishopric for my sake'; Pierson was granted a further two months to conform.[27]

Sir Robert took an active role in trying to mediate and drafted several letters to Bennet, stressing Pierson's unwillingness to disturb the peace of the Church: 'what he cannot comfortably submit to he is willingly silent of', wrote Sir Robert. The issue was complicated because the only person complaining about Pierson was Sir Robert's own father, Thomas Harley,

---

[26] Marriage Settlement, 12 February 1602/3, Brampton Bryan, Harley Mss., Bundle 30a; Venn, *Alumni*, III, 332; Life of Pierson, BL Harl. Mss., 7517 ff.3r–38v; W. Hinde, *A Faithful Remonstrance of the Holy Life and Happy Death of John Bruen of Bruen Stapleford in the County of Chester, Esquire* (1641), 148–52; John Bruen to Harley, 4 May 1619, 2 January 1622/3 and 10 September 1624, BL Loan 29/202 ff.1r, 93r, 138r, and *idem* to Harley, 17 August 1621, 9 February 1621/2 and undated, Loan 29/119. Amongst the works of Perkins edited by Pierson are *A Godly and Learned Exposition upon the First Three Chapters of Revelation* (1606), *The Combat between Christ and the Devil Displayed* (1606), *Commentary on the 11 Chapter of the Epistle to the Hebrews* (1607), *A Godly and Learned Exposition of Christ's Sermon on the Mount* (1608). Pierson was himself the author of two works, *The Cure of Hurtful Cares and Fears* (1636) and *Excellent Encouragements Against Afflictions* (1647). The Epistle Dedicatory of the former of these two works was written by Pierson's step-son, Christopher Harvey the Younger, and reveals the family relationship between the two men.

[27] Harley to Bishop Bennet, 1 September 1615, BL Loan 29/202 f.145r; Hereford and Worcester County RO (Hereford), Hereford Diocesan Court Book 69 (18 January 1615/16), 132 (24 November 1613), 133 (19 July 1615), 134 (5 September 1615) (I am grateful to Dr Kenneth Fincham for these references to the Diocesan Court Records and for the reference cited in the following footnote); Thomas Pierson to Harley, 29 January 1613/14 and 8 September 1615, BL Loan 29/202 ff.138r and 146r.

who was resident at Brampton, Sir Robert being then resident at nearby Stanage Lodge. Pierson complained to Harley about 'your father's violent prosecution' and explained that Thomas Harley was 'implacable'. Sir Robert's solution was to suggest a conference to settle the matter, to be attended by Pierson, Mr Bright a minister from Shrewsbury, and two Shropshire gentlemen, Mr Humphrey Lee and Sir Francis Newport, Sir Robert's then father-in-law. The bishop was clearly sympathetic to Pierson's scruples and in February 1616 Pierson reported that he had dined with Bennet, who had been very kind to him. Bennet died in 1617 and in 1621, during the episcopate of Francis Godwin, Pierson was presented for never wearing the surplice and cutting and chopping the prayer book at his pleasure. By 1629 it appears that Thomas Harley had become reconciled to Pierson, and under the terms of his last will bequeathed the sum of £5 to Pierson, who also acted as a witness to the will.[28]

In general Sir Robert was able to organise the religious life of Brampton to his own liking, without too much interference from the successive bishops of Hereford. This may have been partly because of the geographical situation of Brampton, in the extreme north-west of the county well removed from the diocesan centre of Hereford, but Sir Robert's status as a leading local magnate also served to protect him from outside intervention. Sir Robert's ability to protect non-conformist ministers in the county was clearly spelt out in a letter from the London lecturer John Stoughton, when he urged Peter Thatcher to accept the living at Brampton after Pierson's death in 1633: 'you shall find a worthy, religious, and loving patron and friend of Sir Robert, and such as I have not found many like in all these respects, and beside potent in his country for your countenance and protection'.

Under Sir Robert's guidance Brampton became a centre of zealous puritan worship. In one of his draft letters to Bishop Bennet on behalf of Pierson, Sir Robert explained that at Brampton they had 'never had any such settled preaching ministry here before'. Harley went on to describe his rector's 'diligent and faithful course of preaching Christ crucified, his desire to instruct the youth in the true grounds of religion by catechism and his painful endurance before a communion by going sometimes from house to house to prepare them that should come to the Lord's table'. A later history of his life describes Pierson's evangelical efforts in setting up a combination lecture at Leintwardine, some two miles from Brampton, where Sir Robert was also the patron, and in organising exercises for the local ministers. Pierson made

[28] Harley to Bishop Bennet, 1 September 1615, Thomas Pierson to Harley, 8 September 1615, Harley to Bishop Bennet, 1 September and 3 November 1615, and Thomas Pierson to Harley, 3 February 1615/16, BL Loan 29/202 ff.145r, 146r, 145r, 148r, 151r; Hereford and Worcester County RO (Hereford), Hereford Diocesan Court Book 137 (11 October 1621), Hereford Probate Records, Wills Series, AA.20 no.115, Will of Thomas Harley, dated 30 May 1629.

further provision for the training of the local clergy in his will by bequeathing his personal library of well over 400 books for the use of 13 named ministers.[29]

The godly believed that understanding the gospels, which they regarded as the word of God, was a vital step in the process of salvation and they stressed the evangelical, preaching role of the ministry above all else. Preaching was regarded as one of the main functions of the clergy, but it was only one aspect of the minister's vital role as a teacher. Other aspects included catechising and holding exercises, both for the training of ministers and for the edification of the laity. A preaching ministry was not only important for the salvation of the individual, it was also seen by puritans as an effective antidote to catholicism. Sir Robert was thus always careful to choose well-educated, preaching ministers for the livings in his gift, particularly since Herefordshire was part of what has been characterised as 'the dark corners of the land' in respect of both preaching and religious teaching. This was a view that was endorsed by contemporaries living in the county. At the start of the reign of King James, Rowland Vaughan, a Herefordshire JP, complained that of the twenty-four parishes in the hundred of Webtree not one contained a preaching minister. A survey drawn up in 1641 by Stanley Gower revealed that the problem still persisted. There were only three or four 'constant and conscionable preachers' in Webtree and only twenty such preachers in the whole county, 'yet it is to be feared', continued Gower, 'that there are more in this county than are to be found in all the thirteen shires of Wales, upon which it bordereth'.[30]

Gower had become rector of Brampton in 1634. In 1621 he had been admitted to Trinity College, Dublin and in 1627 became chaplain to James Ussher, the Bishop of Armagh, who was widely respected across the religious spectrum. Sir Robert had been acquainted with Ussher since at least 1621,

---

[29] John Stoughton to Peter Thatcher, 13 February 1633/4, BL Loan 29/172 f.79r, Harley to Bishop Bennet, 25 January 1613/14, Loan 29/123/39b; Life of Pierson, BL Harl. Mss., 7517 ff.21v; PRO PCC/PROB 11/164/358.

[30] Richardson, *Puritanism in North-West England*, 41, 38–39; Collinson, *Puritan Movement*, 168–76; P. Collinson, *The Religion of Protestants: The Church in English Society, 1559–1625* (1982), 128–40; C. Hill, *Change and Continuity in 17th Century England* (1974), 3–47; E. B. Wood, ed., *Rowland Vaughan, His Book* (1897), 43–4; Corpus Christi Mss., 206 ff.3v, 9r. Thomas Harley acquired the advowsons of Brampton Bryan, Wigmore and Leintwardine in 1603 as part of the purchase of the manor of Wigmore, and transferred them, along with the advowson of Clun, to Sir Robert Harley on the occasion of his marriage to Ann Barrett. In 1622 Sir Robert presented Thomas Doughty to the living of Leintwardine and presented John Yates in 1638. William Stephenson was presented to the living of Wigmore in 1624 by the Bishop of Hereford. Sir Robert Harley was also the patron of the living of Aylton in the south-east of the county, where he presented Richard Broughton to the living in 1619: see Marriage Settlement, 12 February 1602/3, Brampton Bryan, Harley Mss., Bundle 30a, and A. T. Bannister, *Diocese of Heefod: Institutions, AD 1539–1900* (Hereford, 1923), 29,30.

probably through their mutual friendship with Lady Vere, and in 1635 Harley informed the bishop that Gower's 'relation to your grace invited me to a diligent inquiry of him and his own worth persuaded me to give him a full and cheerful call'. Once at Brampton, Gower's non-conformity was even more extensive than that of his predecessor. A document in the state papers drawn up in 1638 charged him with omitting the absolution and litany from the prayer book service and only rarely reading the Lord's Prayer and the Ten Commandments. Gower was also accused of not allowing his parishioners to stand during the readings from the gospels nor to bow at the name of Jesus; using his sermons to exhort his congregation not to kneel in prayer on entering the church and to persuade them to wear their hats throughout the lessons and the sermon. Gower was further accused of omitting the sign of the cross in baptism, catechising the local youth on the subject matter of his sermons, and of not wearing the surplice.

These were all long-standing non-conformist practices, which reflected the desire to strip away catholic ceremonies and religious garb regarded as superstitious pre-Reformation relics by puritans. Failure to kneel in church was a common expression of lay puritanism in the early seventeenth century. It is rarer to find examples of laymen refusing to remove their hats in church. The Quakers' refusal of 'hat-honour' in the 1650s is well known, but there were also scattered cases in the diocese of Chester between 1604 and 1633. Refusing to wear the surplice or to use the sign of the cross, and curtailing the prayer book services were all signs of clerical non-conformity which can be traced back to the earliest years of Queen Elizabeth, or before.[31] There was thus clear continuity between the puritanism of the Harley circle and the earliest expressions of puritanism in Elizabethan England. Gower was also guilty, however, of a new religious offence, which had been instigated under the aegis of Archbishop Laud. The charges stated that the communion table was not railed in at Brampton and on communion days was 'brought down out of the chancel into the body of the church'. This was in accordance with the injunctions of 1559, which stipulated that the communion table be kept at the east end of the church and carried into the body of the church for the service, but from 1633 onwards there was an official campaign to eradicate the Elizabethan practice by railing the altar at the east end of the church.[32]

[31] G. D. Burtchaell and T. U. Sadleir, *Alumni Dublinienses* (Dublin, 1935), 337; S. Gower, ed., *Eighteen Sermons Preached in Oxford, 1640, by James Ussher, Lord Primate of Ireland* (1659), Preface; W. D. G. Fletcher, 'Institutions of Shropshire Incumbents', *TSANHS*, 3rd Series, V (1905), 359; Harley to Archbishop Ussher, 29 January 1634/5, BL Loan 29/123/39k; PRO SP16/381/92; Richardson, *Puritanism in North-West England*, 76, 80–1; Collinson, *Puritan Movement*, 71–83; Davies, *The Worship of English Puritans*, 67–9, 263–7. On the subject of hat honour see P. J. Corfield, 'Dress for Deference and Dissent: Hats and the Decline of Hat Honour', *Costume: The Journal of the Costume Society* (1989).
[32] C. Russell, *The Crisis of Parliaments* (Oxford, 1971), 216.

The charges against Gower were accompanied by charges against Sir Robert Harley for allowing Gower's offences and for maintaining Richard Symonds, a suspended minister, as his schoolmaster. Harley was further accused of dominating the parish to such an extent that 'every year his own servants or tenants at the least' were always chosen as churchwardens. The final charge was that 'they do often appoint fasts of their own creating', when Gower showed formidable endurance in remaining in the pulpit from morning till late afternoon:

upon such a day Mr Gower will go into the pulpit between eight and nine of clock in the morning and there pray and preach *ex tempore*, till past one of the clock following. They then sing a psalm, but Mr Gower cometh not forth the pulpit till it be past five of the clock following, if daylight continue so long.

Private fasts have been described by Professor Collinson as 'invariably indicative of advanced, radical puritanism', and they had been proscribed by the canons of 1604, which reserved the appointing of fasts to the bishops. Moreover, Charles I even seemed to disapprove of having too many authorised fasts. In January 1629, in response to the Commons' petition for a fast, he warned that 'this custom of fasts every session is but lately begun and I confess I am not fully satisfied with the necessity of it at this time . . . I do willingly grant your requests herein, but with this note, that I expect that this shall not hereafter be brought into precedent for frequent fasts, except upon great occasions.'[33]

Sir Robert Harley was one of the MPs eager to hold public fasts, and at the start of the 1628 Parliament he declared: 'I joy to see the sense of this House to join to humble ourselves to God. If the King grant it the House and this city may have a set day and the kingdom another day afterward.' In 1629 Harley was a member of the committee which drew up the petition to the King for a fast and during the Short Parliament he was a member of the committee chosen to organise a public fast by the members. Sir Robert was also involved in private fasts both in London and at Brampton. In 1626 the Bishop of London was alerted by a rumour that a private fast had been held on St Andrew's day. He concluded that the fast had been kept by 'the meaner sort of people', but was worried that the 'richer sort', such as the Earl of Warwick, were also involved. He had also heard that Sir Robert Harley had said 'that there were divers who would take the opportunity of the many sermons

[33] P. Collinson, 'Lectures by Combination: Structures and Characteristics of Church Life in Seventeenth Century England', *BIHR*, XLVIII (1975), 190; *Sermons or Homilies, Appointed to be Read in Churches in the Time of Queen Elizabeth of Famous Memory: To which are Added the Articles of Religion and the Constitutions and Canons Ecclesiastical* (1840), 671–2; W. Notestein and F. H. Relf, eds., *Commons Debates for 1629* (Minneapolis, 1921), 28–9.

preached that day to humble themselves to almighty God in a holy fast'. Sir Robert probably did fast on that occasion, since days of prayer and fasting formed a regular part of the religious life at Brampton. The Harleys regularly observed such a day during the quarterly ember weeks and in January 1629 the day appointed for a public fast by the Parliament was also observed by Thomas Pierson at Leintwardine.[34]

As well as observing these authorised days of abstinence, the Harleys also kept private days of prayer, which Sir Robert called 'our exercises'. Several lists setting out 'matter of request to God' and 'matter of thanksgiving' have survived from the meetings held by Sir Robert at Brampton and in London during the 1620s and early 1630s. The lists are also a rich source for the religious problems which most concerned Sir Robert, and they not only contain prayers for the royal family and the members of the Harleys' extended family, but they are also strongly anti-catholic and anti-Arminian in tone. Lady Brilliana's letters also describe the days of prayer and fasting held at Brampton in the late 1630s and early 1640s. She wrote of a 'private day' which the Harleys observed in February 1639, and a similar day was kept when Sir Robert was elected to the Short Parliament in 1640. Such days not only provided an occasion for the expression of religious zeal, they also provided an excellent opportunity for puritans to gather together whilst excluding the ungodly from their midst. Those who gathered to worship at Brampton explicitly bound themselves with a formal covenant and at their meetings prayed 'that God would enable us to keep covenant with him'. In January 1641 a 'private day' was kept at Brampton and was attended by several local clergy – Stanley Gower, William Stephenson, the vicar of Wigmore, William Voyle, the curate of the Shropshire parish of Llanfairwaterdine, and Harley's own appointee at Leintwardine, John Yates. Lay visitors included a Mr More, who was probably Samuel, the eldest son of Richard More of Linley in Shropshire. The lists of prayers drawn up by Sir Robert reveal that he was also in contact with a widespread network of groups holding similar religious 'exercises' in Herefordshire, Shropshire, Cheshire and Lancashire as well as in London, and in 1633 the Harleys prayed for 'the ministers of the word and sacraments, particularly of this place and of these parts and for the continuance of our exercises'. Amongst the ministers named in these prayers were Julines Herring, the lecturer at St Alkmond's, Shrewsbury, who was suspended 'by the violence of bishops' for ignoring certain ceremonies and subsequently fled to Amsterdam; and John Cotton, the minister of Boston, Lincolnshire, who emigrated to America later

[34] *1628 Debates*, II, 35, 36; *CJ*, I, 922; II, 4; *CSPD, Addenda, 1625–1649*, 175; Lewis, *Letters of the Lady Brilliana Harley*, 15, 16, 38, 43, 82; Thomas Pierson to Harley, 14 January 1628/9, BL Loan 29/202 f.247r.

that year. At the beginning of 1634 the Harleys prayed for 'those that are gone out of the land'.[35]

Not only did the Harleys worship on occasion with other puritans, they also tried to draw the godly into other areas of their daily lives. The godly were, of course, a minority on earth and Lady Brilliana noted that 'God's elect must be considered two ways, simply of themselves and comparatively with others. Simply of themselves they are a great number not to be numbered, but comparatively with the wicked, in respect of them they are but few.' In practical terms this meant that the wicked outnumbered the elect on earth and the only safe refuge was to consort with the godly and shun the sinners. For the Harleys one of the most important factors in human relationships was therefore the ability to recognise other members of the godly community. The Harleys thus applied religious criteria to relationships with their own kindred, ignoring their catholic relatives and maintaining a close friendship with the puritan Veres, for example. Even within the confines of their own household the Harleys strove to surround themselves with godly servants. In 1612 Thomas Pierson recommended a cook to the Harleys who was 'a very proper manner of person, religious and sufficiently qualified for his place'. Pierson was later advised by Julines Herring of a man who could serve as horsekeeper for the Harleys, if Sir Robert desired 'one religious'. In 1633 Lady Brilliana informed her husband that she had heard of a gentlewoman who would make a suitable servant: 'she, they say, is religious and discreet'; and when Ned Harley was in need of a manservant in 1641 Lady Brilliana hoped that 'God send you a religious and good natured servant'. These were the sort of qualities that many puritan gentry would have looked for in their servants. Puritan authors were at pains to point out the benefits of being served by godly servants, who could be relied upon not to corrupt the children of the household or each other, and who would not spread scandalous stories about their masters.[36]

Sir Robert was even prepared to lease land to a godly tenant, even though the man could not afford to pay the highest rent. In 1628 Sir Robert was persuaded by Thomas Pierson to rent out a cottage and orchard at Brampton to Edward Pinner. Pierson argued that 'I would fain have him or some honest man be your tenant to it. Mere worldlings will give the most, but such will not further the gospel among us.' The choice of friends was also governed by the

---

[35] Lewis, *Letters of the Lady Brilliana Harley*, 28, 29, 87, 108; Lists of prayers, 17 December 1624, BL Loan 29/52/93, 30 March 1627, Loan 29/202 f.238r, 22 February 1632/3, and 24 January 1633/4, Loan 29/27 part 1; for Herring see William Rowley and others to Harley, 12 May 1642, BL Loan 29/121, *DNB*, IX, 710–11, and S. Clarke, *A General Martyrology* (1651), 462–72; for Cotton see S. Clarke, *The Lives of Ten Eminent Divines* (1662), 55–84.

[36] Commonplace Book ff.66r, 176r; Thomas Pierson to David Harper, 4 July 1612, BL Loan 29/121, Julines Herring to Thomas Pierson, undated, Loan 29/124/71; Lewis, *Letters of the Lady Brilliana Harley*, 6, 131; Cliffe, *Puritan Gentry*, 32–3.

question of religious sympathies. The Harleys regarded religion as the touchstone of friendship and Lady Brilliana recorded in her commonplace book that friends were 'those that are of the same religion, affection and disposition'. Similarly Sir Robert wrote in one of his draft letters to Sir Edward Herbert, 'religion . . . makes friends at first sight'.[37]

Among the Harleys' lay contacts in other counties and in London were a number of men who would later be staunch Parliamentarians during the Civil War. These included the puritan peers Lord Saye, who seems to have been distantly related to Sir Robert, and the second Lord Brooke, who had family links with Lady Brilliana, and the Harleys regularly prayed for the families of the two peers. Saye and Brooke were both founder members of the Providence Island company, set up in 1630 with the intention of colonising the islands of Providence and Henrietta in the Caribbean. The original membership of the company was almost exclusively puritan and the two lords were both very active members, Brooke's London home, Brooke House in Holborn, being the usual meeting place for the company.[38] Harley was also acquainted with Saye's son, Nathaniel Fiennes, another future Parliamentarian. In February 1637 Fiennes wrote to Harley from Brooke House thanking him for the loan of a book and inquiring

if you are to go out of the town, whereby I shall be deprived of the opportunity of waiting upon you and enjoying your good company, which upon divers occasions you have so freely imparted unto me and with such expressions of love and affection as have improved the relation of kindred and put upon me the quality of your most humble servant and kinsman.

Another of Sir Robert's lay contacts was Sir Thomas Wrothe, the Somerset puritan who would side with the radical independents during the Long Parliament. During the 1628 Parliament, Wrothe represented Bridgwater in Somerset and the two men formed a strong attachment. In March 1629 Wrothe invited Harley to a 'lenten dinner', referring to his 'extraordinary affection' of Sir Robert's company. Wrothe further suggested that they should 'go together to Mr Damport's [*sic*] in the morning, where I will provide a seat for you'. Presumably this was an invitation to hear the

---

[37] Thomas Pierson to Harley, undated, BL Loan 29/121; lease, 20 August 1629, Brampton Bryan, Harley Mss., Bundle 70; Commonplace Book f.105r; Harley to Sir Edward Herbert, 12 January 1617/18, BL Loan 29/119.

[38] Lists of prayers, 17 December 1624, 8 June 1625, BL Loan 29/52/93, and 22 February 1632/3, 12 April 1633 Loan 29/27 part 1; Lewis, *Letters of the Lady Brilliana Harley*, 49, 129, 170; A. P. Newton, *The Colonising Activities of the English Puritans* (New Haven, 1914), 58–67. Robert Greville, second Lord Brooke, had been adopted by his cousin Fulke Greville, first Lord Brooke, who was himself a cousin of Sir Edward Conway; for this complicated family background see *DNB*, VIII, 606 and G. E. Cockayne, *The Complete Peerage*, II, 331; III, 400.

preaching of Lady Vere's protegé, John Davenport, vicar of St Stephen's, Coleman street.[39]

His visits to London not only gave Harley the opportunity to hear puritan preachers, but also to cultivate their friendship. Many of the clergymen known to Sir Robert were also non-conformists who had attracted the notice of the Church authorities. Sir Robert's friendship with these men did not go unnoticed and probably contributed to his loss of court office in the 1630s. In London Sir Robert took lodgings or stayed with relatives in areas where puritan preachers were to be heard. In 1611 and 1612 he lodged in Blackfriars, one of the most notoriously puritan parishes in London. In *The Alchemist*, first published in 1612, Ben Jonson satirised the inhabitants of Blackfriars as 'sober, scurvy, precise . . . that scarce have smiled twice since the King came in'. Here Harley swiftly became friendly with William Gouge the puritan lecturer at St Anne's church, Blackfriars, who was to become one of the most popular puritan authors of the day. In June 1613 Gouge wrote to Harley and asked him to mediate in a dispute between a Mr Emerson and Lady Savile, his letter referring to 'our little state in the Blackfriars'.[40]

It was probably in London that Harley also became acquainted with a number of other puritan ministers including Thomas Gataker, Nathaniel Ward and the Brinsleys. In 1621 Harley approached Gataker, the rector of Rotherhithe, and asked him to consider some of the points of disagreement between the English Church and Rome for the benefit of an unknown gentleman. Gataker drew up some arguments for Harley and indicated that he was willing to help further. Two years later Gataker was chosen to preach the sermon at Sir Robert's wedding.[41] In 1621 Harley was in correspondence with Nathaniel Ward in an effort to get Ward's brother Samuel released from prison, where he had been sent for having drawn a cartoon satirising the Spanish ambassador, the King of Spain and the Pope as being in league with the Devil. We do not know when Harley first made the acquaintance of the Brinsleys. John Brinsley the elder was a schoolmaster who was described by the astrologer William Lilly, a former pupil, as 'very severe in his life and conversation, and did breed up many scholars for the universities. In religion he was a strict puritan, not conformable wholly to the ceremonies of the Church of England.' When he was prevented from teaching by the Church authorities Brinsley went to London and took up a lectureship. In the mid-

[39] Fiennes to Harley, 23 February 1636/7, BL Loan 29/119; Barnes, *Somerset, 1625–1640*, 16; *1628 Debates*, I, 63; Sir Thomas Wrothe to Harley, 28 March 1628/9, BL Loan 29/202 f.248r; for Lady Vere's patronage of Davenport see Adams, 'Thesis', 254.

[40] Harley to Thomas Peacock, 18 November 1611, Thomas Pierson to Harley, 30 March 1612, BL Loan 29/202 ff.125r, 129v; B. Jonson, *The Alchemist* (1612), sig., B3r; William Gouge to Harley, 24 June 1613, BL Loan 29/202 between ff.131 and 135.

[41] Thomas Gataker to Harley, 18 June 1621, BL Loan 29/119, 22, 25 June, BL Loan 29/202 ff.49r, 50r; Gataker, *Wife in Deed*, Epistle Dedicatory.

1620s his son John was accused before the High Commission of 'inconformity and factiousness', but this did not deter Harley from recommending him to Lord Herbert of Cherbury for the living of Montgomery in 1631. In his letter to Herbert, Harley explained that his acquaintance with the two Brinsleys was 'ancient'.[42]

Between December 1626 and February 1634 Sir Robert had lodgings in Aldermanbury, another strongly puritan parish where he was well known to two successive lecturers at St Mary's, Thomas Taylor and John Stoughton. Taylor dedicated one of his printed sermons to Sir Robert in 1630, just before he retired from the parish. He was replaced by Stoughton, who was charged by the High Commission in 1635 for collecting money for puritan ministers who had emigrated to New England. As the case against him progressed, a paper was discovered amongst his possessions setting out 'the duty of all God's people to separate themselves from the Church or churches of England, as they now are'. Sir Robert accompanied Stoughton on his appearance before the High Commission and at the same time visited John Workman, the puritan lecturer of Gloucester, in the Gatehouse prison. Workman was charged before the High Commission on an array of charges including preaching against dancing and images, and advocating the election of ministers by their congregation. He was suspended from the ministry in April 1635 and subsequently presided over a seminary of scholars at his home in Tewkesbury. In 1636 he wrote to Sir Robert suggesting a match between one of Harley's daughters and a Mr Thomas Estcourt, who was anxious to find a good wife and 'chiefly to prefer religion in his choice'. Since the Harleys' oldest daughter, Brilliana, was no more than six at the time nothing came of this offer. In 1638 Workman was helping Sir Robert in his inquiries for a suitable tutor at Oxford for young Ned.[43]

Harley's support for these non-conformist ministers was undoubtedly a factor in his loss of office in the mid-1630s. Harley himself thought it was the principal reason and a document written circa 1645 amongst his papers describes the loss of the Mint in the following terms:

in the tenth year of the King, Sir Robert Harley, falling under disfavour of those who were then powerful at court, especially the late Bishop of Canterbury, and as Sir

---

[42] Nathaniel Ward to Harley, 6 August 1621, BL Loan 29/202 f.52r; *DNB*, XX, 790; II, 1256; Shipps, 'Thesis', 221; Harley to John Brinsley, 8 December 1631, BL Loan 29/172 f.42r–v.

[43] *CSPD, 1625–1626*, 488; *CSPD, 1627–1628*, 242; Peter Thatcher to Harley, at his house in Aldermanbury, 11 February 1633/4, BL Loan 29/172 f.78r; T. Taylor, *The Progress of Saints into Full Holiness* (1630), Epistle Dedicatory; J. C. Whitebrook, 'Dr John Stoughton the Elder', *Congregational Historical Society Transactions*, VI (1913–15), 89–107, 177–87. PRO SP16/280/65; 'The State of Sir Robert Harley's Case Concerning his office of Master and Worker of His Majesty's Monies, and his present condition', undated, BL Loan 29/122/5 (internal evidence suggests a date of 1645); PRO SP16/261 ff.206v, 207r; Gardiner, *History of England, 1603–1642*, X, 225; John Workman to Harley, 13 February 1635/6, BL Loan 29/172 f.101r, *idem* to Harley, 23 August 1638, Loan 29/121.

Robert conceives, for that he did appear in the High Commission court at Lambeth with Doctor Stoughton, preacher at Aldermanbury, London, and for entertaining Mr Workman, preacher at Gloucester, into his house, and visiting him in the Gatehouse where he was imprisoned by sentence of the said High Commission court, a *scire facias* was brought against Sir Robert Harley's patent by Mr Noy, then Attorney-General.

During the 1630s Sir Robert was also in contact with William Prynne and Henry Burton, whose harsh punishment for criticising Church and State was to become a *cause célèbre*. Prynne was a puritan polemicist who was committed to the Tower of London on 1 February 1633 for his work *Histriomastix: A Scourge of Stage Players*, which was regarded as being aimed directly at the Queen herself for the roles that she had taken in court masques and other entertainments. At this time Sir Robert was still Master of the Mint and he would have had access to the Tower, where the Mint was sited. Other inhabitants of the Tower testified that Harley had visited Prynne and that his visits coincided with those made by Burton, who was rector of the church of St Matthew in nearby Friday street: 'Mr Burton met with Mr Prynne almost every day in the Tower, and . . . they sat in consultation half days together, sometimes alone, and sometimes with company, naming Sir Robert Harlowe for one of the company.'[44] In 1637 Prynne, Burton and John Bastwicke were all sentenced by Star Chamber to be mutilated, fined and imprisoned for life for their various writings. Harley was thoroughly sympathetic to their plight and at the start of the Long Parliament he moved that Burton and Bastwick should be allowed to come to the House of Commons and present their cases to Parliament in person. The sentences on all three men were reversed by the Long Parliament and they were offered substantial monetary compensation.[45]

Although Sir Robert had a widespread set of contacts with puritans from London and elsewhere, there was little of practical consequence that these individuals could do to force the pace of Church reforms. One recent study has described Sir Robert himself as acting as 'a kind of clearing house for puritans seeking livings and patrons seeking preachers'. This conclusion is based on a misreading of secondary information and gives a distorted picture of the way in which puritan ministers found suitable preferment. Sir Robert did on occasion recommend ministers for certain livings, but it would be wrong to regard his interest in godly ministers as being either highly organised or uniquely influential. Sir Robert and many other puritan gentry used traditional sources of patronage, such as friends and relatives, in order

[44] 'The State of Sir Robert Harley's case . . .', BL Loan 29/122/5; *DNB*, XVI, 432; Gardiner, *History of England, 1603–1642*, VII, 14, 328–30; Microfilm of the Coventry Mss., Cases in Star Chamber, 1616–37, BL M874/13 f.209r–v; I am grateful to Frances Condick for this reference.

[45] Gardiner, *History of England, 1603–1642*, VIII, 226–34; *D'Ewes (N)*, 5 n.13.

to find places for their nominees. Thus in 1627 Harley wrote to his father-in-law, Secretary Conway, on behalf of William Cradock, a former chaplain with the Cadiz expedition, for a 'benefice void, which is in his Majesty's gift'. Within weeks Cradock had been instituted as vicar of the Warwickshire parish of Nuneaton, which was in the gift of the King. Whether Harley was responsible for this we do not know, for Cradock had already approached the Duke of Buckingham asking for a benefice and it may have been the Duke who secured Nuneaton for him. Sometimes Sir Robert's efforts failed altogether; his unsuccessful attempt to persuade Lord Herbert of Cherbury to take on John Brinsley the younger has already been discussed. A similar failure occurred in 1638, when Sir Robert approached Sir Sampson Eure of Gatley Park in Herefordshire about the local living of Burrington. Eure told Harley that he had already recommended someone for the living, which was in the gift of the King.[46]

Other puritan gentry were just as enthusiastic as Sir Robert in the recommendation and patronage of godly ministers. Lady Brilliana herself recommended William Voyle to her brother-in-law Sir William Pelham when the living of Brocklesby fell vacant in 1641. She desired to have 'a good man there', but was dismayed to hear that the living was worth only £30 per annum and Voyle did not pursue the matter. Lady Vere had more success in helping her nominees. In 1624 James Ussher had been elevated to the see of Meath with the help of Lady Vere and the influence of her brother-in-law, Secretary Conway. Ussher subsequently wrote to thank her for the 'effectual means' which she had used and asked her to convey his thanks to Conway, whom he had not met, for his 'extraordinary kindness'. Lady Vere used similar channels of influence to promote John Davenport. In the 1630s when the second Lord Brooke was in the process of renting Ragley Hall from the Conways he suggested a suitable minister for the living there to Sir Robert, describing him as 'very honest and able, but I am content that he be balked so as a sufficient man be put in'.[47] It was probably in such circumstances and with similar sentiments that the majority of recommendations of puritan ministers were made. The puritan laity were able to promote and support godly ministers using their own private sources of patronage and influence and their assistance was exercised in a piecemeal fashion using traditional lines of social contact. It was only rarely that they organised themselves on a more systematic basis.

---

[46] P. Seaver, *The Puritan Lectureships: The Politics of Religious Dissent, 1560–1662* (1970), 50–51; Levy, 'Thesis', 157–8; PRO SP16/70/22; PRO Bishops' Institution Books, Ser.A, 1556–1660, IV, Com. War. p.143 (Round Room Press Mark 19/62); *CSPD 1625–26*, 338; Sir Sampson Eure to Harley, 5 January 1637/8, BL Loan 29/119; Corpus Christi Mss., 206 f.9r.

[47] Lewis, *Letters of the Lady Brilliana Harley*, 107; BL Add. Mss., 4274 f.32r; *CSPD, 1625–26*, 196; PRO SP16/196/84.

One of the very few puritan organisations set up before the Long Parliament was the short-lived Feoffees for Impropriations, founded in London by four ministers and eight laymen. The founders intended to buy impropriated tithes and return them to ecclesiastical use. The need to increase the incomes of the parish clergy was endorsed by the very highest political and religious circles in the early Stuart period. Both King James and Archbishop Laud outlined schemes to restore tithes to the clergy, but did nothing to put them into practice, while some individuals, such as Viscount Scudamore in Herefordshire, restored tithes in their own possession to the Church. The activities of the puritan Feoffees had a distinctly ideological flavour, however, since they intended to use the tithes specifically to support preaching ministers and lecturers; and in 1633 the Feoffees were thus dissolved after Attorney General Noy filed an information against them in the court of the Exchequer. During the course of their activities the Feoffees were able to raise over £6,000 and they bought up thirteen impropriations. Sir Robert was not an immediate member of this group, but he did have contacts with them and he certainly supported their aims. He knew one of the original clerical members, Richard Sibbes, and his friend William Gouge later replaced another member who died in 1626. Perhaps it was because of these personal contacts that Harley sold the tithes of Presteigne to the Feoffees in 1627. Harley did, of course, make a profit on this sale, but his interest in the Feoffees was more than just commercial. He actively supported measures in Parliament to pay higher stipends to the ministry and in 1632 was himself considering a plan to turn over his tithes from Leinthall Starkes to Thomas Pierson. In 1633, when the Feoffees were under legal scrutiny, Harley prayed for the 'case for the Feoffees'. Even after they were disbanded the Feoffees remained a model for puritan reform; and at the start of the Long Parliament Stanley Gower wrote to Sir Robert with a plan for Church reformation, which included the advice that 'the Feoffees plot' should 'go forward'.[48]

The suppression of the Feoffees illustrates the divide which was being created within the Church during the reign of King Charles. When Ned Harley went to university in 1638 the religious atmosphere in Oxford was very different from the religious life at Brampton. Indeed within three months of his arrival Ned complained to his eldest sister Brill that he had 'not the word of God preached . . . in a right manner'. Of course there was no lack of

[48] R. O'Day, *The English Clergy: The Emergence and Consolidation of a Profession, 1558–1642* (Leicester, 1979), 103, 86; I. M. Calder, *Activities of the Puritan Faction of the Church of England, 1625–1633* (1957), *passim*; Zagorin, *The Court and the Country*, 180; Sibbes to Harley, undated, BL Loan 29/121; Howse, 'Contest for a Radnorshire Rectory', 70; *1628 Debates*, III, 557, 586; paper dated 29 September 1632 in Harley's hand and list of prayers 22 February 1632/3, BL Loan 29/27 part 1; Stanley Gower to Harley, 28 November 1640, Loan 29/119. For the schemes devised by King James and by Archbishop Laud see above, chapter 1, n.33. For Scudamore see *DNB*, XVII, 1093.

preaching at the university, but preachers did not have the liberty to pray extempore and at such length as did Stanley Gower at Brampton. Furthermore the doctrine of predestination had been effectively outlawed by royal proclamation in 1626.[49] While Gower could preach more or less what he liked at Brampton, in Oxford divines were very much in the public eye and were thus more restricted.

The Harleys were also alarmed at the Laudian innovations in Church worship, such as the railed altar and bowing to the altar, which were evident at Oxford. In January 1639 Lady Brilliana voiced her opposition to the adoption of these practices there:

I hope there will be no such things imposed upon your house as in some others [she wrote to Ned] and I hope, if it should be, you will keep to the truth in everything; and in my opinion, he who stands for the truth in a small thing (as we think, for none of God's truths in his service is small), is of a more courageous spirit than one that will only show themself in great matters.

Later, on hearing that her nephew Edward Pelham had arrived to study at Oxford, she warned Ned that

I believe he thinks all well done that is new to him and that he sees gentlemen do with a good grace, which he thinks they do when they bow to the altar, but I pray God teach him another lesson.

Sir Robert shared his wife's opinions about Laudian alterations in religion. During the Short Parliament he supported John Pym in his call to have such innovations denounced as 'crimes', and in the same session he complained that 'are we not brought almost to idolatry in bowing' to the altar.[50] The Harleys along with many other puritans regarded the Arminian clergy as innovators, who were forcing the Church towards an accommodation with Rome in matters both of theology and the externals of Church worship. The fact that the Harleys regarded themselves as being in the mainstream of the traditional Church is further highlighted by their attitudes towards separatists. It is sometimes difficult to discern the fine line between extreme puritans, who wished to exclude the ungodly from their private worship, and separatists, who believed that church congregations should only consist of the godly. The Harley circle was, however, quite adamant that there was a distinction. In her commonplace book Lady Brilliana disparagingly referred to the Brownists as a group who would have the Church 'nowhere, but in their parlour at Amsterdam'. In 1639 she followed the establishment of a

---

[49] Brilliana Harley to Edward Harley, 25 January, 15 February 1638/9, 7 May 1639, BL Loan 29/172 ff.211r, 216r, 232r; Cliffe, *Puritan Gentry*, 150.

[50] Lewis, *Letters of the Lady Brilliana Harley*, 18, 96–7; E. S. Cope and W. H. Coates, eds., *Proceedings of the Short Parliament of 1640*, Camden Society, 4th Series, XIX (1977), 181; J. D. Maltby, ed., *The Short Parliament (1640) Diary of Sir Thomas Aston*, Camden Society, 4th Series, XXXV (1988), 89.

separatist group at nearby Llanfairwaterdine with great interest. She described their leader, Walter Cradock, as 'a worthy man, but sometimes he does not judge clearly of things'. In November 1639 the Harleys' schoolmaster, Richard Symonds, became increasingly involved with this group, which resulted in his refusal to join in a public fast with the Harleys and his departure from Brampton. Lady Brilliana related all these events to Ned in her letters and revealed that she herself had some reservations about the prayer book: 'I fear we shall be so earnest in beating down their too much villifying of the common prayer book that we say more of it than ever we intended.' At the beginning of the Long Parliament, when religious changes seemed to many to be inevitable, puritans were at pains to disassociate themselves from the more extreme ideas of the separatists. Stanley Gower went so far as to compare them to the hated catholics: 'on the one side papists that erect their Babel amongst us; on the other side Brownists that discourage your reformation of our Zion, whilst they contend for their independent government'.[51]

Prior to the calling of the Long Parliament, the Harleys' puritanism revolved around an emphasis on the faith and godly life of the individual, combined with attempts to eradicate what they perceived as any surviving catholic influences from the Church. They did not want to separate from the Church and they did not see themselves as opponents of the established Church. The Harleys shared these attitudes with other puritans and they made a conscious effort to seek out the friendship and company of like-minded puritan laity and ministers. This approach to religion certainly predated the rise of Arminianism in the English Church. Sir Robert's support for non-conforming ministers dates back to at least 1612, when he presented Thomas Pierson to the living at Brampton Bryan. Similarly, Lady Brilliana's commonplace book, which reveals so much about the puritan understanding of godly behaviour, was started in 1622, well before complaints about Arminian clergy were first raised in Parliament in 1624. The Harleys' puritanism should not therefore be regarded simply as a response to Arminianism. The Harleys' perceptions of their godly community as a beleaguered minority were, however, strongly reinforced by the belief that the Arminians intended to reintroduce catholicism to England and thus overthrow the existing Church and state. Their experience of the growth of Arminianism in the 1620s and 1630s was undoubtedly the stimulus which led the Harleys to press openly for reform of the Church hierarchy in the Long

[51] P. Collinson, 'Towards a Broader Understanding of the Early Dissenting Tradition', in C. R. Cole and M. E. Moody, eds., *The Dissenting Tradition: Essays for Leland H. Carlson* (Athens, Ohio, 1975), 11; Commonplace Book f.66r; Lewis, *Letters of the Lady Brilliana Harley*, 26, 31, 74, 76, 77, 78, 84, 69; Stanley Gower to Harley, 9 August 1641, Bl. Loan 29/173 f.157r.

Parliament. The Harleys' long-term desires for a range of reforms, which would finally purge the Church of catholic usage and influence, would also be central to their opposition to the crown in the 1640s.

※ *4* ※

Religion and politics before the
Long Parliament

Surviving personal documentation about the Harleys' attitudes towards
national politics during the 1620s and for much of the 1630s is patchy in
comparison with the detailed information that exists for the years 1638–43.
For the 1620s the Harleys' papers can be supplemented, however, by reports
of Sir Robert's speeches in Parliament, which reveal that his antipathy
towards Arminians and catholics in England was the counterpart of his
sympathy for the reformed churches abroad. Although Harley was
outspoken in the House about religious matters, he rarely made direct
criticism of royal policies on other issues. His relationship with Secretary
Conway undoubtedly restrained Harley from direct political opposition in
these years and he was also genuinely concerned to see priority given to
problems of a religious nature, and in particular to the successful prosecution
of war against Spain, which he regarded as a part of the struggle to maintain
the international protestant cause against the machinations of its catholic
foes.

As an MP Sir Robert was also expected to represent the concerns of his
constituents to the House, and he did raise points of purely local importance
in the Commons, such as the state of salmon fishing in the Wye and the price
of grain in Herefordshire in 1624.[1] More often, however, he spoke about
issues of wider concern relating to religion, finance and warfare. The
impression that he concentrated on these larger issues may possibly be a
distortion created by the scribes and diarists who recorded the debates in the
Commons. Diarists in particular were apt to omit routine business from their
notes, and Professor Russell had concluded that 'it appears unlikely that, even
on the best-reported days, more than about a quarter of the words spoken in
the Commons are preserved'. If the men who reported procedure in the

---

[1] *CJ*, I, 704, 711; Nicholas Diary, 12 April 1624. See also the letter from the Mayor and
Aldermen of Hereford to Harley, 5 April 1624, BL Loan 29/50/71; an identical letter was
sent to Sir John Scudamore, the senior knight of the shire, PRO C115/M21/7636.

House were biased, they nevertheless shared that bias with a good number of people outside Parliament. The circulation of news in the early Stuart period indicates that people increasingly wanted to hear about topics of national and international importance; local events tended to be widely reported only if they had some direct bearing on national news. Furthermore, the frequent Parliaments of the 1620s undoubtedly helped both to arouse and to shape public opinions.[2]

Parliament itself was regarded not simply as a body designed to grant taxation and to pass legislation, it was a meeting place for King and people, where grievances could be aired and resolved and where royal policies could be endorsed by the representatives of the political nation. It was a natural and vital forum for the discussion and resolution of a wide range of issues, 'the soul of the commonwealth, that only is able to apprehend and understand the symptoms of all such diseases which threaten the body politic', as John Pym phrased it in a speech to the Short Parliament. The existence of Parliament was also seen as a barrier to tyranny. In 1610, when the future of the institution itself seemed under threat, the lawyer James Whitelocke described Parliament as 'the storehouse of our liberties', and in 1624 Sir Benjamin Rudyerd told the Commons that 'as long as we have Parliaments we shall have liberties'. Service in Parliament was therefore an important public duty, a 'great and weighty employment', so Thomas Pierson wrote in a letter to Harley at the start of the 1626 session. Moreover, election to Parliament, especially to one of the prestigious county seats, was a validation of local influence and could also be a stepping stone to the patronage of the court, and was thus tenaciously pursued by the more ambitious of the greater gentry.[3]

Parallel with the belief in the importance of Parliament ran an undercurrent of fear that the institution itself was in danger of extinction at the hands of the first two Stuart monarchs. Such fears had first escalated in 1610 in connection with plans for the Great Contract, which would have ensured the crown a set annual income, thus raising the question of whether the King would continue to call Parliaments if he no longer needed to rely on them for the vote of subsidies. The political methods of both James I and Charles I subsequently reinforced such alarms, and in particular the benevolence raised by James in 1614 and the forced loan of 1626 were perceived, as Dr Cust notes, as threats to the 'principle of parliamentary taxation'. The experience of the 'Personal

---

[2] Russell, *Parliaments and English Politics*, xviii; Cust, 'News and Politics in Early Seventeenth-Century England', 69–72.

[3] Cust and Lake, 'Sir Richard Grosvenor and the rhetoric of magistracy', 46–53; E. S. Cope, *Politics Without Parliaments, 1629–1640* (1987), 27–32; Cope and Coates, *Proceedings of the Short Parliament*, 149; E. Foster, ed., *Proceedings in Parliament, 1610*, II (New Haven, 1966), 109; C. Thompson, ed., *The Holles Account of Proceedings in the House of Commons in 1624* (Orchard Press, Essex, 1985), 29 (11 March 1624); Thomas Pierson to

Rule' appeared to be a further vindication of the belief that the crown was hostile towards Parliament. During the debates in the Short Parliament Sir Benjamin Rudyerd, who was one of those MPs who was particularly sensitive to this issue, warned: 'let us beware of having the race of Parliaments rooted out'.[4]

King Charles' determination to rule without Parliament during the 1630s left such an obvious gap in the traditional political process that many people would have agreed with Pym's assertion to the same Parliament that 'the intermission of Parliaments have been a true cause of all these evils to the commonwealth, which by the law should be once every year'. Although statutes dating from the reign of Edward III did provide for annual Parliaments, it was not expected that they should meet so frequently, but nor was it anticipated that a whole decade should pass without an assembly. In the early 1630s the Harleys prayed for 'a happy meeting in Parliament', and later the war against Scotland caused widespread speculation that a Parliament would be called both to fund and to endorse the war. The absence of Parliaments in the 1630s robs us of an important source of knowledge about Sir Robert's political and religious attitudes, but the relative lack of evidence can be further overcome by examining Sir Robert's role as one of a group of Herefordshire governors called upon to execute contentious policies during Charles I's reign. The county's response to the forced loan, the collection of ship money and the prosecution of the war against the Scots is particularly revealing. In examining these issues we can trace the ways in which local governors could show disapproval of royal policies without open resistance. The frustrations of the county magnates in their attempts to accommodate the wishes of both the crown and their local community are also increasingly apparent and reached an unprecedented level in the summer and autumn of 1640, when the drive to defeat the Scottish Covenanters reached its peak. Not only were local communities expected to provide an army to fight the war, they were also forced to make payments of ship money and were charged with a further bewildering array of military levies including 'army money, waggon money, horse money, conduct money', as a disgruntled petition from Northamptonshire complained to the Short Parliament.[5] The need to finance the

Harley, 24 March 1625/6, BL Loan 29/121; M. Kishlansky, *Parliamentary Selection: Social and Political Choice in Early Modern England* (Cambridge, 1986), 23–31.

[4] J. S. Levy, 'Why Was it Feared That Parliament Might be in Danger of Extinction Between 1610 and 1614?', unpublished paper; Cust, *Forced Loan*, 68, 152–62, 305; Cope and Coates, *Proceedings of the Short Parliament*, 140. Rudyerd was responsible for the famous speech of 1628 in which he declared, 'this is the crisis of Parliaments; we shall know by this whether Parliaments live or die', cited in Russell, *Crisis of Parliaments*, 299.

[5] Cope and Coates, *Proceedings of the Short Parliament*, 155 (the editors of this work cite 4 Edw. III, c.14 and 36 Edw. III, c.10, as the relevant statutes); lists of prayers dated 22 February 1632/3 and 12 April 1633; and 24 January 1633/4, BL Loan 29/27 part 1; Cope, *Politics Without Parliaments*, 178; *CSPD 1640*, 7.

war against Scotland was the decisive factor which induced the King to call Parliament in the spring of 1640, but the session was abruptly terminated after three weeks when it became obvious that the grant of subsidies would not go ahead without lengthy discussion of the accumulated grievances of the 'Personal Rule' of the previous eleven years. The debates did, however, outline a plan of reform which would be undertaken more thoroughly by the Long Parliament in an attempt to uncover the links between arbitrary taxation, religious changes and a descent into tyranny, which critics of the royal government firmly traced to the start of the reign of Charles I.

SIR ROBERT HARLEY'S PARLIAMENTARY CAREER, 1604–1629

Sir Robert Harley's first experience as an MP was in the Parliament of 1604–10, where he sat as burgess for the borough of Radnor. As might be expected from a new member, his initial service in Parliament was not overly distinguished. He was clearly interested in the major topics under discussion, including the proposed union between England and Scotland and the Great Contract of 1610, but he rarely joined in the debates.[6] It is also possible that, since he was a new and relatively unknown member, the diarists did not take pains to record Harley's comments. He did not sit in Parliament in either 1614 or 1621 and his absence in those years remains unexplained. Competition for a seat was intense and he may simply have been unable to find a constituency which would accept him. He did, however, play a prominent part in the county election in Herefordshire for the Parliament of 1621. At the end of 1620 Sir Robert circulated members of the leading local gentry asking them to delay giving their support to any candidate for the county seats 'till we shall meet to deliberate and resolve of the fittest for that service, wherein I desire that neither faction nor affection, but discretion and true understanding may point us out the men'. As this letter indicates, the election was not a simple matter to be decided at the polls by the electors. It was subject to negotiation and power-broking amongst the local elite, who commanded the votes of tenants, clients and other dependents. Most candidates were elected unopposed, because any potential rivals had already been persuaded to withdraw and a contested election was undesirable, since it meant the public rejection of one or more candidates and a subsequent loss of esteem for those who had failed to be returned. A disputed election could also lead to a public

---

[6] Harley was a member of the committee appointed on 14 April 1604 to consult with members of the House of Lords about the union and he spoke on the subject of the Great Contract on 20 July 1610: see *CJ*, I, 172, 453. There are copies of the main parliamentary speeches concerning the union in 1607, and of the debates of 5 and 6 November 1610 concerning the Great Contract, among Harley's papers: BL Loan 29/202 ff.93r–107r, 49r–72r, 75r–86r. I would, however, query the assertion made by D. H. Willson and E. Foster that some of these notes are in Harley's hand: see Levy, 'Thesis', 72 n.96; for Harley's interest in the Great Contract see also a draft letter to Sir Edward Herbert from Harley,

rift amongst the gentry and even to violence amongst their rival groups of supporters.[7]

At this date Sir Robert was probably not putting himself forward as a candidate, for he was not yet in a position to challenge the predominance of the leading county families. He was, however, taking a prominent role in orchestrating the choice of representatives, doubtless in the hope that this would help his prospects of sitting for the county in the future. Following the despatch of his letter, Harley and eighteen other prominent Herefordshire gentlemen, including Sir John Scudamore (the later Viscount) and Fitzwilliam Coningsby, met at Hereford. Here they signed a document in which they agreed that whenever an election was held they would meet in advance 'to point out two fit men to be proposed to the freeholders of the same county to elect if they please to approve of them'. The leading gentry would thus effectively decide the outcome of the county elections in advance. There was nothing to stop other candidates putting themselves forward, but if they did not have the backing of the majority of the local magnates then they would have little chance of success. Such prior selection was a system which worked along similar lines in other English counties, including Shropshire, Dorset and Cheshire.[8] It was based both on the county gentry's shared assumptions about their roles as the natural leaders of local society and on their distaste for election contests. The Herefordshire agreement seems to have remained in force at least until October 1640, when Harley informed the Earl of Essex that he and Fitzwilliam Coningsby had

been invited by divers gentlemen of the best quality in this county to stand to be knights for this shire at the next Parliament, the knowledge whereof we understand ourselves much obliged to represent to your lordship, in reference to the great interest your lordship hath in Herefordshire, and our humble thankfulness for your lordship's former favours, well knowing what lustre your lordship's approbation would put upon us, and what eclipse we should suffer without it in that employment.

Herefordshire was without a resident peer and the Earl's landholdings there gave him some influence within the county. His endorsement was thus desirable, but clearly secondary to the choice of the local magnates.[9]

    undated, BL Loan 29/119; for an assessment of Harley's role in the 1604–10 Parliament see W. Notestein, *The House of Commons 1604–1610* (New Haven, 1971), 2, 315–17, 424; and D. R. L. Adams, 'The Parliamentary Representation of Radnor, 1536–1832' (Wales MA Thesis, 1970), 548.

[7] Lewis, *Letters of the Lady Brilliana Harley*, xliii–xliv (these letters are undated, but internal evidence clearly indicates that they relate to the 1621 Parliament); D. Hirst, *The Representative of the People? Voters and Voting in England Under the Early Stuarts* (Cambridge, 1975), 109–31; Kishlansky, *Parliamentary Selection*, 9–21.

[8] Folger Library, Scudamore Mss., Vb2 (21); Thomas Pierson to Harley, 16 February 1627/8, BL Loan 29/202 f.237r; Kishlansky, *Parliamentary Selection*, 27.

[9] Hirst, *Representative of the People?*, 15; Draft letter from Harley and Fitzwilliam Coningsby to Essex, 9 October 1640, BL Loan 29/172 f.300r.

In 1621 Sir John Scudamore and Fitzwilliam Coningsby were returned to Parliament as the knights of the shire. In the subsequent Parliament of 1624 Harley made a remarkable breakthrough when he was returned as junior knight for Herefordshire with Sir John Scudamore as his senior partner. Sir Robert had been able to break the traditional hegemony of the Crofts and the Coningsbys, partly because of Sir Herbert Croft's much publicised conversion to catholicism in 1617 and partly because of Sir Robert's own marriage to Brilliana Conway in 1623.[10] As a result of this union Sir Robert had assumed full control of his father's Brampton estate, making him one of the wealthiest gentlemen in the county. His acquisition of a powerful court patron in the person of his father-in-law, Secretary Conway, had further enhanced his local influence, but it is unlikely that Conway had intervened directly in the election. The selection of county Herefordshire representatives lay firmly in the hands of the gentry elite, as the agreement of 1620 suggests. In 1625, however, there is once again an unexplained gap in Harley's parliamentary service, but in 1626 he was returned as senior knight for Herefordshire for the first time. In 1628 Harley sat for the borough of Evesham in Worcestershire and on this occasion his father-in-law played a documented role. Conway had himself represented Evesham in 1621 and 1624, and in 1628 wrote directly to the borough requesting that they return Harley as their burgess.[11]

During the 1620s Sir Robert emerged more confidently as a 'Parliament man'. He was now linked to the court as the son-in-law of Secretary Conway, and in 1626 became a holder of court office himself as Master of the Mint. Sir Robert also acted as Secretary Conway's aide in the Commons, even to the extent of trying to shield Conway's patron, the Duke of Buckingham, against impeachment in 1626 and against parliamentary censure in 1628. At first sight Buckingham appears to have been an unlikely candidate for Sir Robert's political support, but the Duke had previously cultivated a wide group of clients including puritans. His clientage had narrowed after the accession of Charles, when Buckingham realised that the new King favoured the religious leanings of men like Laud and Neile. The York House conference of 1626 clearly revealed the Duke as a promoter of the Arminians, and he had well-known connections with the English catholics, his own mother being an open professor of the old faith.[12] Sir Robert may perhaps have hoped that the Duke would reverse his policy and return to a broader-based patronage, and it was

---

[10] Williams, *Parliamentary History of the County of Hereford*, 41–4; PRO SP14/93/129; Ham, *The County and the Kingdom*, 279.

[11] Lease, 6 May 1623, Brampton Bryan, Harley Mss., Bundle 83; Folger Library, Scudamore Mss., Vb2 (21); *Return of the Names of Every Member*, 469, 479; R. E. Ruigh, *The Parliament of 1624* (Cambridge, Mass., 1971), 85, 135–6; *Return of the Names of Every Member*, 454, 461; PRO SP16/93/32.

[12] Lockyer, *Buckingham*, 306–8, 468–9.

clearly the royal favourite's support for a war to recover the Palatinate which was the crucial factor that drew Harley into his clique. Sir Robert's backing for the Duke was, in fact, highly guarded and not totally uncritical and it is almost certain that Harley regarded his primary allegiance as lying with Conway.

As Secretary of State, Conway was sometimes with the King and unable to attend Parliament in person and he relied on Harley, amongst others, to keep him informed about debates in the House, as a letter to Harley, dated from Windsor on 29 April 1624 reveals. 'I pray you,' wrote Conway, 'if you be upon any royal points in Parliament, or have passed any, either concerning the subsidies or otherwise, to give me an accompt thereof, that I may labour to dispose humours, and make such answers as shall be most requisite.' Harley noted three points on the back of Conway's letter. First, the insertion of the names of the council of war in the subsidy act; secondly, that the session should not end before the passage of 'our good bills' nor should it be delayed, because then the levy of subsidies might suffer; thirdly, the House desired the expedition of a proclamation to banish Jesuits.[13]

When Conway was elevated to the peerage in March 1625 he had all the more need of an ally in the Commons to keep him abreast of developments there. Harley was also a useful advocate for policies supported by Conway, particularly the prevention of attacks on the Duke of Buckingham in 1626 and 1628, and the grant of taxation in the same parliaments. As Lord Admiral the Duke was held responsible in the 1626 Parliament for the decision to allow France to use English merchant ships against the Protestant stronghold at La Rochelle and the bungled expedition against Cadiz, which had failed to engage the enemy. His opponents in the Lords and Commons used these failures to launch a sweeping condemnation of the Duke, which culminated in an attempted impeachment.[14] Within the Commons Sir Robert Harley was one of Buckingham's most energetic defenders and repeatedly tried to divert the opposition led by Sir John Eliot, a former Buckingham man. On one occasion Harley urged the Commons to consider that the danger from both English and continental catholics was a more pressing matter than the miscalculations of the Duke: 'to fight with two kinds of enemies, within the kingdom and without. Not to dispute at the errors past'. A few days later Sir Robert urged the Commons not to blame Buckingham, but to set about considering what remedies could cure the ills of the kingdom. His words were, however, both ambiguous and barbed, suggesting that Harley was highly critical of the conduct of the court under King Charles, and his speech contained the warning that Buckingham could only be protected if he was

[13] Conway to Harley, 29 April 1624, BL Loan 29/202 ff.122r, 123v.
[14] Lockyer, *Buckingham*, 281–331; G. C. E. Tite, *Impeachment and Parliamentary Judicature in Early Stuart England* (1974), 178–220.

able to prosecute the war successfully: 'we have neither lost honour, liberty, seas. The effeminateness of this kingdom and riotous excess the greatest cause. Single council not to be condemned if it have success. It depend upon success. That we should make haste to our remedies and call for an accompt.'[15]

In 1628 Harley, along with Sir Benjamin Rudyerd and Sir James Perrott, spoke against naming the Duke in the Remonstrance listing the grievances to be presented to the King. In these debates Harley did not attempt to exonerate the Duke, but tried to deter the House from taking extreme action against him, openly declaring: 'I stand not up to acquit him, but only that we do not name his name. Let us make him an instrument of good to the commonwealth.' In protecting Buckingham it is clear that Harley was not acting directly as the Duke's client, but rather on behalf of Conway, who was anxious to help his patron. The complex hierarchical structure of such patronage relationships is revealed by the course of the supply debates during an earlier Parliament. In 1624 Conway had urged the Commons to abandon their demand that the King should declare war on Spain before they would grant him any subsidies. The King was adamantly opposed to any grant of subsidies being conditional on a declaration of war and in this instance Conway was acting as a mouthpiece for King James, as would be expected of the Secretary of State. It would come as no surprise if Sir Robert had supported Conway in the Commons, but in fact Harley was one of the most vociferous advocates of the contrary policy, which was also favoured by Prince Charles and the Duke of Buckingham. Here Sir Robert was almost certainly acting on behalf of Conway, who was in no position to support his own patron directly in the House.[16]

Sir Robert's actions in 1624 contrast strongly with his behaviour in subsequent Parliaments, when he adopted the opposite line and tried to persuade his fellow MPs not to attach any conditions to the grant of money. Once again this seems to be a reflection of Harley's relationship with Conway. As a principal servant of the crown one of Conway's chief concerns in Parliaments was the need to expedite grants of subsidies, which in 1624 he referred to as 'the wheel [which] must move all'. Thus in 1626 Sir Robert spoke out against making the grant of subsidies conditional upon redress of grievances and he advocated that the subsidy bill should be passed at the same time that the Commons presented their grievances to the King. In 1628 Sir Robert again tried to speed up the subsidy bill and on 28 April he called for

---

[15] For Eliot see Russell, *Parliaments and English Politics*, 278–309, *passim*; Whitelocke Diary, 24 February, 28 February, 16 March, 27 March, 2 May 1626; Grosvenor Diary, 2 May, 4 May 1626.

[16] *1628 Debates*, 247–8; Russell, *Parliaments and English Politics*, 177–8; Spring Diary, 11 March, 19 March 1624; *CJ*, I, 733, 742.

the report of the bill from committee in order to 'endear his Majesty to us'. On 3 June he declared that the King would accept their Remonstrance of grievances if it was framed in the right manner, proposing that the preamble should begin, 'Sir, we will supply you'. In the subsequent session of 1629 Sir Robert called for the reading of the tonnage and poundage bill, 'because the King has sent for it'. This was a particularly sensitive issue, because in Charles' first Parliament the Commons had voted that the King be allowed to collect tonnage and poundage for one year only, instead of the traditional grant for life.[17]

The close nature of the relationship between Conway and Harley was recognised by others, who used Harley as an avenue of approach to the Secretary. In 1624 the Cheshire puritan John Bruen asked Harley to persuade Conway to present a petition on behalf of two Cheshire justices who had received an 'affront' because of their zeal for the 'reformation of profanations'. In the same year Sir Robert Heath, the Solicitor General, wrote twice to Harley asking him to secure Conway's approval for a bill to ban the import of Spanish tobacco and for a letter to the Eastland merchants concerning the import of foreign ashes for the manufacture of soap. In 1627 Sir Henry Marten approached Harley and asked him to use either his own influence or that of Lord Conway to gain permission for a book by Stephen Dennison to be dedicated to the King.[18] Sir Robert's position as a client and close relative of Conway should not be read as evidence that he only acted on Conway's business in the Commons. His commitment to war against Spain and his speeches concerning religion give ample evidence of Harley's freedom of thought in the House. A further example is provided by his insistence in 1626 that the imprisonment of Sir Dudley Digges and Sir John Eliot for their speeches against Buckingham touched the 'liberties of the House'. On that occasion Harley boldly demanded that the King should inform the House of the reasons for the arrests.[19]

During the 1620s Sir Robert's support for an aggressive policy of war against Spain in order to recover the Palatinate from catholic hands was dictated almost entirely by his religious convictions. In 1620 he had been active in raising money in Herefordshire to pay for the cost of the volunteer force raised to serve under Sir Horace Vere and in 1624 he was drawn into the circle of pro-war advocates in Parliament headed by Buckingham. The Duke's policy had attracted a disparate group whose motivations were varied

[17] Nicholas Diary, 1 May 1624; Whitelocke Diary, 27 March 1626; *1628 Debates*, III, 130, 139; IV, 65; Notestein and Relf, *Commons Debates for 1629*, 108; Gardiner, *History of England, 1603–1642*, V, 364–5.
[18] John Bruen to Harley, 10 September 1624, BL Loan 29/202 f.138r; PRO SP14/165/5, 167/46; Sir Henry Marten to Harley, 11 April 1627, BL Loan 29/202 bound between ff.211 and 223.
[19] Grosvenor Diary, 12 May, 17 May 1626.

and were not based solely on the religious ideals exhibited by Harley. Sir Dudley Digges, for example, possibly hoped that by supporting a war he could establish himself as a client of the Prince of Wales, and Sir Edwin Sandys, as a member of the Virginia company, may have had economic reasons for wanting war. Secretary Conway was another prominent member of this grouping and his approach to the war was more consciously guided by *raison d'état*, for he was disturbed by the strategic implications of the spread of Spanish influence in Europe.[20] Harley, however, viewed the war more consciously as a struggle to preserve English protestantism against a major religious enemy. When a joint committee of the two Houses drew up a list of reasons for terminating diplomatic discussions with Spain, Harley brusquely complained that the principal reason for the breach with Spain, the need to maintain the security of English protestantism, had been omitted: 'the main thing left out – the maintenance of our religion at home'. In his diary of proceedings in this debate Sir William Spring noted:

some would have had religion put in, and laboured much that it being the principal motive it ought not to be omitted, but answer was made that these reasons being perhaps to be published for satisfaction of the christian world, it was not fit to publish anything that should cause it to be said that the war (if a war must follow) was in any respect for religion. This was allowed of, and was that thing for which the King afterwards gave thanks to the committee that went to him to Theobalds.

Spring clearly states that the omission was designed to make the resolution acceptable to the King, and apart from Sir Robert's outburst there was little opposition to this formulation in either the Commons or the Lords.[21]

Sir Robert's speeches in the Parliaments of the 1620s consistently reveal his deeply felt anti-catholicism, which also led him to speak against the English Arminians in the sessions of 1628 and 1629. At the start of the 1624 Parliament Sir Robert had supported Sir John Jephson's demand for a 'guard for our persons' to be supplied by the Mayor of London to deter any catholic plot against Parliament. Distrust of the native catholic population had been fuelled by the proposals for war against Spain and by rumours that if the Prince of Wales married a catholic princess the laws against Roman catholics would be suspended.[22] In the Commons, during the debates whether England

---

[20] For the financing of the volunteer force see S. L. Adams, 'Thesis', 294–303; Harley was actively engaged in collecting money for the force: see his papers dated June to November 1620, BL Loan 29/202 ff.3–46 *passim* and lists of contributions; and Baron Dohna to the county of Hereford, 4 June 1620, BL Loan 29/123/36; Russell, *Parliaments and English Politics*, 168–71; T. Birch, *The Life of Prince Henry of Wales* (Dublin, 1760), 389–90. Harley himself joined the Virginia Company with the holding of one share in February 1623: S. M. Kingsbury, ed., *The Records of the Virginia Company of London*, II, (1906), 243.

[21] Spring Diary, 1 March 1624; *CJ*, I, 729; Spring Diary, 5 March 1624.

[22] Nicholas Diary, 26 February 1624.

should join the continental war against Spain, many MPs voiced the commonly held belief that English catholics would support an invasion by a foreign catholic power. When the House first considered the breach of the negotiations with Spain about the marriage treaty and the recovery of the Palatinate, Sir John Strangeways suggested that 'all the great papists should be confined, for the Spanish will for matter of invasions rely on the papists here'. Later in the course of the debate Sir Robert also drew attention of the dangers from English catholics at a time when war was being planned against the continental catholic powers. He insisted that the King would have to break off all diplomatic negotiations with Spain, especially if England were to retain the alliance of the Dutch:

> Sir Robert Harley moves consideration of our foreign enemies to be great, but those at home much more, who lie in our bosoms and are not distinguished or known of us, but are familiar and conversant in all companies and councils; shews that it is impossible that the King can break off the treaty of the marriage and continue that for the Palatinate, that it must join with the other, and that the care and ease of the King's grandchildren does concern us chiefly; that it is high time to make sure with the Hollander, who wants not offers and will assuredly join with support and friends elsewhere, if they should be still made jealous of us by continuing the treaties, either of them.

Fears that the native catholics would support a foreign invasion have been characterised as 'a long-standing habit among those who remembered Elizabeth's reign'. Sir Robert was certainly old enough to remember the Spanish Armada; he had also been a Member of Parliament in November 1605 when the Gunpowder Plot had been uncovered, and at their prayer meetings the Harleys regularly gave thanks to God for England's deliverance from these two major offensives against the protestant cause.[23]

Sir Robert, together with other influential speakers such as John Pym and Sir Robert Phelips, was often able to summarise the views of the House of Commons on religion in succinct fashion, and his speeches on this topic were generally well heeded. At the start of April 1624, for example, he called for strict and specific measures to be taken against the English catholics: 'that the recusants may be disarmed and confined, that Jesuits and all seminaries to be banished and the receivers of them to be had under the law. For such as resort to ambassadors, that the law may be inflicted upon them not only in this, but that their revenues be employed for the wars.' Most of the points raised by Harley in this speech were incorporated into a petition from the Houses to King James on 23 April, which prompted the King to issue a proclamation banishing Jesuits and seminary priests a few days later. James also promised

---

[23] Nicholas Diary, 1 March 1624; Spring Diary, 1 March 1624; Russell, *Parliaments and English Politics*, 82; *Return of the Names of Every Member*, 448; for the lists of prayers see below, n.47.

to execute all laws against recusants and to take suitable action against catholics attending mass at the homes of catholic ambassadors.[24] The King was, however, still being pressed by the French to make concessions to his catholic subjects and before the year was out he and the Prince had given a secret undertaking to the French to release the English catholics from persecution. Subsequent royal policy on the matter of anti-catholic legislation was both clumsy and contradictory. At the start of his reign King Charles ordered the suspension of the penal laws against the catholics, but the arrival of Princess Henrietta Maria and her household in England in the summer of 1625 and the escalation of preparations for war against Spain coincided to produce a wave of anti-catholic feeling in the Parliament of that year. In response the King rapidly withdrew his protection of the catholics and agreed that the laws should be executed against them.[25]

Sir Robert did not attend that Parliament, but in 1626 he expressed his opinion to the House that the 'growth of popery' be included as one of the grievances of the kingdom to be presented to the King, a subject to which he returned in the Long Parliament.[26] This was a period when the influence of the Arminians was also seen to be growing in England, and Sir Robert was one of the small but vociferous group of MPs who linked the dangers of catholicism with the spread of Arminianism. In 1626 he joined in the Commons' attempts to censor the writing of Richard Montagu, one of the most notorious of the Arminian clergy, and suggested that the King should prevent Montagu publishing anything while he was under investigation by the House. In 1628 Harley went onto the offensive and named four more Arminian theologians in the House, demanding that their writings should also be scrutinised:

I will add another to Montagu, no less dangerous. 'Tis one Dr Jackson. They would introduce popery. They pretend they are the reformed religion and Church of England. They do introduce a supremacy. They are possessed of churches amongst us. The new way is to bring in popery. Let there be a committee named to consider of the books of Cosin, Sibthorpe and Manwaring.[27]

Harley's attack had been in preparation well before the opening of the session in March 1628. In the previous February he had written to his rector at

[24] Spring Diary, 2 April 1624; PRO SP14/159/32, 34; a proclamation was issued on 6 May 1624 banishing Jesuits and seminary priests: see J. F. Larkin and P. L. Hughes, eds., *Stuart Royal Proclamations: Royal Proclamations of King James I, 1603–1625* (Oxford, 1973), 591–3.
[25] Lockyer, *Buckingham*, 209; PRO SP16/2/1; Russell, *Parliaments and English Politics*, 207–12; Gardiner, *History of England, 1603–1642*, VI, 32–3.
[26] Whitelocke Diary, 27 February, 1626; *D'Ewes (N)*, 91. For Harley's attitude towards the catholics in the Long Parliament see below, pp. 119–22.
[27] Russell, *Parliaments and English Politics*, 29–32; Dr Tyacke has identified Harley as one of a group of 31 'anti-Arminian activists' who spoke in the Commons on doctrinal subjects between 1624 and 1629, and concludes that it was 'largely those with a late Elizabethan university experience who defended a Calvinist interpretation of the thirty-nine articles': N.

Brampton, Thomas Pierson, asking for his opinion of a work by Thomas Jackson, a royal chaplain and protégé of Archbishop Neile. At the end of that month Sir Robert held a prayer meeting at his London lodgings in Aldermanbury, where he prayed 'for the Churches of Great Britain, and the gospel, in one purity and against sects'; in the margin of this list of prayers he noted 'popery' and 'Arminianism'.[28]

Fears that there might be a change in the established religion were quickly linked to the spectre of arbitrary government in debates in the House. The Petition of Right, which was delivered to the King at the end of May 1628, was an initial attempt to address the issue raised by the forced loan and by the disastrous policy which had led to war against the two greater continental catholic powers, Spain and France. Enforcement of the loan had led to the confinement of refusers and the infamous Five Knights case, in which five prominent opponents of the loan had been unable to obtain release from imprisonment 'by his Majesty's special commandment'. The loan itself had been intended to raise revenue for the war, which had culminated in the failure of the 1627 expedition to the Isle de Rhe intended to relieve the Huguenots, in which at least 5,000 Englishmen had perished. The Petition thus denounced both arbitrary taxation and arbitrary imprisonment, as well as forbidding compulsory billeting.[29]

The King's first reply to the Petition was regarded by the Commons as inadequate, and Sir John Eliot moved that they should embody their grievances in a Remonstrance, which was presented to King Charles two weeks later. This was a far-ranging document, which dwelt at length on the 'subversion of religion' at the hands of both catholics and Arminians, linking this to the 'innovation and change of government' evidenced by the forced loan, and the employment of foreign mercenaries who 'may unite with the popish party at home if occasion serve, or join with an invading enemy to do extreme mischief'. The links between innovation in religion and oppression of the subject had first been raised in the Remonstrance debates on 5 June by Christopher Sherland in censuring the Arminians who 'run in a string with the papists and flatter greatness to oppress the subject'. Hampden had followed in joining 'an innovation of religion suspected' with 'alteration of government' and asked 'can you forbear when it goes no less than the subversion of the whole state?' Sir Robert Harley was present during this

---

Tyacke, 'Arminianism in England, in Religion and Politics, 1604–40' (Oxford University, D.Phil. Thesis, 1968), 168–9; Whitelocke Diary, 17 April 1626; *1628 Debates*, II, 86.

[28] Thomas Pierson to Harley, 16 February 1627/8, BL. Loan 29/202 f.237r; list of prayers, 30 March 1627 and 29 February 1627/8, BL. Loan 29/202 f.238r–v. For Jackson see *DNB*, X, 544–5.

[29] Cust, *Forced Loan*, 58–62; Lockyer, *Buckingham*, 401; the Petition of Right is printed in Gardiner, *The Constitutional Documents of the Puritan Revolution: 1625–1660* (Oxford, 1968), 66–70.

debate and followed the arguments put forward. The next day he called for the Remonstrance to proceed and itemised the heads of their grievances which had been hammered out the previous day: 'yesterday we collected divers heads and named a subcommittee. Moved to have those heads read and, where we like not, we may alter. The heads: fear of

1 Innovation of religion.
2 Innovation of government.
3 Disasters in all our designs abroad.
4 Causes of all these.'[30]

Although religious disputes were clearly stirring up discontent against royal policies and were being linked to politically sensitive debates about the extent of the royal prerogative, the Commons' attack on the Arminians went unheeded by the crown. After the prorogation of Parliament at the end of June, Montagu was appointed Bishop of Chichester. Roger Manwaring, a royal chaplain, who had been impeached by Parliament for preaching in favour of the forced loan and stood accused of trying 'to infuse into the conscience of his majesty the persuasion of a power not bounding itself with law', was granted a royal pardon and presented with the living of Stanford Rivers by the King. Robert Sibthorpe, another pro-loan preacher, was made a royal chaplain and was included in Manwaring's pardon to prevent future action being taken against him. In 1629 the parliamentary assault on the Arminians was renewed with vigour and Sir Robert was in the vanguard of the attack. At the start of the session he called for a public declaration by the Commons of their religion and a Remonstrance to be presented to the King asking once again for the punishment of the Arminian apologists. During the course of this debate Sir Robert outlined what he called 'our religion' in the following terms: 'the articles made in 1562 in Queen Elizabeth's time, the articles made at Lambeth, the articles in Ireland. King James also by his wisdom and pen in the Synod of Dort being solely guided by our example'.[31]

Archbishop Whitgift's Lambeth Articles of 1595 had never been officially adopted by the Church, but they supported the Calvinist position on predestination much more clearly than the 39 Articles. The same was true of the Articles of the Irish Church promulgated in 1615 and the declaration of the Synod of Dort, which King James had approved in 1619. Harley's insistence that 'our' religion was based not only on the 39 Articles, but also on these subsequent definitions, was incorporated into the resolutions drawn up by a sub-committee for religion on 24 February 1629, which have been described by Professor Kenyon as 'the most extreme pronouncement on religion made by the Commons during this period'. A week later the

[30] Russell, *Parliaments and English Politics*, 377; *1628 Debates*, IV, 120, 121, 155, 311–17.
[31] *DNB*, XIII, 715; XII, 989; XVIII, 192; Notestein and Relf, eds., *Commons Debates for 1629*, 116.

Parliament was dissolved after the dramatic scenes involving the forcible detention of Speaker Finch in the chamber and the reading by Sir John Eliot of the Commons' Protestation, which denounced 'innovation in religion' and the collection of tonnage and poundage without the consent of Parliament.[32]

The subsequent abeyance of Parliaments until 1640 removed a focus of contact between the court and individuals who were influential in their local communities. Men who had previously served in Parliament were also cut off from a source of local prestige for over a decade. For the Harleys this loss was compounded by the death of their major court connection, Viscount Conway, in 1631 and by Sir Robert's removal from office as Master of the Mint in 1635.[33] There is thus a world of difference in Sir Robert's confident assertion in a draft letter to Conway written from the Mint in early June 1627 that 'to begin with news were to play my city part' and his plea to George Rawdon in 1636: 'if you will make me partake of your news at court, you know how much it will make a country gentleman beholding to you'. In describing himself as a 'country gentleman', Harley was drawing on a wealth of imagery which at its simplest level contrasted the purity of the 'country' with the corruption of the 'court', but which also encompassed complex ideologies about politics and right religion.[34] By the latter half of the 1630s Sir Robert clearly no longer identified himself with the court and its interests. His personal sense of isolation from the court was undoubtedly reinforced by royal policies which the local gentry in general found to be both extremely cumbersome and highly unpopular in their execution.

THE HARLEYS, HEREFORDSHIRE AND REACTIONS TO THE PERSONAL RULE

During the 1630s King Charles was able to govern without Parliament because he embarked on a policy of peace and because of the drive in the 1630s to further exploit extra-parliamentary sources of revenue. Peace had been concluded with France in April 1629 and the war with Spain was terminated some eighteen months later. This relieved the tensions caused by billeting and reduced government expenditure, but the deficit caused by the wars still had to be met. The solution lay in such measures as distraint of knighthood (fining those who were eligible for, but had failed to take up, the

---

[32] Russell, *Crisis of Parliaments*, 211–12; J. P. Kenyon, *The Stuart Constitution, 1603–1688, Documents and Commentary* (Cambridge, 1973), 149; Russell, *Parliaments and English Politics*, 415–16; the Resolutions on religion and the Protestation are printed in Gardiner, *Constitutional Documents*, 77–83.

[33] *CSPD 1629–1631*, 495; *CSPD 1636–1637*, 445; for the history of Harley's career as Master of the Mint, see chapter 1, n.16 above.

[34] Harley to Viscount Conway, June 1627, BL Loan 29/27 part 1; PRO SP16/319/48; for the debate on 'court' and 'country' see chapter 1, n.28 above.

order of knighthood), the revival of forest fines and, most notoriously, because it affected the largest number of individuals, the collection of ship money from 1634 onwards. Resort to extra-parliamentary revenue was by no means new to the 1630s; what was new was the level of such taxation, which had been heralded by the experiments with the free gift, a benevolence and the forced loan all within the space of a few months at the start of Charles' reign. Such measures were invariably met with a certain measure of obduracy combined with pleas to be allowed 'to give in a parliamentary course', as Lord Saye had said in response to King James' demand in 1622 for a benevolence to pay for the recovery of the Palatinate.[35] On that occasion the Herefordshire magistrates, including Sir Robert Harley, had informed the privy council that local people were both unable and unwilling 'to answer your lordships' expectation in this way'. This lack of co-operation contrasts sharply with Sir Robert Harley's energetic efforts in 1620 to collect voluntary donations for the same cause. In a second letter about the benevolence in 1622, the Herefordshire justices made clear their preference for parliamentary taxation and described themselves as being

not a little grieved to understand from your lordships that his Majesty's great and important occasions found not supply more answerable to his Majesty's expectation in Parliament, the way of our desires, wherein we shall be always ready to supply his Majesty to the uttermost of our abilities, as any of our ancestors ever were his Majesty's most royal progenitors.[36]

It is difficult to interpret the exact beliefs which lay behind such protests. Calls for parliamentary taxation could perhaps indicate a principled and constitutionally based preference for raising revenue with the consent of a representative body, and this explanation cannot be lightly dismissed. At the same time they were clearly part of a conscious delaying process, which gave local governors a bargaining counter to use against the central authorities. In their letter, the Herefordshire JPs tactfully refused to supply a list of those who had refused to contribute to the benevolence. Doubtless they hoped that the council would accept the county's contribution without taking the matter further.[37] Similar delaying tactics were employed in Herefordshire at the start of the new reign in response to both the free gift and the forced loan. In October 1625 the county's lord lieutenant, the Earl of Northampton, wrote to his deputies and to the Herefordshire justices asking them to supply a list of

---

[35] Cope, *Politics Without Parliaments*, 21; Morrill, *Revolt of the Provinces*, 27; Cust, *Forced Loan*, 2; Saye is quoted in M. L. Schwarz, 'Lord Saye and Sele's Objections to the Palatinate Benevolence of 1622: Some New Evidence and its Significance', *Albion*, IV (1972), 16.

[36] PRO SP14/130/34, 132/40.

[37] Cust, *Forced Loan*, 153–64, 7; PRO SP14/132/40; in Oxfordshire Lord Saye thought that 'the requiring of the names of those that would not give . . . might be taken for a kind of pressing': cited in Schwartz, 'Lord Saye and Sele's Objections to the Palatinate Benevolence of 1622', 15–16.

those able to loan money to the King and the amounts they could pay. The Earl's letter went unheeded and a little less than two months later one of his deputies, John Rudhall, informed Sir John Scudamore of Holme Lacy that 'in the business of the privy seals we have done nothing, but left every man to make his own excuse'.[38] Northampton fired off a second letter and received a reply at the start of January 1626 from a number of Herefordshire magnates, including Sir Robert, who argued that the King's original instructions related solely to Wales. On this occasion dilatory tactics removed the immediate problem. By virtue of his position as Lord President of the Welsh Council, Northampton acted as lord lieutenant in the four English marcher counties and in most of the counties of Wales. With the privy council breathing down his neck for information from so many counties the Earl simply forwarded the Herefordshire letter to the council with a list of names for the county which he had compiled himself. Demands were subsequently sent out under the privy seal and Sir Robert is recorded as being assessed at the sum of £30.[39]

Later that year the crown turned to the expedient of the forced loan in order to raise further revenue. The organisation on this occasion was much more efficient than that for the free gift. Commissioners were named in each county and the Earl of Northampton himself appointed a meeting of the Herefordshire commissioners, which he attended with Sir John Bridgeman, Chief Justice of Chester. Sir Robert Harley was chosen for this service, but he did not attend the meeting with the Earl and there is evidence that less than three weeks later he was in London attending to business at the Mint. His attitude towards the loan is unknown, but he certainly played no active part in its collection, which continued throughout 1627.[40] Dr Cust's research on the forced loan has uncovered a widespread desire amongst local governors to 'steer a course, which, whilst not involving open opposition at the same time avoided indicating any positive approval for the levy', and this seems to have been the strategy adopted by Harley. Moreover, one of the perquisites of the Master of the Mint was freedom from payment of subsidies and other taxes, and Harley was probably not liable to pay the loan either. At least one Mint official, Thomas Knyvett of Ashewellthorpe, did appeal to this privilege in order to claim exemption.[41]

There was constitutional opposition to the loan in other counties, which in some cases was linked to puritanism, but in Herefordshire opposition seems to have centred on financial arguments, the chief of which was the claim that defaulters were unable to pay because they were too poor to do so. The plea of

---

[38] BL. Add. Mss., 11051 f.31r; PRO C115/N2/8523.
[39] BL. Add. Mss., 11051 f.21r; PRO SP16/18/72 (1) and 18/72; PRO E401/2586.
[40] Cust, *Forced Loan*, 99–101; BL. Add. Mss., 11051 f.32r; PRO SP16/54/2(1), 54/28, 56/10.
[41] Cust, *Forced Loan*, 240; Nottingham University Library Mss. Dept., Portland Mss., Welbeck Collection, Pw2 Hy 1(60); Cust. *Forced Loan*, 139.

poverty would also be made by ship money defaulters in Herefordshire in the later 1630s. Inability to pay was the basic argument used in two petitions from the county JPs to the privy council in 1637 and 1638 and in a grand jury petition of 1638. These documents all alluded to the high charges on the county in the form of relief payments to areas hit by the plague. Outbreaks of pestilence had also affected the wool trade with Worcester, 'stopping wholly our commerce there this year', as Sir Robert Harley and his fellow JPs insisted in 1638. Such economic arguments would have been far more palatable to the council than any directly constitutional arguments, and it is not until September 1640 that there is evidence that anyone in Herefordshire challenged the legality of the ship money levies.[42]

Yet behind these assertions lay the realisation of the Herefordshire gentry that they were being called upon by the crown to administer increasingly unenforceable policies and perhaps this, as much as any constitutional argument, helps explain why the Long Parliament embarked upon its monumental platform of reformation. The collection of ship money had started in 1634 and by 1639 its payment was sliding into unmanageable arrears throughout the country. The complaints of sheriffs and their assistants, who were facing intractable problems in their attempts to collect payments, had become a prominent theme in the state papers of 1639 and 1640 as arrears multiplied throughout the country. Only two-thirds of the sum demanded in the 1638 writs was collected, whilst only a fifth of the total was forthcoming in response to the writs of 1639.[43] The onus of assessment and collection lay firmly with the sheriff, who was responsible for any arrears even after his term of office was at an end, and Professor Cope has written of 'the all-consuming nature of dealing with the levy', which faced individual sheriffs such as Sir Thomas Danby in Yorkshire and Sir Peter Temple in Buckinghamshire. In common with officials in other counties, the Herefordshire sheriffs encountered increasing difficulties in collecting ship money as each annual writ went out and even the money that came in was extracted under duress. William Scudamore, the first of the county's ship money sheriffs, complained to the privy council that he had spent ten months assessing the amounts due before he could even begin the levy. Henry Lingen, sheriff in 1638, reported that he had met with opposition from the leading JPs, naming Sir Richard Hopton as the ringleader, although he did not specify the nature of their objections. He later complained that the petition sent to the council

[42] Cust, *Forced Loan, passim*; PRO SP16/73/29, 78/46(1), 79/81, 80/18(1, 2); Lord Saye opposed the loan on constitutional grounds: Schwarz, 'Lord Saye and Sele's Objections to the Palatinate Benevolence of 1622', 18; PRO SP16/376/133, 407/42; Nottingham CRO, Portland Mss., DD.4P 68/12; PRO SP16/466/77.

[43] Gordon, 'The Collection of Ship-Money in the Reign of Charles I', 141–62; see also M. A. Faraday, 'Ship Money in Herefordshire', *TWNFC*, XLI (1974), 219–29.

from the justices had made people even more backward in paying the tax as they waited for a reply.[44]

Burdensome though it was, the collection of ship money was not the only problem facing local governors immediately before the meeting of the Long Parliament. The war against Scotland was another crucial factor in arousing grievances against the crown amongst the English, for it provoked disapproval for aggression against a fellow protestant nation and also presented the gentry with mounting problems of administration. The conflict started as the direct result of the introduction of the English prayer book into Scotland by royal proclamation in the summer of 1637. Scottish opponents of the book drew up a Covenant at the start of 1638, which bound all who took it to oppose religious innovations 'till they be tried and allowed in free assemblies and in Parliaments'. The subsequent withdrawal of the book and the convention of a Church assembly failed to secure a compromise and both sides resorted to raising an armed force.[45] The religious beliefs of people like the Harleys naturally made them sympathetic to the Calvinist Scots, whom Sir Robert had referred to as 'our brethren of Scotland' in the Commons in May 1628. Lady Brilliana's letters, written in the late 1630s, display a similar sympathy for the Scots and her distaste for the war against them. In May 1639 Lady Brilliana reported the journey of the Marquis of Hamilton into Scotland with 7,000 English soldiers and reflected: 'these things are of the Lord, and as none thought of such a business as this is, so we are ignorant what the issue will be: the Lord give us hearts of depentances [*sic*] upon him'. Following the conclusion of the Treaty of Berwick in June she wrote to Ned Harley of the 'so good news of peace'.[46]

War against protestant Scotland was a complete contradiction of the foreign policies favoured by the Harleys in the 1620s and 1630s, when they saw continental politics as the outcome of the battle between the true Church on the one hand and its foes on the other. At the end of 1624 they had prayed at Brampton Bryan for 'the good estate of God's Church everywhere. The defeating of the plots of all the enemies of it. The distressed Churches of Bohemia, France, the Palatinate, Low Countries. In the King's dominions.' These prayers were repeated during the ensuing decade with some minor variations. In 1627 La Rochelle, Denmark and Germany were included, as well as the conversion of Queen Henrietta Maria. In 1633 the Harleys prayed for 'a worthy general to succeed the King of Sweden', following the death of Gustavus Adolphus at the battle of Lutzen, and at the same time they

[44] Cope, *Politics Without Parliaments*, 108; PRO SP16/407/49, 392/56, 410/23.
[45] G. Donaldson, *Scotland: James V – James VII* (Edinburgh, 1978), 309–28; the Covenant is printed in Gardiner, *Constitutional Documents*, 124–34.
[46] *1628 Debates*, III, 58–9; Lewis, *Letters of the Lady Brilliana Harley*, 51–2, 58–9.

optimistically prayed for the conversion of the King of France.[47] These lists, usually drawn up in Sir Robert's own hand, encapsulate the Harley's view that national and international affairs were dominated by the fight to maintain the protestant religion in the face of the assault of its adversaries. This belief is further reflected in Sir Robert's active support for the English volunteer force sent to the Palatinate in 1620 and by his speeches in the Parliaments of the 1620s, in which he had advocated war against Spain to recover the Palatinate on religious grounds, and repeatedly emphasised the dangers posed by catholics and Arminians at home. Moreover, Sir Robert regarded the struggle for the Palatinate as a manifestation of the final conflict between good and evil. In 1621 he sent the commander of the Palatinate volunteer force, Sir Horace Vere, a tract on the Book of Revelation by Robert Parker, which had been circulating amongst the godly in manuscript form, although it was not published until 1651 at the direction of the Lincolnshire gentleman, Sir John Wray, under the title *The Mystery of the Vialls Opened*. Harley informed Vere that 'I have had it by me many years and, as I take it, the author hath been dead 7 or 8 years and though these times begat it not, yet it may now be best produced wherein God doth seem to fulfil that which it foretells.'[48]

A similarly apocalyptic interpretation of the continental war can be detected in Lady Brilliana's letters to her son Edward, which date from October 1638. In November of that year commenting on the capture of Prince Rupert and the Earl of Craven at the battle of Lingen, she wrote:

in all these things we must remember the warning, which our Saviour has given us, when he told his disciples that there must be wars and rumours of wars . . . great troubles and wars must be, both to purge his Church of hypocrites, and that his enemies at the last may be utterly destroyed, but you my servants be not careful for yourselves, you are my jewels, and the days of trouble are the days when I take care of jewels; and my dear Ned, though I firmly believe there will be great troubles, yet I look with joy beyond those days of trouble, considering the glory that the Lord will bring his Church to; and happy are they that shall live to see it, which I hope you will do.

The Harleys were certainly not alone in their belief that they were experiencing the final phases of the struggle between Christ and Antichrist during the 1602s and 1630s. From the early years of the Reformation English writers began to identify the Pope as Antichrist and to argue that the Book of Revelation foretold the downfall of the catholic Church, which would be

---

[47] Lists of prayers dated 17 December 1624 and 8 June 1625, BL Loan 29/52/93; dated 30 March 1627 and 29 February 1627/8, Loan 29/202 f.238r–v; dated 22 February 1632/3 and 12 April 1633, Loan 29/27 part 1.
[48] Draft letter from Harley to Vere, 14 February 1620/1, BL Loan 29/202 ff.47r–48v; Cliffe, *Puritan Gentry*, 207.

accompanied by the Second Coming of Christ.[49] The Harleys were doubtless familiar with numerous eschatological works and Lady Brilliana was probably referring to the writings of the Scot, John Napier, who had calculated 1639 to be the year in which there would be 'loud threatenings against the antichristian empire', when she wrote in April of that year to Ned with rumours of Reformation in Spain and other news from Germany:

we hear that the King of Spain begins to deal with the monasteries in Spain, as Harry the 8 did in England. My dear Ned, let me upon this put you in mind that this year 1639 is the year in which many are of the opinion that Antichrist must begin to fall. The Lord say amen to it: if this be not the year, yet sure it shall be, in His due time. What news I hear concerning Germany you may see by this enclosed, which I received this morning.

The Scottish war was similarly interpreted by Lady Brilliana as part of a divinely ordained plan. 'If we fight with Scotland', she wrote to Ned at the start of March 1639, 'and are engaged in that war, then a foreign enemy may take his time of advantage. The cause is the Lord's', she concluded, 'and He will work for His own glory.'[50]

In 1639 the recruitment of troops for the Scottish campaign and the exaction of coat and conduct money to pay for them also placed further strain on the creaking local administration, which was already overburdened by the collection of ship money. In March the Herefordshire deputy lieutenants had been ordered to press 200 men to rendezvous at Ashby on 1 April, but at the start of that month Lady Brilliana reported, 'all the lusty men are afraid and hide themself'. In their desperation to avoid the draft some of the pressed men killed their conductor on the road to Ludlow and escaped. Violence against men in authority continued throughout the ensuing year. In October one of the bishop's secretaries was murdered whilst serving a process on a man opposed to the bishop granting what was believed to be common land to the secretary. In January 1640 the under-sheriff was murdered in the course of executing a suit of outlawry, which served to make other local officials nervous about collecting ship money.[51]

In April 1640 there was renewed pressing of men for the war and early in May the pressed men from Herefordshire rioted at Presteigne and almost killed their captain, who was saved by the men of the trained band. It was rumoured that the men had refused to serve under the captain because he was a catholic, and similar mutinies against allegedly catholic officers also took

---

[49] Lewis, *Letters of the Lady Brilliana Harley*, 10; C. Hill, *Antichrist in Seventeenth-Century England* (Oxford, 1971), 1–40; P. G. Lake, 'The Significance of the Elizabethan Identification of the Pope as Antichrist', *Journal of Ecclesiastical History*, XXXI (1980), 161–78.

[50] Lewis, *Letters of the Lady Brilliana Harley*, 41, 30.

[51] *Ibid.*, 37, 38, 44; PRO SP16/466/77; Lewis, *Letters of the Lady Brilliana Harley*, 67; PRO SP16/454/10.

place in Berkshire, Gloucestershire, Wiltshire and Northamptonshire.[52] The fear that catholics were fomenting the war against the Scots had initially been prompted by the plan to use catholic forces from Ireland, Scotland, England and the Continent against the Scots, which had been promoted by the catholics at court in the summer and autumn of 1638 and partially adopted by the King in the following year. In that year a satirical broadside, entitled *Reasons That Ship and Conduct Money Ought to be Paid*, had contended that the war was an attempt to enforce popery on the Scots and that 'captains and lieutenants must be all papists, for none will go but them'; and the Harleys certainly believed that the King was using catholic troops against the Scots.[53] Such crude anti-catholic material echoed the more sophisticated documents produced by the Scots Covenanters themselves, who linked the attempt to introduce English religious observance into Scotland with the rise of Arminianism and tyrannical government across the border.

Increased government measures were taken to censor information from Scotland during the Bishops' Wars. Christopher Hill has noted that 'when the Scottish war came, the government's monopoly control over pulpit and press was used to the fullest extent. All Scottish manifestos were suppressed; but the royal proclamation against the Scots was ordered to be read in all the churches of England'. Despite these moves by the crown, information about the Scottish wars did circulate in England. Edward Lord Montagu had copies of the 'principal acts of the Parliament of the Scots the 11 June 1640', and of the interchanges between the King and the Scots later that summer. Pro-Covenanter documents were also available in London and the Harleys were able to obtain manuscript copies of restricted items.[54] Amongst Sir Robert's papers and endorsed in his own hand is a handwritten copy of one of the Scottish manifestos that the King had tried to have suppressed in England, entitled 'an information to all good christians within the kingdom of England from the noblemen, barons, burroughs, ministers and the kingdom of Scotland for understanding their intentions and actions from the unjust calumnies of their enemies'. The 'information' had been printed in Edinburgh, but it was circulated in manuscript form in England, since this circumvented the orders against printed material from Scotland. The 'information' dwelt in detail on the Arminian innovations in religion which had

---

[52] Lewis, *Letters of the Lady Brilliana Harley*, 95; R. Clifton, 'Fear of Popery', in C. Russell, ed., *The Origins of the English Civil War* (London 1973), 158.

[53] Hibbard, *Charles I and the Popish Plot*, 96, 126; the Harleys certainly believed that Charles was using catholic troops against the Scots: see Lewis, *Letters of the Lady Brilliana Harley*, 31 and young Brilliana to Edward Harley, 24 May 1639, BL Loan 29/172 f.234r.

[54] Hill, *Society and Puritanism*, 43–4; E. S. Cope, *The Life of a Public Man, Edward, First Baron Montagu of Boughton, 1562–1644* (Philadelphia, 1981), 175; Hibbard, *Charles I and the Popish Plot*, 127–8.

already taken place in England and accused the Arminian clergy of subverting the government of England:

> we regret together with our dear christian brethren of our neighbour nation that we should have so evident and sensible experience of the dangerous plots set a foot and entertained by the churchmen of greatest power in England, for introducing innovations in religion, by corrupting the doctrine, changing the discipline, daily innovating the eternal worship of God, pressing publicly and maintaining points of Arminianism and heads of popery, defending and advancing preachers and professors of that judgement and allowing books stuffed with that doctrine. Fining, confining, and banishing all such as in conscience of their duty to God labour to oppose the doctrine, discipline, or worship of the Church of Rome, by their encroaching and usurping upon his Majesty's prerogative, tyrannising over the consciences, goods, and estates of persons of all qualities within that kingdom.[55]

The accusations that the Arminian church leaders were responsible for introducing popery and tyrannical government into England must have struck a fearful note for Harley, who had been an enthusiastic supporter of the 1628 Remonstrance which had similarly emphasised the Commons' fears of 'the undermining of religion and these things tending to an apparent change of government'; and Sir Robert could not have failed to understand the connection between the two documents.[56]

The circulation and availability of such statements and of news items was obviously crucial to the Harleys' analysis of events both at home and abroad throughout this period. Both Sir Robert and Lady Brilliana were eager to hear about matters of state importance and they obtained information in a number of ways. Printed sources were licensed by the privy council and were subject to censorship, but handwritten sources were exempt from such rigid restrictions. Dr Cust's research points, however, to the fact that 'the commonest method of passing on news remained word of mouth'. This he concludes was to be expected in a society which was 'only partially literate', whilst also avoiding the dangers of writing about anything controversial.[57] During the late 1630s the Harleys obtained printed news sheets known as corantoes, which dealt mainly with foreign news and which had first appeared in England in the early 1620s. In October 1632 the corantoes had been suppressed by order of the privy council and were re-licensed in December 1638. As soon as Lady Brilliana heard this news she informed Ned that 'now the corantoes are licensed again you will weekly see their relation', and during the ensuing months she regularly sent him the corantoes which she received as well as a number of printed newsbooks.[58]

---

[55] 'An Information to all Good Christians', BL Loan 29/46/30; H. G. Aldis, *A List of Books Printed in Scotland before 1700* (Edinburgh, 1970), 138.

[56] *1628 Debates*, IV, 315.

[57] Cust, 'News and Politics in Early Seventeenth-Century England', 62, 65.

[58] Siebert, *Freedom of the Press in England, 1476–1776*, 148, 155–6; Lewis, *Letters of the Lady Brilliana Harley*, 19, 27, 32, 26, 51, 62, 66.

The Harleys also relied on manuscript sources of news such as separates, which were transcripts of reports of parliamentary speeches, state trials and other news of national importance. They might be produced privately by MPs for circulation amongst friends and relatives and they were also produced commercially by scriveners. During the Short Parliament Ned sent a number of separates home to his mother, who was delighted since it was difficult for her to obtain exact reports of the debates: 'I have heard of many bold speeches that have passed there; and that passage between the Archbishop and my Lord Saye is diversely reported, but I believe that which I received from you.' Ralph Goodwin, the burgess of Ludlow and former protégé of Secretary Conway, also sent separates to Lady Brilliana, which she had copied and sent on to Ned.[59] Another popular source was the written newsletter, a commercial product which first appeared in the late sixteenth century and which was becoming increasingly common by the 1620s. A few newsletters from the early 1620s have survived amongst the Harley papers and relate mainly to events in the Palatinate.[60]

Personal letters provided another source of news, but these might well fall into the wrong hands and the quality of news in letters could be very variable, since correspondents were aware that their letters might be intercepted. Most writers thus chose to present the news as bare statements of fact with no political or constitutional analysis, but this should certainly not be interpreted as evidence that they were unaware of or uninterested in the broader implications of the news they were reporting. As the daughter of a former diplomat and a courtier, Lady Brilliana was highly conscious of the need to avoid writing anything contentious in her letters. At the very start of Ned's time at Oxford she warned him: 'when you write by the carrier, write nothing but what any may see, for many times the letters miscarry', and she was to remark that if she could talk to Ned she would be able to tell him 'more of my mind'. In April 1639 she made a veiled reference to the need to use a code: 'I have told you if you remember of a paper that some statesmen make use of, when they would not have known what they write of. Write me word whether

---

[59] Notestein and Relf, *Commons Debates for 1629*, xxx, xxxi; Cust, 'News and Politics in Early Seventeenth-Century England', 62–4; Lewis, *Letters of the Lady Brilliana Harley*, 90–1, 93; for Goodwin see M. F. Keeler, *The Long Parliament, 1640–1641: A Biographical Study of its Members* (Philadelphia, 1954), 190–1; a number of separates are preserved amongst the Harley papers, including a petition from William Prynne to the Star Chamber in 1632; a letter from the Council of Scotland to the King concerning their inability to establish the prayer book in Scotland in 1637; a description of the Scottish assembly held in Glasgow in 1638; and the speeches of the King and the Lord Keeper from the opening of the Short Parliament: see BL Loan 29/172 ff.57r–v, 157r–158v, 195r–198v, 275r–278v.

[60] Cust, 'News and Politics in Early Seventeenth-Century England', 62–4; for newsletters and other news items amongst the Harley papers see, for example, newsletters dated October 1621 and July 1622, BL Loan 29/202 ff.56r–59r; 'Proceedings of the Princes of the Union since 2 October 1620', BL Loan 29/46/39; information about the 'states army', 1631, BL Loan 29/172 ff.44r–48v.

you understand what I mean.' In May she sent Ned a copy of a Scottish sermon with the admonition, 'you must take care who sees it, you never read such a piece'.[61]

It might be supposed that the Harleys were unusual in their pursuit of information, and indeed the general extent of public interest in news has been the subject of recent debate.[62] If we compare the Harleys with other leading gentry it is clear that the desire for news was widely shared at this social level. Viscount Scudamore, for example, was English ambassador in Paris from 1635 until 1639, and his personal papers attest the deep interest that he had for events beyond the confines of Herefordshire, employing no less than nine newsletter correspondents during the 1620s and 1630s.[63] The women of the Harley circle were similarly keen to receive news. Lady Vere, who had spent much time on the continent with her husband Sir Horace, remained in England during the campaign to recover the Palatinate of 1621–2, but Sir Horace ensured that she received regular information, which she in turn passed on to Sir Robert. This particular interest was also inherited by the Harleys' eldest daughter, Brilliana, whose letters written to her brother Edward at Oxford between 1638 and 1640 are full of observations about the war between England and Scotland and the Short Parliament, which were presumably culled from the opinions of her parents.[64]

The news of the calling of a Parliament in the spring of 1640 was greeted by widespread enthusiasm, and electioneering was certainly coloured by issues such as ship money, the Scots war and religion, but the unusually high number of contested seats in this election cannot be ascribed solely to divisions over these issues. Pressure also mounted at the polls as men who had never sat before jockeyed for places with experienced Parliament men and an unusually high number of seats were contested.[65] The Harley papers give a clear account of the excitement generated by the meeting of a Parliament after so many years without an assembly. Lady Brilliana busied herself with

[61] Cust, 'News and Politics in Early Seventeenth-Century England', 88–9; Lewis, *Letters of the Lady Brilliana Harley*, 11, 37, 40, 55.

[62] For the suggestion that there was a marked lack of interest in political news in the 1620s and 1630s see Hirst, *Representative of the People?*, 145 and Morrill, *Revolt of the Provinces*, 22–3; Dr Cust's article on the circulation of news convincingly puts the opposing view: Cust, 'News and Politics in Early Seventeenth-Century England', 60–90.

[63] For Scudamore's papers see, for example, BL Add. Mss., 11044 ff.57–169 *passim*; evidence of his use of news correspondents is cited in Cust, 'News and Politics in Early Seventeenth-Century England', 63 n.9.

[64] HMC, Thirteenth Report, Appendix, part 2, *Mss. of His Grace the Duke of Portland Preserved at Welbeck Abbey*, II (1893), 110–17; a newsletter amongst Sir Robert's papers is endorsed in his hand 'from my Lord General Vere to his Lady, news', BL Loan 29/46/39; Brilliana Harley to Edward Harley, 27 March, [. . .] April, 29 April, 24 May and 9 November, 1639, BL Loan 29/172 ff.227r, 229r, 230r, 234r, 244r.

[65] Hirst, *Representative of the People?*, 217–22; Cope, *Politics Without Parliaments*, 177–87; Cope and Coates, eds., *Proceedings of the Short Parliament*, 7–8.

relaying the results of the spring elections in Herefordshire and the surrounding counties to Ned at Oxford. In Herefordshire Sir Robert Harley and Sir Walter Pye 'were chosen with a unanimous consent', and

> Mr Francis Newport and Sir Richard Lee are burgesses of Shrewsbury. My cousin Andrew Corbet and Sir John Corbet and Mr Peierpoint [*sic*] contend, who shall be knights for Shropshire. Ludlow have made choice of Mr Goodwin to be burgess, having refused my Lord President his letters for Sir Robert Nepper, his son-in-law. Mr Harbert is chosen for Montgomeryshire.

Richard More and Sir Robert Howard were returned for Bishop's Castle in Shropshire and Lady Brilliana remarked, 'I much rejoice that in all places they are so careful to choose worthy men for so great a business, as the Parliament.' Her letters continued to express her hopes for 'a happy issue of this Parliament' and even on 4 May, the day before the Short Parliament was dissolved, Lady Brilliana wrote lengthily to Ned at Magdalen Hall,

> I thank you that you make me partake of what you hear; for your father has not time to write many particulars. The state of the Parliament which I received from your father I send you here enclosed, and that which I had from you. Return mine again. I believe you have the Lord Keeper's speech, and the Speaker's, and therefore I do not send them to you. I pray God give a happy success to this Parliament; if not we may fear worse effects than has been yet. You and myself have great reason to be earnest with our God for your father. I believe this week will show what they will do, as all our expectations are upon the Parliament, so I desire all our prayers may be for it.

It was not until 10 May that Lady Brilliana received a letter from Sir Robert, 'by which I found the news of the dissolution of the Parliament to be true'.[66]

THE FAILURE OF THE SHORT PARLIAMENT

Surviving parliamentary diaries reveal that Harley was an active participant in the debates of the Short Parliament, calling for the House to examine the Star Chamber records relating to ship money and agreeing with speakers who proclaimed the levy to be illegal. In the subsidy debate of 4 May Harley expressed his dislike for the Scots war, with the hope that 'we might advert this threat without shedding of blood'. The *Commons Journals* show that he was named to a number of committees, including that of privileges and the committee chosen to investigate the commission of the convocation, which met at the same time as the Parliament and which had been authorised by the King to make canons for the first time since 1604.[67] Sir Robert's religious concerns are further reflected in his preferment of a petition from Peter Smart,

[66] Lewis, *Letters of the Lady Brilliana Harley*, 85, 86, 87, 90, 92, 94, 95.
[67] Maltby, *The Short Parliament*, 24; Scottish Records Office, Hamilton Mss., G. O. 406/1/ 8253, 4 May 1640 (I am grateful to Professor Conrad Russell for allowing me to use his transcript of this debate); *CJ*, II, 4, 8.

who had suffered at the hands of the High Commission for criticising the ceremonies introduced at Durham by Archbishop Neile. His case had become a *cause célèbre* when he lost his prebend at the cathedral and subsequently refused to pay a fine of £500. His refusal led to his imprisonment in King's Bench and he was not released until 1641 following the intervention of the Commons.[68]

The important place which Harley accorded to religious reforms is also reflected in a list of 27 queries sent to the Parliament which have survived among his papers. The list is not in his hand, but was doubtless compiled for Harley to take with him to Westminster. The majority of questions dealt with religious matters, including whether altars and church decorations such as pictures and crucifixes were legal. The document suggested that if the King needed revenue then he should annexe the profits of bishoprics to the crown, and also that monopolies be removed and ship money 'cleared' in order to take away doubts about the levy. The central importance of religion was also accepted by John Pym in his speech of 17 April to the Commons, when he declared 'religion is in truth the greatest grievance to be looked into'. His speech contained a blueprint for an attack on the conduct of the royal government over the past decade; it started with 'the breaches of our liberty and privileges of Parliament' in 1629, itemised religious complaints, and ended with the grievances of 'civil government', which included the collection of tonnage and poundage without the consent of Parliament, distraint of knighthood, ship money and monopolies. The Commons decided to deal with these accumulated grievances before turning to supplying the King with subsidies, but after a brief three weeks the King's annoyance at the delay in securing a grant of money led to a dissolution without the passage of any legislation or the grant of subsidies.[69]

The assembly of the Short Parliament had done nothing to ease the difficulties encountered by local officials, not just in Herefordshire, but in every English county. The need to supply money and men for the war continued to pose problems for the greater gentry as they struggled to regulate the behaviour of the pressed men and to continue the collection of ship money. The logistics of moving hundreds of often unwilling combatants around the English countryside was a continued cause of disruption in the English counties during the summer and autumn of 1640. Once the pressed men were assembled in Herefordshire the privy council twice delayed their

[68] Maltby, *The Short Parliament*, 22–3, 24. The petition was not in fact signed when Harley offered it to the House and its reading was deferred until the next day; *CJ*, II, 8. For Smart see *DNB*, XVIII, 392–3.

[69] List of 'queries' dated 1639, BL Loan 29/172 ff.251r–252r; Cope and Coates, *Proceedings of the Short Parliament*, 149–57; Cope, *Politics Without Parliaments*, 188–90.

march north, and the deputies decided to disband the men rather than pay for their maintenance at the county's expense. In July the men finally set off, but when they reached Leominster to the north of Hereford they refused to move until they were properly paid. The townsfolk, reluctant to continue billeting unruly soldiers in their homes, took matters into their own hands and beat the unwelcome troops out of the town. Lady Brilliana sent a most vivid report of the incident to Edward Harley:

the soldiers from Hereford were at Lemster last Thursday on their march to their rendezvous; the captain not paying them all of their pay, they would have returned into the town again, but all the town rose, and those that were come out of church, and with those arms they had, beat them back, but there being a great heap of stones out of town, the soldiers made use of them as long as they lasted, in which time the townsmen did but little good, till that powder was spent, and then the townsmen were too hard; many were hurt on both sides. The captain would have come into the town, but he was kept out.[70]

A few days later three of the county's deputies – Sir John Kyrle, Roger Vaughan and John Scudamore – wrote to their lord lieutenant, the Earl of Bridgewater, and informed him that 'we passed through great and eminent dangers both of our lives and fortunes, in regard of the mutinous disobedience and insolent behaviour of the soldiers never before known or heard of in this county in our times'. Reports of similar outrages perpetrated by the pressed men in other counties amounted to nothing less than widespread mutiny. In June and July 1640, stories of assault, desertion, desecration and even murder were commonplace, and the Herefordshire deputies blamed the 'news of the great misdemeanours' committed in other counties for making the Herefordshire men 'most dangerously insolent and mutinous'.[71]

In the summer of 1640 a secret commission given to the catholic Earl of Worcester by the King revived fears about the native catholics. In July King Charles ordered the Earl of Bridgewater, the President of the Welsh Council, to instruct his deputy lieutenants of Herefordshire, and the south Wales counties of Radnor, Monmouth, Brecknock, Glamorgan, Carmarthen and Pembroke, to obey Worcester, 'who hath been entrusted with some secret service'. The service appears to have been the levy of troops, but the Earl's religious sympathies meant that he was suspected of levying catholics. In the following month the Herefordshire deputy lieutenant, John Scudamore of Ballingham, wrote to his cousin Viscount Scudamore and told him: 'we are in

---

[70] PRO SP16/456/69; Lewis, *Letters of the Lady Brilliana Harley*, 98.
[71] PRO SP16/459/86; similar disorders were experienced amongst the pressed men from other counties: see for example, Barnes, *Somerset 1625–1640*, 276–7.

great amasement what my Lord of Worcester his commission may be . . . the puritans fear it may concern their religion and the courtiers their pockets'.[72]

Ship money was also a continuing cause of concern in the county. The sheriff for 1640, Thomas Aldern, reported in September 1640 to Secretary Nicholas that most of the gentry were refusing to pay that year's assessment. The under-sheriff had refused to have anything to do with that year's writ because of the murder of his predecessor, and the constables and collectors would not distrain the goods of defaulters. Aldern was reduced to using his own servants to execute the writ and was weary with having to imprison his own constables for refusing to obey him. Such problems were duplicated throughout the country. The war against Scotland was also going badly; on 20 August a Scottish army 25,000 strong crossed into England at Cold-stream, and within ten days Newcastle had fallen to the invaders.[73]

The failure of the war thus combined with growing domestic discontents to renew the pressure for Charles to summon another Parliament. At the start of September he was petitioned by twelve peers, including the Earls of Bedford, Essex and Warwick, and Lords Brooke, Saye and Mandeville, to call a Parliament to remove 'the great distempers and dangers now threatening the Church and State and your royal person'. The signatories were in contact with the Scottish Covenanters; and the Scots war and 'innovations in matters of religion' headed the list of 'evils and dangers' enumerated in the petition, closely followed by the increase of popery, the 'great mischiefs' attendant upon the use of Irish and foreign troops, 'the urging of ship money', and 'the heavy charges upon merchandise'. Finally the peers noted 'the great grief of your subjects by the long intermission of Parliaments and the late and former dissolving of such as have been called without the happy effects which otherwise they might have procured'. Gardiner ascribes the authorship of the petition to Pym and Oliver St John, and its delivery was timed to coincide with a supplication from the Scots for an English Parliament to help redress their own grievances.[74]

Other petitions were also drawn up: one from Yorkshire was drafted, but was never delivered; a draft petition from Herefordshire has survived amongst Sir Robert Harley's papers and it too was undelivered, because it was organised too late to be presented before the King's meeting with an

---

[72] *CSPD 1640*, 483; PRO C115/M13 part II/7265; at the start of the Long Parliament Worcester and his son Lord Herbert were accused of levying forces in the Welsh Marches, which were to join with an Irish army levied by Strafford: see Gardiner, *History of England, 1603–1642*, IX, 289.

[73] PRO SP16/466/77; Lake, 'Collection of Ship Money in Cheshire', 63–4; *CSPD 1640*, 229–30, 244, 245–6, 253; Gardiner, *History of England 1603–1642*, IX, 189–95.

[74] Gardiner, *Constitutional Documents*, 134–6; V. Snow *Essex the Rebel* (University of Nebraska Press, 1970), 229–30; Gardiner, *History of England 1603–1642*, IX, 198–9.

assembly of the peers arranged for 24 September. It was feared that 'if it come to his Majesty after that day it will savour of faction'. A petition from London, similar to that of the peers, was delivered to the King at York on 22 September, two days before the meeting of the Great Council of peers, at which Charles announced that writs would be sent out for another Parliament.[75] In the new assembly the King would face a parliamentary opposition which had forged strong links with the Scots, and the presence of the invading Covenanter army on the northern borders of the realm would make it impossible for Charles to ignore the demands for reform put forward by the Long Parliament.

[75] Gardiner, *History of England, 1603–1642,* IX, 204; 'a Draft of a petition for the County of Hereford to His Majesty, 1640', BL Loan 29/50/73; Gardiner, *History of England 1603–1642,* IX, 205–8.

5

The opening of the Long Parliament, 1640–1641

The Parliament that met at Westminster on 3 November 1640 rapidly launched a comprehensive investigation into the royal government and its supporting institutions, which triggered nation-wide excitement and provoked further demands for reforms from London and the provinces. MPs were inundated with petitions and letters to such a degree that one historian has written of 'this new relationship of the Long Parliament man with his politically aroused constituents'. Herefordshire was no exception, and the letters which Sir Robert Harley received from the county and elsewhere clearly illustrate the interaction between events at the centre and the development of public opinions in the localities before the outbreak of the Civil War.

Sir Robert Harley had been elected as senior knight of the shire for Herefordshire in October 1640 and his support for reforms was initially widely endorsed within the county.[1] He was described as 'the mouth of this country' by Stanley Gower and was encouraged by a broad spectrum of local gentry, including the mayor and the members of the city council of Hereford, and the JPs, Sir William Croft, a future royalist, and James Kyrle of Walford, who would support Parliament during the Civil War.[2] Such enthusiasm for reform was widespread in 1640, but it was by no means universal. There were pockets of resistance and scepticism from the very start of the Long Parliament, which were later augmented by the reactions of the moderates and conservatives, who became increasingly hostile to the Parliament throughout 1641. By the spring of 1642 Sir Robert Harley's uncompromising stance was no longer widely endorsed by his county. The confidence which had led the

[1] Hirst, *Representative of the People?*, 184; Harley and Fitzwilliam Coningsby to the Earl of Essex, 9 October 1640, BL Loan 29/172 f.300r. Harley's junior partner, Fitzwilliam Coningsby of Hampton Court, was expelled from the House of Commons in October 1641 for his part in the soap monopoly and would be strongly royalist during the war. Coningsby was replaced by his 19-year-old son Humphrey, who was himself disabled in May 1643 for deserting Parliament: Keeler, *Long Parliament*, 139–40.

[2] Stanley Gower to Harley, 23 January 1640, BL Loan 29/119, Edmund Aston and others to Harley, 1 February 1640/1, Sir William Croft to Harley, 1 January 1640/1, Loan 29/173 ff.63r, 7r–v, James Kyrle to Harley, undated, Loan 29/120.

local gentry to select him as their representative in October 1640 was lost and within the country at large two ideologically opposed parties were beginning to take shape. The polarisation which created these parties can be traced throughout the opening months of the Long Parliament. It was accelerated by the critical events which started at the beginning of the second session of the Long Parliament in October 1641, and culminated in the King's attempt to arrest the Five Members in the first week of January 1642.[3]

Once Sir Robert had taken his seat at Westminster he rapidly emerged as one of the most active supporters of the reform group, whose main leaders were John Pym, Oliver St John and John Hampden in the Commons and the Earls of Bedford, Warwick and Essex, and Lords Brooke and Saye in the Lords. These men, and their allies in Parliament, pursued an energetic policy of bringing the King's 'evil counsellors' to book by a thorough investigation of their misdemeanours in all spheres of public life, in the hope that by bringing down the King's chief ministers they could replace them with their own nominees. They also planned sweeping reforms, designed to restrict the King's actions in the future, and to purge existing corruptions of both the State and the Church.[4] Before the end of 1640 the Commons had impeached Strafford and Laud for high treason and voted both ship money and the Church canons of 1640 to be illegal. The army, the judiciary, and the universities were being scrutinised by various parliamentary committees, and the prerogative courts and regional royal councils in Wales and the North were also under investigation. Such was the volume of business undertaken by MPs that on 8 January 1641 a separate committee was appointed to consider which were the most important issues under discussion and which could be temporarily disregarded. Four days later, following a report by Sir John Hotham, the House of Commons ordered that only sixteen major committees and the five grand committees should continue in session, while all other committees and sub-committees were suspended and were not revived until the beginning of March.[5] As the Long Parliament progressed, fundamental differences in the objectives of the King's critics emerged, which not only led to the creation of a royalist party, but which also created splits amongst the parliamentarians. Initially, however, the opponents of the King appeared united and their plan that members of the reform group should be appointed to the privy council was described as 'the news of the town' in London in December 1640.[6]

[3] Gardiner, *History of England, 1603–1642*, X, 32–151.
[4] P. Christianson, 'The Peers, the People, and Parliamentary Management in the First Six Months of the Long Parliament', *JMH*, XLIX (1977), 575–99.
[5] Kenyon, *Stuart Constitution*, 189–92, 251; *CJ*, II, 66, 84. I am grateful to Professor Conrad Russell for drawing my attention to the work of the 'committee for committees'.
[6] C. Roberts, 'The Earl of Bedford and the Coming of the English Revolution', *JMH*, XLIX (1977), 600.

William Voyle, curate of a Shropshire parish close to Brampton, hoped that Harley would be amongst those to gain office, but it is doubtful whether he was included in these plans, although he did have connections with some of the 'reform network' peers. Lord Brooke, for example, was distantly related to Lady Brilliana and he was regarded with great esteem by the Harleys, who had a similar opinion of Lord Saye which can be traced back as far as 1624. During his campaign to be elected to the Long Parliament, Sir Robert had also been in contact with the Earl of Essex, but this appears to have been a formal acknowledgement of the Earl's influence within Herefordshire rather than evidence of any significant personal connection between the two men. Harley's links with the Earl of Warwick may have been of a more personal nature, and in 1641 and 1642 Warwick wrote to Harley asking for his help in the House concerning the sequestration of the office of Postmaster, in which the Earl had a legal interest.[7] Harley, however, did not have any obvious patronage links with these peers and cannot be regarded simply as a client of any individual member of the House of Lords. His actions during the Long Parliament were largely those of an independent MP, and his standing in the House was based both on his active support for the reformers and on his own long service as a Parliament man.

Sir Robert was one of a handful of men whose parliamentary experience stretched back to the first Parliament of James I or beyond and, as a long-serving member, he was ensured a place on the committee for parliamentary privileges, traditionally appointed at the start of each Parliament. He was also named to many of the committees set up to investigate grievances against the royal government and the Church, amongst them the committee which drew up charges of impeachment against Archbishop Laud, and the select committee of twenty-four, chosen to report on the state of the kingdom. The latter contained a high proportion of those who managed the attacks on crown policies in the Commons, including Pym, Hampden and Clotworthy.[8] Harley himself acted as chairman of both the committee considering abuses in the civil and religious government of the universities and, temporarily, of the grand committee for trade. Harley clearly supported the programme proposed by Pym, including the passage of reform legislation and the removal of the King's two chief ministers, Strafford and Laud, and he was one of the

---

[7] Anonymous paper headed 'General Things' in Voyle's hand, BL Loan 29/172 f.363v; Levy, 'Thesis', 65 n.76; Harley and Fitzwilliam Coningsby to the Earl of Essex, 9 October 1640, BL Loan 29/172 f.300r, the Earl of Warwick to Harley, 3 February 1640/1 and 26 March 1642, Loan 29/173 ff.67r, 233r. See also Warwick's letter to Harley attempting to explain his intervention in the recruiter election for Sandwich on behalf of his son, Charles, BL Loan 29/121. Harley also had contact with Stephen Marshall, the vicar of Finchingfield in Essex and a Warwick protégé; see Levy, 'Thesis', 189 n.12. For Harley's links with Lords Brooke and Saye see chapter 3, n.38 above.

[8] Keeler, *Long Parliament*, 15–16; *CJ*, II, 20, 34, 44, 52, 25; Christianson, 'The Peers, the People and Parliamentary Management', 584–5.

back-bench members who undertook much of the routine work in the Commons to secure those policies. He was a conscientious and hard-working MP, who raised points of order in debates, reported from committees and frequently went to the House of Lords bearing messages or bills for the consideration of the upper House.[9] During the course of 1640 and 1641 Harley's stature increased to the point where he was regarded as a natural deputy for John Pym in various offices. In January 1642 he replaced Pym as chairman for the standing committee for Irish affairs, after Pym had taken refuge in the City of London following the King's abortive coup against Parliament. When Pym died in December 1643 his place on the committee for the Assembly of Divines was also taken by Sir Robert.[10]

Sir Robert's status as senior knight of the shire and his position as an experienced and active MP meant that he was contacted by local people for various reasons. At the start of 1641, for example, the Mayor and city council of Hereford asked for Harley's help in getting rid of weirs on the river Wye, which impeded salmon fishing. Sir Robert's activities at Westminster were clearly known and widely endorsed in the county at this stage and their letter ended by commending Harley for his 'approved endeavours for the good of the Church and commonwealth'.

The work of the Parliament was similarly welcomed by others in Hereford-shire, and the jurisdiction of the Welsh Council was condemned in a grand jury presentment made at Hereford in January 1641, which also explicitly endorsed the work of the Long Parliament by denouncing ship money as 'a burden and a grievance', and by declaring the levy of coat and conduct money to be 'unlawful'. At the start of 1641 the JP, Sir William Croft, also approved of the attack on ship money, although a year later he would be one of Sir Robert's fiercest critics in Herefordshire. Between January and August 1642 Croft opposed the Parliament in public and privately tried to persuade the Harleys to abandon the parliamentarian cause. Yet in January 1641 he wrote to Harley about the investigation in progress into the jurisdiction of the Welsh Council in terms that showed his approval of Parliament.

'It is like the long argument about ship money,' observed Croft.

It is plain we are injured by authority and when that may be persuaded to do us right we shall be restored to our liberty, which I doubt we are not so near as we deserve,

---

[9] *CJ*, II, 92; Report from the Committee for Trade, 16 February 1640/1, BL Loan 29/46/36; BL Harl. MSS., 163 f.605r; *CJ*, II, 32,57,85. For the work of the universities committee in Cambridge see D. Hoyle, 'A Commons Investigation of Arminianism and Popery in Cambridge on the Eve of the Civil War', *Historical Journal*, XXIX (1986), 419–25.

[10] W. H. Coates, A. S. Young and V. F. Snow, eds., *The Private Journals of the Long Parliament, 3 January to 5 March 1642* (New Haven and London, 1982), 14 n.3; *CJ*, III, 341. In April 1642 Harley was named to a commission for Irish affairs which included, amongst others, Pym, Holles, Cromwell, Sir Henry Vane and 7 members of the Lords, including Essex, Northumberland and Lord Saye: see V. F. Snow and A. S. Young, eds., *The*

since his Majesty is desirous to have power to show mercy to the worst of malefactors. He hath done that long enough and if he be not gotten from that, he is not come home to us. If the firebrands be not put out, all our houses will be set on fire; it is not well those little sparks Windebank and Finch are but hid in embers, they may be raked out to make a new fire.[11]

The 'firebrands' were the King's advisors during the Scottish war, including Strafford, who had been dubbed the 'incendiaries' by their opponents. Croft was writing in response to Sir Robert's request for information about the earlier drive against the status of the Welsh Council led by Croft's father between 1604 and 1614, when Sir Herbert Croft had argued that the Council should have no power in the four English marcher counties. Although not involved in the earlier campaign, Sir Robert had spoken against the Council in Parliament in 1628, and in 1640 was an active member of the committee set up to examine the two regional royal councils of Wales and of the North.[12] Sir Robert's efforts on behalf of religious reform were also applauded by prominent puritans in Herefordshire, such as the justice, James Kyrle, who asked Harley for help in removing the vicar of Walford, a Mr Buckley, whom Kyrle described as 'a most scandalous vicar' and 'our drunken, debauched guide'. Kyrle told Harley that he wished 'the Lord' would 'prosper your pains and holy endeavours in his work, that we may see the reformation we hope, and pray for'.[13]

Harley's most regular correspondents during the first session of this Parliament were Lady Brilliana and Stanley Gower. Although his replies are apparently lost, the letters which he received demonstrate that the two major concerns of Sir Robert's puritan circle in Herefordshire at the start of the Long Parliament were their desire for Church reforms and their fear that the King had fallen victim to a 'Catholic plot'. This latter belief carried with it an implied concern for the constitution, and in his first great set speech to the Commons of 7 November 1640 John Pym had declared that there was a 'design to alter the kingdom both in religion and government'.[14] Those who

---

Private Journals of the Long Parliament, 7 March to 1 June 1642 (New Haven, 1987), 403–69.

[11] Edmund Aston and others to Harley, 1 February 1640/1, BL Loan 29/173 f.63r; J. and T. W. Webb, *Memorials of the Civil War Between King Charles I, and the Parliament of England as it Affected Herefordshire and the Adjacent Counties*, II (1879), 335–6; Sir William Croft to Harley, 1 January 1640/1, BL Loan 29/173 f.7r-v. For Croft's later royalism see below, chapters 6 and 7, *passim*.

[12] Gardiner, *History of England, 1603–1642*, IX, 242; Ham, 'The Four Shire Controversy', 381–99; HMC, *Dovaston Manuscripts*, 270; *CJ*, I, 684; *1628 Debates*, III, 473–4; *CJ*, II, 216. In 1624 Harley had been actively involved in promoting draft legislation to exempt the four English marcher counties from the jurisdiction of the Welsh Council: see *CJ*, I, 684, 767.

[13] James Kyrle to Harley, undated, BL Loan 29/120.

[14] *D'Ewes (N)*, 8.

believed that there was a plot to force catholicism upon the English nation also believed that traditional liberties were being eroded in the process.

Lady Brilliana's letters reveal that she was in complete support of Parliament's actions and was pleased, for example, to learn of the progress of the attainder bill against Strafford and his execution in May 1641: 'I am glad that justice is executed on my Lord Strafford, who I think died like a Seneca, but not like one that had tasted the mystery of godliness.' Like so many other puritans Lady Brilliana believed that Parliament would remove 'all these things and persons, that have been such a hindrance to the free passage of His glorious gospel', and she was delighted to hear of the bill to abolish the Court of High Commission, which received royal assent in July 1641. The Court had been a major instrument in silencing and punishing godly ministers; Sir Robert knew at least two ministers, John Workman and John Stoughton, who had been interrogated by the Court in the mid-1630s, and Workman was subsequently suspended from the ministry by the Court. During the summer of 1641 Lady Brilliana was also eager to follow the progress of the 'root and branch' bill, which would have abolished bishops in England and Wales.[15]

Stanley Gower's letters to Harley show similar enthusiasms. He was interested in the national constitutional debate and was well informed about proceedings in Parliament, particularly Harley's committee work. Only six days after the opening of the Parliament Gower wrote: 'it joys us much to hear that the King has referred the full trial of offences and offenders to you'. Furthermore he was not only aware of current constitutional arguments, he was also versed in the recent Scottish manifestos aimed at the English:

I have not had leisure this last week to transcribe the words of Bilson and other writers, *de iure regio*, but I shall do it, God willing, by the next. Meanwhile I have read a testimony from King James in his speech at Whitehall 1609, which is a stronger testimony than any other, *in propria causa*, his distinction there of kingdoms is the same with the Scots: into absolute, as the Turks; and pactional kingdoms, as ours, and his words are better than their (viz.).

The King of England doth by pact or covenant, and that by oath, enter upon the kingdom to govern it according to the laws thereof, which if he cease to do, he is perjured and ceases to be a King, and degenerates into a tyrant, whosoever counsels him to that course they are vipers and pests.

Gower also offered his patron a steady flow of advice about Church reforms, which included tighter controls on English catholics, the pulling 'down' of the bishops, and the removal of Church ceremonies and subscription, 'two great clogs which must be removed else we are still under their

---

[15] Lewis, *Letters of the Lady Brilliana Harley*, 131, 115, 140, 132–3, 135, 138, 140, 141, 143. For Workman and Stoughton see above, pp. 63–4.

insupportable yoke'. Gower further urged Harley to seek ways of establishing a 'faithful ministry', one of the traditional concerns of the puritans.[16]

The contacts which Sir Robert had with his constituents in Herefordshire were not exceptional during the Long Parliament, but he was also approached by many puritan clergy from the marcher counties of England and Wales; their letters indicate that not only was Harley's reputation for godliness well known, but that many people looked to him to lead the way in Parliament for religious change. In December 1640 John Tombes, the vicar of Leominster, complained to Harley about the low stipends which he and his curate received and about the actions of the local JP, Wallop Brabazon, who five years previously had used his power as churchwarden to turn the communion table at Leominster 'altar-wise and to be railed'. Tombes took the opportunity to link the problems which he had encountered locally with the growing demands for wider reforms and suggested that the lack of preaching in the county was the direct result of the low levels of pay of the parish clergy. Tombes confessed to Harley that he could no longer support himself, 'unless this Parliament take some course for providing for the ministry'.[17]

Welsh ministers also regarded Harley as their natural spokesman, and in June 1641 he was asked to present a petition from Wales to Parliament by the Shropshire cleric Oliver Thomas, who argued that 'if the care of provisions for us be committed to our Welsh parliamentary knights and burgesses, our hopes are gone', and asked Harley for help in the encouragement of 'my Welsh ministry'. Harley delivered a petition later that month on behalf of the separatist ministers Walter Cradock and Henry Walter, in which they described the plight of the godly in the counties of Glamorgan, Monmouth, Brecknock and Radnor, who had been arrested and 'molested by mulcts' for attempting to hear sermons outside their own parishes.[18]

Harley also received letters from clerics in the English marcher counties bordering on Wales. The charged atmosphere of expectation and uncertainty generated by the debates of the Long Parliament is caught in a letter to Harley from the Shropshire curate William Voyle, who wrote in November 1640 that

human wisdom will say: in the business of reformation, content yourselves at this time to go so far. This voice did prevail in the beginning of Queen Elizabeth.

[16] Stanley Gower to Harley, 9 November, 20 November 1640, BL Loan 29/172 ff.308r, 309 r–v, *idem* to Harley, 28 November 1640, Loan 29/119.

[17] John Tombes to Harley, 12 December 1640. BL Loan 29/172 f.344r; Tombes had been trying to persuade the Bishop of Hereford to restore the impropriated tithes of Leominster for some years: see PRO C115/D13/1723. For the dispute with Brabazon see the petition of the borough of Leominster, undated, BL Loan 29/50/73.

[18] Oliver Thomas to Harley, 5 June 1641, BL Loan 29/121; BL Harl. MSS., 163 f.740v.

But the present way (sayth Duns Scotus) is, not a horse left in Egypt. Exodus 10, v. 26 and we know not, what invitations and encouragements, and opportunities you may have beyond the common expectation.

In a separate plan of reform Voyle urged that Parliament should meet every three years, and that all 'ecclesiastical laws, constitutions, rules etc.' should be void unless 'established by his Majesty with the advice of his Parliament'. He also voiced long-standing puritan demands, including the abolition of surplices and kneeling at communion: the removal of signing with the cross at baptism and the destruction of 'monuments of idolatry' such as altars, holy water, crucifixes, images, pictures and stained glass.[19]

In June 1641 John Hall, a Worcestershire cleric, enthusiastically praised Harley's renown for godliness: 'your countenance hath refreshed many, your kindness invited many to seek your favour, and your zeal for the cause of religion hath ministered strength to them that droop'. Hall annotated his letter with the words 'anno renovationis' – the year of renewal or perhaps restoration, and praised the House of Commons with the following words:

how is the glory of God sufficiently to be admired, in the wisdom, righteousness and integrity of that honourable House; the Lord add to your lustre more and more, to the daunting of the enemy, and raising up of feeble spirits to give thanks. How many mouths have you opened, that were sealed up, yea many spirits have you enlarged that were straitened, yea many congregations give abundant thanks to God on your behalf.[20]

The fervour of men like Voyle and Hall was matched, however, by parallel evidence amongst the Harley papers that some people in the marches were opposed to any moves against the Church from a very early date. In December 1640 Samuel Fisher, another Shropshire curate, wrote to Harley about a 'seminary priest' in his county who had reputedly slandered the twelve peers who had petitioned the King to hold a Parliament in the summer of 1640. Fisher recorded that the man had declared: 'those Lords who had put up the petition to his Majesty were a company of puritan rascals, base fellows and scabs'. At the start of January 1641 Gower recorded that Sir Paul Harris, a Shropshire gentleman, and later a staunch royalist, was saying 'the Parliament hath not the King as fast as they think'. Gower lamented that 'the vulgar comfort themselves with assured confidence that bishops will get up again. I tell you but the language of Babel's bricklayers.' In the same month young Thomas Harley wrote from Brampton to his brother Edward in London and informed him that 'some men jeer and cast forth reproachful words against

---

[19] William Voyle to Harley, 23 November 1640, and anonymous papers in Voyle's hand headed 'General Things', undated, BL Loan 29/172 f.315r, ff.363r–367v.

[20] John Hall to Harley, 21 June 1641, BL Loan 29/173 f.116r.

the Parliament, and others that might forward the proceedings of the Parliament are very backward'.[21]

One of the major divisions in opinion throughout the country centred on the Church hierarchy. The majority of Sir Robert's correspondents blamed the ills of the Church squarely on the bishops, and the great recurrent theme in the Harleys' dealings with other puritans in 1640 and 1641 was the need for changes in Church polity. William Bourne, a fellow of the collegiate church of Manchester, urged Harley to 'remove whatsoever savours of Antichrist from amongst us'. Edward Harley's tutor at Oxford, Edward Perkins, also equated the bishops with Antichrist and wrote to his pupil with 'all due respect to your noble father', adding 'the Lord make him an instrument to pull off this little horn from off the head of the beast. The Lord confound the bishops.'[22] In November 1640, Stanley Gower informed Sir Robert that a number of ministers in the diocese of Hereford had not been notified of the elections for the convocation. He complained enigmatically that 'in the most general business that concerns all the clergy, the bishops' party are alone and exempt us from our votes that they make up that number of 666, which in that agrees to them as well as in other names'. The aggrieved diocesan ministers drew up two petitions, one against the irregular conduct of the elections and the other against the Church canons of 1604 and 1640, which Gower forwarded to Harley. They had also sought legal advice from Mr William Littleton and Justice Littleton of Shropshire who, wrote Gower, 'both like exceeding well what we have done, assuring us (what we hope) that Parliament will both take due notice of us and that it will be a good remonstrance against the corruption of that hierarchy, whose downfall we expect daily'. This is the first direct reference to the 'downfall' of the bishops in the Harleys' surviving papers, and Gower's letter demonstrates that people in the localities were discussing reforms of the episcopacy well in advance of the presentation in the following month of the London 'root and branch' petition, which called for the government of the Church by 'archbishops and lord bishops, deans and archdeacons etc. . . . with all its dependencies, roots and branches' to be abolished.[23]

The most comprehensive indictment of the bishops received by Harley was contained, however, in a survey of the ministry of Herefordshire compiled by

[21] Samuel Fisher to Harley, 18 December 1640, BL Loan 29/172 ff.352r–353v, Stanley Gower to Harley, 2 January 1640/1, Loan 29/273 f.9r; Fletcher, *Outbreak of the English Civil War*, 359–60; Thomas Harley to Edward Harley, 29 January 1640/1, BL Loan 29/173 f.62r. The slander described by Fisher was later reported to Lords Saye and Brook: see HMC, *Fourth Report, Appendix, pt I, Manuscripts of the House of Lords* (1874), 56 and *LJ*, IV, 188.

[22] William Bourne to Harley, 8 January 1640/1, BL Loan 29/119, Edward Perkins to Edward Harley, 23 November 1640, Loan 29/172 f.317r.

[23] Gower to Harley, 12 December, 20 November 1640, BL Loan 29/172 ff.346r, 309r; the root and branch petition is printed in Gardiner, *Constitutional Documents*, 137–44.

the most active puritans in his home county and written up by Stanley Gower.[24] The survey was undertaken in response to an order of the Commons of 19 December 1640, which called for all MPs to inform the House of the state of the ministry in their counties within six weeks. The information that was subsequently received by the Commons provided the basis for the proceedings of the committee for scandalous ministers. Sir Robert sent a copy of the order to his wife, who acted promptly and was, as Gower noted, 'very active in so great a business'. On the advice of Edward Broughton, a local gentleman, copies of the order were sent out 'to men well effected to this service of God, King, Church, kingdom and country, inhabiting the hundreds, entreating them to bring unto the quarter sessions at Hereford a true and their best intelligence, such as might rightly inform the Parliament'.

A total of fourteen laity and clergy, including Lady Brilliana, the JP James Kyrle of Walford, Stanley Gower and John Tombes, were involved in collecting information for the survey and it was this group which would also form the core of parliamentarian resistance in the county from the earliest stages of the Civil War. The survey covered the whole of the county and was conducted parish by parish; it supplied the names of the parish clergy, 'their means, manners, labours and patrons'. Some of the ministers were commended as good preachers, but the majority were condemned mainly for not preaching, for being ill-educated or being of 'lewd conversation' or 'scandalous' life. Mr Shaw, the vicar of Birley, who 'hath set up a stone altar', was branded 'as both vicious and superstitious' and the parish of Sarnesfield was described as 'a nest of papists'. The clergy of Hereford cathedral were found to be at best 'but civil and formal, no examples or encouragements to piety and conscionable painfulness'. The cathedral service was denounced as the 'fountain of superstition throughout the whole county. Metamorphosing itself into strange gesticulations, crouching, ducking, shifting from place to place . . . with a world of other ceremonial trinkets and fopperies devised to make gaze upon the outside of empty ceremonies and superstitious pomp.' Not one cleric was openly tainted as an Arminian, which suggests that at parish level in Herefordshire the issue of doctrine was not the most pressing. The central arguments of the survey ran against the authority of the bishops, who were singled out as the greatest cause of the ills of the kingdom and were, as Gower phrased it, 'the main atlases which uphold the babel of confusion both in Church and Commonwealth and amongst the rest, they are the greatest causes of the scarcity of a painful, constant and conscionable

---

[24] Corpus Christi Mss., 206. My use of this document has been greatly helped by the existence of an annotated transcript made by F. C. Morgan, the former archivist of Hereford Cathedral: see Hereford Cathedral Muniments Room, Ms. 6A. vi. For Gower's role in drawing up the survey see Stanley Gower to Sir Robert Harley, 23 January 1640/1, BL Loan 29/119.

ministry, themselves being none such'. According to the survey, the cure for these problems lay in the foundation by Parliament of a presbyterian Church system with election of ministers vested in the presbytery. The Church was to be purged of 'the trash and trumpery of massing ceremonies, altars, images, crucifixes, copes, surplices, organs etc., instead of which to make God's worship as plain and decent as may be'.[25]

The puritans were, however, a distinct minority in Herefordshire and their resolutions found little favour in the county. Indeed a few months later, in May 1641, John Tombes informed Sir Robert that 'I find that I am very odious to the cathedral, non-preaching, scandalous ministers of this country for my endeavours to certify you of the estate of the ministry in this county.' Divided opinion was running so high on the subject of religion that contemporaries concluded that 'parties' were already forming around the issue of the Church hierarchy by December 1640, when Stanley Gower had referred to the 'bishops' party' in his letter to Harley. In a letter dated 25 January 1641, John Pyne, MP for Poole, also referred to 'episcopacy, which has so many advocates and so strong a party in our House'. The opponents of the bishops saw the Scottish Covenanters as their natural allies and at the end of February 1641, when objections were raised in London against a statement from the Scots confirming that they wished to see episcopacy abolished in England, Lady Brilliana expressed her fears that 'the Scots' declaration would give the contrary party occasion to show themselves'.[26]

Lady Brilliana's letters also reveal the strength of her own feelings against the bishops. In January 1641 she wrote to Edward Harley: 'I believe that the hierarchy must down and I hope now.' Two months later she wrote: 'I am glad that the bishops begin to fall, and I hope that it will be with them as it was with Haman; when he began to fall, he fell indeed.' In June 1641 Lady Brilliana was elated to hear that the 'root and branch' bill had received two readings in the Commons and wrote to her son how

I much rejoice that the Lord has shewed Himself so mightily for His people in hearing their prayers, that it is come so far as that the bishops and all their train is voted against. I trust in God they will be enacted against, which I long to hear, and I pray God take away all those things, which have so long offended.

Yet it would be incorrect to interpret her statements as evidence of an unqualified support for a Scottish-style presbyterian Church in England. During the early months of the Long Parliament the Harleys, and many other

---

[25] *CJ*, II, 54; Stanley Gower to Harley, 23 January 1640/1, BL Loan 29/119; Corpus Christi Mss., 206 ff.6r, 7r, 10r, 12v, 11v, 12r. For the later activities of those involved in collating the survey see Levy, 'Thesis', 207.

[26] John Tombes to Harley, 3 May 1641, BL Loan 29/173 f.99r, Stanley Gower to Harley, 12 December 1640, Loan 29/172 f.346r; Pyne's letter is quoted in Fletcher, *Outbreak of the English Civil War*, 97; Lewis, *Letters of the Lady Brilliana Harley*, 118.

puritans, would probably have accepted an episcopate with greatly curtailed powers, largely because they were unsure just how much reform they could expect to achieve. Stanley Gower, for example, clearly preferred the total abolition of episcopacy, but a letter from him to Sir Robert written in December 1640 demonstrates that he would tolerate an episcopate, provided there was 'much alteration at least, of the government by bishops'. The survey of the Herefordshire ministry, drawn up by Gower with the aid of other prominent local puritans, also advised that episcopacy should be abolished altogether or reduced to its 'first order'. The decision should rest with Parliament, but if bishops were retained they should have no temporal powers and the ultimate authority in the Church would be shared with the 'presbyters'.[27]

Similarly in December 1640, William Voyle suggested that it should be considered whether it would be best to 'yield (in part) to the bishops'. Sir Robert himself probably shared the views of these ministers in early 1641. The Ministers' Petition and Remonstrance, which Harley presented to the House of Commons in January of that year, were not 'root and branch' documents, although they did call for 'reformation in matters of religion and the government of the Church'.[28] The 'root and branch' bill for the 'utter abolishing and taking away' of the Church hierarchy received its first reading at the end of May 1641. By that time the Parliament had already engineered the execution of Strafford and had secured the passage of a bill which prevented Charles dissolving Parliament without its own consent. Under such circumstances the more extreme measure of 'root and branch' must have appeared an achievable aim to the Harleys, who now gave their wholehearted support to this bill. A similar process of radicalisation has been detected in other MPs, such as Sir John Wray, Sir William Brereton and Sir Thomas Barrington.[29]

---

[27] Lewis, *Letters of the Lady Brilliana Harley*, 111, 119, 132–3; Stanley Gower to Harley, 28 November 1640, BL Loan 29/119; Corpus Christi Mss., 206 f.13r. In his letter to Harley, Gower stated that he had drawn up the survey at the request of those involved in collecting the information and continued, 'I am persuaded the very reading of this unto the House would give the casting voice, if it should come to that, whether bishops should be certified or removed. I have to my meanness proposed some considerations either way': Stanley Gower to Harley, 23 January 1640/1, BL Loan 29/119.

[28] Anonymous paper headed 'General Things' in Voyle's hand, BL Loan 29/172 f.363r; *D'Ewes (N)*, 335–6, 277; apparently no copies of the Ministers' Petition and Remonstrance have survived.

[29] Gardiner, *History of England, 1603–1642*, IX, 369, 373, 379–83; J. Morrill, 'The Religious Context of the English Civil War', *TRHS*, 5th Series, 34 (1984), 170–1; J. Morrill, 'Sir William Brereton and England's Wars of Religion', *JBS*, XXIV (1985), 311–32. A draft of the 'root and branch' bill survives amongst Sir Robert's papers, Nottingham University Library, Portland Mss., Welbeck Collection, Pw2/Hy/31 (ff.15 and 16 bear minor amendments in Harley's hand). For the history of the bill see A. J. Fletcher, 'Concern for Renewal in the Root and Branch Debates of 1641', in D. Baker, ed., *Renaissance and Renewal in*

Support for 'root and branch' was also widely recognised as a prerequisite for continued Scottish aid to the English Parliament. At the start of 1641 William Bourne wrote to Harley warning him that Parliament should opt for total abolition in order to establish accord between England and Scotland:

because there will be some difference betwixt the conformists and others what discipline shall be raised, I think you may do well to conform the same to the Apostles' times, whereof we have precedents in France, Geneva and Scotland, and other reformed Churches. The which if you do, you shall make a most comfortable and perpetual accord betwixt the kingdoms, but if it so fall out that Christ and Antichrist be comixt together, it will breed a perpetual dissension.[30]

The 'root and branch' bill was, in fact remarkably Erastian in tone and would have set up commissions of nine laymen in each county to replace the bishops, thus giving English gentry greater control than their Scottish counterparts.[31] According to two separate parliamentary diaries, it was Sir Robert who called for the debate on the bill to go ahead on 11 June and the account by Sir Simonds D'Ewes gives us an insight into the backroom tactics which were an important, but largely hidden, aspect of the Long Parliament:

Sir Robert Harley, as I gathered, Mr Pym, Mr Hampden, and others, with Mr Stephen Marshall, parson of Finchingfield, in the county of Essex, and some others, had met yesternight and appointed that this bill should be proceeded with this morning, and the said Sir Robert Harley moved it first in this House. For Mr Hampden, out of his serpentine subtlety, did still put others to move those business that he contrived.

Gardiner drew attention to the fact that D'Ewes' report goes on to include data from 1643 and thus 'has no weight as contemporary evidence'.[32] Yet even if the precise details cannot be trusted, D'Ewes assertion that such meetings took place outside Parliament is undoubtedly correct and is confirmed in a much later letter, dated 1659, from Cornelius Burgess to Richard Baxter, which also casts interesting light on the issue of episcopacy:

Nor did we ministers that appeared against their usurping of sole ordination and sole jurisdiction ... ever speak a word tending to the extirpation of all episcopacy, but only to reduce it to the primitive. This I can more fully assert, perhaps, than any other; because the managing of that business lay with me, both before a number of Lords and Commons, with whom (by their appointment) Mr White of Dorchester, Mr Marshall, Mr Calamy, myself and one or two ministers more, met twice every week at some of their lodgings. Among them was the Earl of Warwick, the Lord Saye, Lord Brooke, with some other nobles, Mr Hampden, Mr Pym etc. and not one was for total abolishing of all, or any, but usurped episcopacy.

Christian History, Studies in Church History, XIV (Oxford, 1977), 279–86. I am grateful to Professor Russell for this last reference.
[30] William Bourne to Harley, 8 January 1640/1, BL Loan 29/119.
[31] University of Nottingham Library, Portland Mss., Welbeck Collection, Pw2/Hy/31 ff.13r–20r.
[32] BL Harl. Mss., 478 f.647r, Harl. Mss., 163 f.691v; Gardiner, *History of England, 1603–1642*, X, 77, n.3.

Burgess, White, Marshall and Calamy were all involved in drafting the ministers' remonstrance, which Harley had presented to the Commons in January 1641, and Burgess may well have been referring to that particular document in his letter, which, as has been noted, did not demand 'root and branch' abolition of episcopacy.[33] Clarendon also later stated that support for 'root and branch' was very limited inside Parliament, but in contrast to Burgess averred that in 1641 both Lord Brooke and Lord Saye were in favour of radical reform: 'in the House of Peers there were only at that time taken notice of the Lord Saye and Brooke, and they believed to be positive enemies to the whole fabric of the Church, and to desire a dissolution of that government'. Given Clarendon's assessment of the limited amount of support in the House of Lords for changes in the government of the Church, why did the Commons press ahead with the bill in the summer of 1641? A bill excluding the bishops from the upper House had already been defeated in the Lords on 8 June, and the 'root and branch' bill could not be passed if the bishops still wielded their votes in Parliament.[34]

Sir Robert was, of course, aware that he was regarded as a prime mover for religious reforms, and in calling for the debate on the bill to go ahead in June 1641 he was sending a clear signal to the godly in the land that he and his fellow reformers were acting decisively against the bishops. Outside Parliament the debates on episcopacy had sparked off a great national movement which embraced thousands of people. The London 'root and branch' petition presented to the Commons in December 1640 was variously said to carry 10,000 or 15,000 signatures, although the number of signatories may well have been inflated by the names of people who did not understand what they were signing. This was an allegation made by the supporters of episcopacy and it was one which deeply worried Lady Brilliana. In February 1641 she asked Edward Harley to

send me word whether those that have put in the petitions against bishops have taken the hands of all such as do not understand what they have put their hands to. I am told it is the way in all countries, and that Mr Mackworths gave such directions. To me it does not seem reasonable; for, in my opinion, such hands should be taken as understand it, and will stand to what they have done.

Despite these allegations it is clear that there was strong opposition to episcopacy, and during 1641 nineteen counties sent 'root and branch' petitions to Parliament. Professor Fletcher concludes that 'it is appropriate to speak of a national petitioning campaign'.[35]

[33] Dr Williams' Library, Baxter Mss., Letters 59/III, f.80r; for reference to the Ministers' Petition and Remonstrance see above, n.28.
[34] Macray, *History of the Rebellion and Civil Wars in England*, I, 309; Fletcher, *Outbreak of the English Civil War*, 101.
[35] D'Ewes(N), 313–14, 138; Lewis, *Letters of the Lady Brilliana Harley*, 113–14; Fletcher, *Outbreak of the English Civil War*, 92.

The question of the fate of episcopacy was, however, highly divisive and in Herefordshire the Harleys' puritan circle had to abandon their promotion of an anti-episcopal petition because of lack of support. The JP, James Kyrle, took the petition to the quarter sessions at Hereford in January 1641, but could not persuade any of the other justices to sign it. Lady Brilliana recorded that 'my young cousin Vaughan' had collected 70 signatures, but Kyrle would not send the petition to Harley for presentation to Parliament until more people had signed. That there was only limited support in Herefordshire for the reforms advocated by the local puritans was a fact which eluded Stanley Gower. He complained to Harley that he was 'ashamed to see the causeless timidity of the justices of our country to subscribe the petition against episcopacy, though they had Gloucestershire and other countries for their precedent'.[36]

The reform group in Parliament was, however, acutely aware that in some regions there was hostility or indifference towards the measures that it was pursuing. In an attempt to counteract such reactions the House of Commons directed its members to mobilise public opinion by promoting parliamentary orders in their constituencies. On 5 May 1641 the Commons ordered that the document known as the Protestation should be printed and MPs should send copies to the county sheriffs, justices and borough officials to encourage them to take the attached oath and to tender it to the local population. Harley had been a member of the committee that had drawn up the Protestation and oath in response to the news of the First Army Plot. The initial information about the plot indicated that King Charles intended to raise an armed force in London against Parliament and the oath thus bound all who took it to defend 'the true reformed protestant religion . . . His Majesty's royal person and estate, as also the power and privilege of Parliaments, the lawful rights and liberties of subjects'.[37]

Harley drafted a letter to Herefordshire reinforcing the contents of the Protestation, which he described as demonstrating the care of the House of Commons in asserting 'the truth of our holy religion from popish innovations, and our fundamental laws and liberties from such pernicious counsels and conspiracies, as threatened their subversion'. Lady Brilliana confirmed that in the areas where the Harleys were influential – Brampton, Wigmore and Leintwardine – the oath was taken on 16 May 'with much willingness'. The oath was also taken in Hereford, Weobley, Leominster 'and in other parts of this county'. Later that summer Sir Robert was instrumental in having another parliamentary order publicised in the counties. On 26

---

[36] James Kyrle to Harley, undated, BL Loan 29/120; Lewis, *Letters of the Lady Brilliana Harley*, 111, 113–14; Stanley Gower to Harley, 23 January 1640/1, BL Loan 29/119.

[37] *CJ*, II, 135, 132; Gardiner, *History of England, 1603–1642*, IX, 351; The Protestation and oath are printed in Gardiner, *Constitutional Documents*, 155–6.

August he moved in the House that 'some course might be taken' to circulate printed copies of the order for a public thanksgiving held to mark the conclusion of peace with the Scots. On the same day the House ordered its members to 'take the best care they can for the dispersing' of the order.[38]

At the start of September 1641 Parliament went into recess for six weeks and Sir Robert was able to return to Brampton Bryan for the first time since the session had started. On his arrival in Herefordshire he set about a campaign to enforce the recent Commons' resolutions on religion, which amongst other things called for the removal of images and crucifixes from all churches. Sir Robert was a member of the committee which had drawn up the resolutions and he now instigated a public drive against what he saw as idolatrous images in the parishes near Brampton. Harley's earlier iconoclasm, described by his daughter Brilliana in 1639, had been a private affair.[39] Now, however, Harley was acting with the full authority of the House of Commons and he was concerned to make his activities as conspicuous as possible. In the last week of September he visited Wigmore, where he was the patron, and destroyed the church cross there. Henry Ecclestone, an official in the Welsh Council, later described 'Sir Ro: Harlowe's vehement course in pulling down the cross at Wigmore . . . and caused it to be beaten in pieces, even to dust, with a sledge, and then laid it in the footpath to be trodden on in the churchyard'.

Four days later Sir Robert visited another parish where he was the patron, Leintwardine, 'and broke the windows in the church and chancell and broke the glass small with a hammer, and threw it into [the] Teme, in imitation of King Asa 2 Chronicles 15: 16: who threw the images into the brook Kidron'. At Aymestry, however, Sir Robert met with opposition from the minister, Mr Lake, and the parishioners who 'withstood him' as Ecclestone politely put it, 'and so he departed for that time'. A draft of a letter to the churchwardens of Leominster also survives, in which Harley complained that two days previously on his return from the quarter sessions at Hereford he had seen

in your churchyard of Lempster, one crucifix upon the great stone cross there, and another crucifix of stone over the church porch, and in the great window in the west end of the church two crucifixes painted, and other scandalous pictures of the persons of the Trinity, and in the great window in the east end of the church one other crucifix painted, all which I require you to abolish, according to the order of the House of

[38] Draft letter from Harley and Fitzwilliam Coningsby to the sheriff and JPs of Herefordshire, 8 May 1641, BL Loan 29/173 f.101r; Lewis *Letters of the Lady Brilliana Harley*, 130; Herefordshire JPs to Harley, 5 March 1641/2, BL Loan 29/173 f.228r; BL Harl. Mss., 164 f.880r; *CJ*, II, 275.

[39] *CJ*, II, 278–9. The Commons' Resolutions are printed in Gardiner, *Constitutional Documents*, 197–8. For Harley's iconoclastic activities in 1639 see chapter 3, n.12 above.

Commons, which I send you herewith, as also to see carefully performed the further directions of the said order.[40]

The brief recess had given Harley ample opportunity to make a dramatic and public avowal of his desire for religious reforms. In general, however, he was restricted in his attempts to influence local opinion by the sheer distance between Westminster and his home. During parliamentary sessions Harley had to rely on personal letters to keep local people informed about proceedings in Parliament, and in May 1641, for example, another Welsh Council official in Ludlow had noted that 'there has some packets been brought of late (one last week) by posts to this town, directed to Mr John Aston, a mercer, and were sent from Sir Robert Harley . . . the business therein being only (as I hear) advertisements of the proceedings in Parliament to the puritan party in these parts'.[41]

Sir Robert was also, of course, writing to his wife and to his rector at Brampton Bryan, and their letters reveal a great amount of information about the impact of the news which they received. Lady Brilliana's immense interest in parliamentary affairs meant that both Edward Harley and his father made efforts to relate important events to her. Edward had accompanied Sir Robert to the opening of Parliament and had abandoned his studies at Oxford in order to stay on in London. He was clearly as interested in the Parliament as were his parents and the first item which he sent home from London was the King's speech at the opening of Parliament. In response his mother asked for the Speaker's speech, and requested that Ned should tell her 'what good men are of the Parliament'. Edward continued to send news items to his mother throughout the first session, but Sir Robert's commitments as an MP meant that he was unable to write to his wife with the same frequency and detail employed by his son. Lady Brilliana understood this and in her letters to Edward she acknowledged the weight of work undertaken by Sir Robert at Westminster, describing him as 'full of business'. Yet, despite all the difficulties, Sir Robert did find time to write to his wife, sending, for example, the seven charges against Strafford which were read to the Commons in November 1640.

The speed with which Lady Brilliana received news could vary considerably. Some of the Harleys' letters were sent by carrier to Hereford or Shrewsbury, where they had to be collected. News contained in letters sent by the carrier could be two weeks old by the time that it reached Brampton, but Lady Brilliana decided that 'the sureness of the carrier, though he is slow, makes me write by him'. In April 1641 a new post was set up at Ludlow and

---

[40] Huntington Library, Ellesmere Mss. 7350; Harley to churchwardens of Leominster, 8 October 1641, BL Loan 29/173 f.165r.
[41] Edward Martyn to the Earl of Bridgewater, 17 May 1641, Shropshire RO, Bridgewater MSS. 212/364.

Lady Brilliana asked Ned and Sir Robert to send their letters there, 'for it will be easier than to send to Shrewsbury'.[42] The Harleys also made use of local people who were travelling to or from London to carry letters privately whenever they could, since this would normally ensure a swifter arrival. Local people continued their normal habits of travelling or sending to London for a variety of reasons and letters were delivered for the Harleys both by local gentry or their servants, and by other messengers, such as the mercer (probably John Aston of Ludlow), and on one occasion the sheriff of Shropshire.[43]

Letters carried by hand could arrive within hours of the events which they described. In December 1640 Sir Robert entrusted a letter for his wife to the hands of an apothecary named Morgan. The letter described the flight of Secretary Windebanke to France in order to escape impeachment by the House of Commons, and it was given to Lady Brilliana late on the night of 11 December, the day after Windebanke had left England. The speed with which Lady Brilliana received this news indicates that people in the localities could be very well informed about events at Westminster and could react to them almost as quickly as people in London. The excitement generated by the receipt of topical news was further heightened by eyewitness accounts. The apothecary, Morgan, who had seen the triumphal entry of Prynne and Burton into London, was able to describe the scene himself to Lady Brilliana, and when Stanley Gower was in London for nearly two months in the spring of 1641 he was most impressed with events in the capital, particularly the trial of Strafford. On his return he regaled all and sundry with the story and Lady Brilliana almost wearily noted at the end of April that 'Mr Gower has not yet made an end of the relation of my Lord Strafford's charge. He is as much taken with the relation, as I think he was with hearing it.'[44]

Lady Brilliana not only knew about past events, she was also informed about future debates in the Parliament, which intensified her desire for further news. In 1641 she was told by Edward Harley and 'others' that 25 January had been chosen by the Commons for the debate about episcopacy. Accordingly that day was observed as a day of prayer at Brampton, 'to sue to our God for His direction of the Parliament', and Lady Brilliana was impatient to hear the outcome of the debate. She was obviously pleased to hear from her husband and elder son, but she also valued their letters because she believed that the information they sent to her was accurate. The problem of sifting truth from rumour was formidable and between 1640 and 1642

---

[42] Lewis, *Letters of the Lady Brilliana Harley*, 100–1, 104, 106, 111, 113, 130–1; Lady Brilliana to Harley, 1 April 1641, BL Loan 29/173 f.91r.

[43] Lewis, *Letters of the Lady Brilliana Harley*, 103, 104, 105, 106, 111, 116, 124, 125, 130, 131, 134, 141, 143; Lady Brilliana to Harley, 20 November 1641, BL Loan 29/173 f.176v.

[44] Lewis, *Letters of the Lady Brilliana Harley*, 105, 104, 113, 115, 118, 126.

there was an enormous amount of inaccurate news in circulation which spread both in print and by word of mouth.[45]

The problems involved in obtaining exact reports are also well illustrated in Lady Brilliana's letters. At the beginning of February 1641 she thanked Edward for sending her a copy of a speech by the King in which he upheld the powers of the bishops. She had seen the speech before, but 'it was various from yours'. At the start of April she complained to Harley that 'the intelligence of this country is very various and I think this country is worse than any for they are averse to all that is good. Yet I do not repent that my lot fell in it, because I am yours, in whom I think myself happy.'[46] Similarly in June she asked Edward to write to her about the outburst in the Commons against the Scots by Herbert Price, because there were such 'various reports' of the incident. The problems of procuring accurate news were compounded by the ease with which falsehoods gained credence. In March 1641 Lady Brilliana noted that 'many rumours are in the country'. A few weeks later she recorded that in the 'country they have in report hanged the Archbishop'. On 8 May, the day on which the attainder bill was passed against Strafford by the House of Lords, which also coincided with the panic at Westminster over the First Army Plot, Lady Brilliana wrote: 'we hear of great matters that have been done at London this week, but I believe nothing till I hear it from a sure hand'.[47] Some rumours were so implausible, however, that Lady Brilliana rejected them out of hand. Three weeks after the Parliament had opened she reported that she had heard that Parliament had adjourned for ten days, 'but I defer my belief', and at the end of April 1641 she informed Edward that 'in the country they had broken the Parliament and beheaded my Lord Strafford', which she wryly noted 'would not hang well together'.[48]

There were, however, other rumours which she did not ignore and which alarmed and frightened many people in the country and at Westminster. These were stories about a national catholic plot, which proliferated in late 1640 and throughout 1641, and which were seemingly verified by the findings of MPs at Westminster. The belief that the King was caught at the centre of a sophisticated catholic intrigue was also a dominant theme in the news which was circulating in the provinces and the Harley papers clearly illustrate how this fear helped to mould public opinion against the crown. The accusation of catholic plotting was repeated in all of the major public statements of Parliament in 1640 and 1641, and thus one of the seven original charges against Strafford accused him of having encouraged the Irish

[45] Lewis, *Letters of the Lady Brilliana Harley*, 111, 136–7; Fletcher, *Outbreak of the English Civil War*, xxviii.

[46] Lewis, *Letters of the Lady Brilliana Harley*, 112; Lady Brilliana to Harley, 2 April 1641, BL Loan 29/173 f.93r.

[47] Lewis, *Letters of the Lady Brilliana Harley*, 135, 118, 129–30.

[48] *Ibid.*, 103, 126.

catholics 'to make them of his party. To promote his tyrannical designs and settle mutual dependence.' The Protestation of May 1641 had similarly declared that 'the designs of the priests and Jesuits, and other adherents to the See of Rome, have of late been more boldly and frequently put in practice than formerly, to the undermining and danger of the ruin of the true reformed religion in his Majesty's dominions established'. The Grand Remonstrance, which catalogued the ills which had beset the nation since the accession of King Charles, 'without the least intention to lay any blemish' upon the King's 'royal person', also asserted that 'those evils under which we have now many years suffered, are fomented by a corrupt and ill-affected party . . . whose proceedings evidently appear to be mainly for the advantage and increase of popery'.[49]

Parliamentary propaganda undoubtedly magnified the power of the catholics in England, but it should not be forgotten that the King had openly favoured catholics. Not only was Queen Henrietta Maria a catholic, but during the 1630s catholicism had been increasingly fashionable at court. Furthermore, many Englishmen regarded catholicism and Arminianism as synonymous and they regarded the spread of Arminianism as further evidence of the strength of the popish plot. The Grand Remonstrance thus insisted that 'the Jesuits and other engineers and factors for Rome . . . have so far prevailed as to corrupt divers of your bishops and others in prime places of the Church, and also to bring divers of these instruments to be of your Privy Council, and other employments of trust and nearness about your Majesty, the Prince and the rest of your royal children'.[50]

During 1642 the statements issued by Parliament continued to stress the existence of a 'popish plot', and belief in the plot was a fundamental tenet of parliamentarianism once war had broken out; and the public denunciation of a conspiracy would have made little impression if there had not been a large body of opinion in the country willing to believe in it. The MPs who investigated the plot were convinced of the truth of their findings and it would be totally incorrect to regard them as manipulating distrust of catholics solely in order to gain support outside Parliament. Pym and his allies did play upon such sentiments in order to sway opinions in the House, but this tactic was successful purely because so many members were genuinely concerned about catholic subversion, as was Pym himself. The anxieties of the MPs were reflected in the number of committees which they set up to investigate the extent of the plot during the first few weeks of the Long Parliament and Harley, who had proved himself fervently anti-catholic in Parliaments in the 1620s, was active both on some of these committees and in the ensuing

---

[49] *D'Ewes (N)*, 61; Gardiner, *Constitutional Documents*, 155–6, 202–32.
[50] Clifton, 'Fear of Popery', in Russell, ed., *Origins*, 144–67; Fletcher, *Outbreak of the English Civil War*, 26, 139; Gardiner, *Constitutional Documents*, 203–4.

debates in the House. He was also amongst those MPs who favoured accepting Alderman Pennington's offer of 300 London citizens to guard Parliament against catholic attack, since Parliament was traditionally regarded as a prime target for catholic assault and tales of bloody designs against MPs at Westminster were rife during 1640 and 1641.[51]

Rumours about catholics did not, however, originate solely in London. They were matched by purely local alarms, news of which travelled to London and fuelled the fears voiced by MPs. Such local stories were interpreted as further evidence of a national plot involving the highest authorities in the land and Sir Robert's own apprehensions were shared at his home. On 9 November 1640, six days after the Parliament was opened, Stanley Gower wrote from Brampton to tell Harley that he had heard that the City of London was expecting a two-pronged attack from the Tower of London and from Lambeth Palace, by royal forces and by forces raised by Archbishop Laud. The Tower was in fact being fortified, and complaints were raised about this in the Commons on the same day that Gower wrote to Harley, which again underlines the rapidity with which key issues were being reported to the localities. In his letter Gower added that there was also local evidence of a plot and noted that 'we apprehend as great fears in the country, papists' houses are so ready for to execute whatsoever plots are hatching'. In order to foil the catholics he advised that 'papists' houses should be searched through the land and their ammunition seized on'. He continued with the ominous news that at Sir Basil Brook's house at Madley, Shropshire, some 35 miles north-east of Brampton, three cooks were preparing as much meat as they could, although it was not known who was to eat it. Gower added that Brook had reputedly said 'he wonders that my Lord of Canterbury should dissemble so long, since it is well enough known he is a papist'. Brook was a known catholic confidant of the Queen, which must have made his supposed comments about Laud all the more alarming.[52] Less than a fortnight later Gower informed Harley that catholics were secretly moving munitions by night to 'red castle' – Powis Castle in Montgomeryshire – the home of the catholic Lord Powis, which was to be a royalist stronghold during the First Civil War. In December and January both Lady Brilliana and Gower reported the 'great resort of papists' at Plowden Hall, the Shropshire home of the catholic Plowden family, 'which makes some fear they have some plots'.[53]

[51] *CJ*, II, 24, 32, 42: *D'Ewes (N)*, 56; Clifton, 'Fear of Popery', in Russell, ed., *Origins*, 159–62. For Harley's anti-Catholic stance in the 1620s and 1630s see above, chapter 4, *passim*.

[52] Stanley Gower to Harley, 9 November 1640, BL Loan 29/172 f.308r; *D'Ewes (N)*, 291–2. I am grateful to Professor Conrad Russell for information about the fortification of the Tower of London: see *D'Ewes (N)*, 16, 24, 29–30.

[53] Stanley Gower to Harley, 20 November 1640, 12 December 1640, BL Loan 29/172 ff.309v, 346, *idem* to Harley, 2 January 1640/1, BL Loan 29/173 f.9r; Lewis, *Letters of the Lady Brilliana Harley*, 105.

A fresh wave of panic broke at the start of the second session of the Long Parliament in October 1641 following news of the Incident, in which Charles was implicated in a plan to assassinate three Scots protestant Lords, and the revelation of the Second Army Plot against the English Parliament, which intensified mistrust of the King. News of the rebellion of the Irish catholics was then broken in Parliament at the start of November 1641 and accounts of the barbaric slaughter of hundreds of protestant men, women and children in Ireland revived fears of catholic uprising in England and Wales, especially in counties with coastlines facing Ireland, where refugees fleeing the insurrection arrived with horrific tales of murder, torture and pillage.[54] The prospect of a catholic revolt was seemingly confirmed on 15 November when the House of Lords questioned a tailor named Beale, who claimed to have overheard a design to kill 108 Members of Parliament, which would be followed by a general uprising on 18 November. Sir Robert took immediate steps to warn both his family at Brampton and other local puritans. Henry Ecclestone recorded the 'stir this last week' in Ludlow, where a nightly watch was set up following the arrival of a letter from Sir Robert to John Aston 'in these words – look well to your town, for the Papists are discovered to have a bloody design, in general, as well against this kingdom, as elsewhere'. At Brampton, 'they were all in arms upon the top of Sir Robert's castle and took up provisions there with them and in great fear'. All of which concluded Ecclestone, 'puts the country in a great amaze'. Bewdley, in Worcestershire, received the same news and the people there were 'up in arms with watch all night in very great fear'.[55]

Following her husband's instructions Lady Brilliana arranged for a good provision of bullets to be made and guns were kept charged against possible attack. She informed Harley that Brampton could not withstand a siege and asked him whether the family should seek safety in a nearby town, perhaps Shrewsbury. This was the first time that Lady Brilliana was to suggest leaving Brampton with her children, but during the next two years she repeatedly asked Harley if she should leave, as the dangers from royalist forces became ever more apparent. In 1641 Sir Robert rejected this course of action, as he was to do again on later occasions. Lady Brilliana, however, remained anxious for some weeks. On 11 December she informed her husband that she hoped 'as you do, that the papists will not attempt anything', but she was prepared to suffer for her faith:

---

[54] Gardiner, *History of England, 1603–1642*, X, 23; Fletcher, *Outbreak of the English Civil War*, 135; Clifton, 'Fear of Popery', in Russell, *Origins*, 159; K. J. Lindley, 'The Impact of the 1641 Rebellion upon England and Wales, 1641–5', *Irish Historical Studies*, XVIII (1972–3), 143–76.
[55] Gardiner, *History of England, 1603–1642*, X, 43, 73; Huntington Library, Ellesmere Mss. 7352.

I thank you that you give me warning not to be afraid, I hope I am not. I desire to place my security in the safe protection of my God and if I suffer anything in professing His name, I hope I shall never be sorry for it, but rather rejoice that I am counted worthy so to do.[56]

Lady Brilliana little realised that in less than a year she would be taking similar precautions against an attack on Brampton by the protestant gentry of her own county. Yet even before the start of 1642 some of the key issues over which the Civil War would be fought had already become matters of debate in Herefordshire. One of the major divisions between royalists and parliamentarians in the county during the course of 1642 would be the question of whether to retain or to abolish bishops, but this division was already evident as early as January 1641, when James Kyrle could not persuade any of his fellow JPs to subscribe the petition against episcopacy.[57] The fact that religious issues lay at the heart of divided opinion, both locally and nationally, was obvious to contemporaries, who were writing of 'parties' in connection with episcopacy as early as December 1640.

Another central division between supporters of the King and supporters of Parliament in 1642 would be the extent to which they were prepared to trust the King to rule according to the laws. The belief that there was a widespread catholic plot, which the King had been unable or unwilling to counter, persuaded the Harleys and many others that the King was untrustworthy. Royalist propaganda in 1642 discounted the existence of such a plot and insisted that the King must be trusted. During the first year of the Long Parliament some of the crucial differences between the future Civil War parties had therefore become starkly apparent. The critical weeks of December 1641, when the Commons impeached twelve bishops, including Bishop Coke of Hereford, and the following January, when the King launched an unsuccessful coup against Parliament, served to clarify the precise issues which led to the establishment of the Civil War parties.[58]

[56] Lady Brilliana to Harley, 20 November, 4 December and 11 December 1641, BL Loan 29/ 173 ff.175r–182r.
[57] James Kyrle to Harley, undated, BL Loan 29/120.
[58] Fletcher, *Outbreak of the English Civil War*, 119–90 *passim*.

6

The formation of parties in Herefordshire

On 10 January 1642 the royal family fled from Whitehall Palace to Hampton Court, and throughout the next two months King Charles travelled uneasily through the southern and eastern counties of England, arriving on 19 March in York, which became the rallying point for loyalists to the royal cause. The King's sudden withdrawal from the capital was prompted both by his earlier failure to arrest Lord Mandeville (later the Earl of Manchester) and five leading oppositionists in the House of Commons, and by his fear that the Commons would impeach the Queen in retaliation for his attempted coup against Parliament. Charles realised that the weight of public opinion in Westminster and the City was firmly in favour of the Parliament and any further attempt at coercion would jeopardise his own safety and that of his family.[1]

As Pym and his fellows went into hiding to avoid arrest, the House of Commons took emergency measures to meet in the City of London, where a committee of twenty-five was named to sit in the Guildhall to consider the King's blatant breach of parliamentary privilege. The select committee for Irish affairs was also ordered to meet at nearby Grocers' Hall, and in the absence of Pym, Sir Robert Harley acted as chairman. The wisdom of this transfer was demonstrated on the night of 6 January when an alarm was raised that the King was coming to the City with 1,500 horse to take the Five Members by force. Although the news proved to be false, the reaction of the Mayor and citizens was rapid. The City gates were shut and chains erected across the streets to stop the troops and within an hour thousands of armed men had taken to the streets. In truth the King was in no position to storm such a stronghold, and instead looked to the localities to provide the military support needed to subdue Parliament. The day after Charles had departed to Hampton Court the members of the House were able to return triumphantly

[1] Gardiner, *History of England, 1603–1642*, X, 137–78.

to Westminster supported by the City trained bands and crowds of well-wishers.[2]

For the most perceptive observers the attempt to arrest and impeach Lord Mandeville, and Pym, Hampden, Holles, Strode, and Haselrig was followed by a further dramatic polarisation of opinion and news of the episode travelled swiftly. Sir Robert avoided his usual carriers and immediately sent word of the incident to Brampton via the post at Worcester, but even before his letter had arrived Lady Brilliana knew that 'many of the House of Commons were accused of treason' and feared that her husband would be amongst them. Though relieved to hear from Harley's own hand that he was not involved, she nevertheless understood the broader implications of this news. She recognised that sides were forming in response to the national crisis at Westminster and identified the cause of Parliament with the cause of the godly in the unceasing struggle between good and evil, as her reply to Harley clearly demonstrates — 'the accusation of my Lord Mandefeeld [*sic*] and the 5 of the House of Commons made all good hearts sad, but the Lord has shewed Himself to be on the side of those that take part with him'.[3]

Following the King's withdrawal to the provinces, local gentry were called upon to execute parliamentary orders which clearly did not have royal sanction; and the exact nature of the authority of Parliament, and in particular of the House of Commons, became a pressing issue for the county gentry, who realised that Parliament was arrogating the executive powers of the crown. The key matter of contention between the King and Parliament in the opening months of 1642 was the control of the militia. The two Houses passed an ordinance on 5 March nominating their own lords lieutenant to replace the royal nominees. The King's response to this was contained in a message of 15 March to Parliament in which he declared 'that His subjects cannot be obliged to obey any act, order or injunction to which His Majesty has not given His consent'. The next day the House of Commons formally claimed supreme legislative power for 'the Lords and Commons in Parliament' and stated that Charles' command that they should not be obeyed was 'a high breach of the privilege of Parliament'.[4]

In Herefordshire the question of whether to accept Parliament's claim to be able to act separately from the crown proved as divisive as the arrival of the royalist commission of array some six months later. This issue was also widely seen as a crucial strand in the development of royalist ideology elsewhere. The Kentish petition of 25 March demanded that 'no order, in

[2] Coates, Young and Snow, *The Private Journals of the Long Parliament: 3 January to 5 March 1642*, xxv, 14; B. Manning, *The English People and the English Revolution* (1976), 111–13.

[3] Lady Brilliana to Harley, 10 January and 15 January 1641/2, BL Loan 29/173 ff.191r, 195r.

[4] *LJ*, IV, 587; Husbands, *Exact collection*, 113–14; Gardiner, *History of England, 1603–1642*, X, 176.

either or both Houses, not grounded on the laws of the land, may be enforced on the subject, until it be fully enacted by Parliament'. Similar doubts were expressed in the statements made on behalf of the crown during the early months of 1642, which linked this specific point to the prospect of arbitrary government by Parliament and the consequent overthrow of the personal liberties embodied in Magna Carta.[5] The problem was also discussed in private; writing from his family seat in Nottinghamshire, Lord Montagu addressed his son William at length on the subject:

I see yet little hopes of accommodation. This word Parliament rightly understood, would make a great turn of peoples' ears. It is most sure he is not of a true English spirit that will not shed life and all that he hath for the maintenance and preservation of Parliaments, consisting of the King, Lords, and Commons. But to have the ordinance of Lords and Commons bind all the subject[s] to England without the consent of the King is of most dangerous consequence, and a violation of all the privileges of Parliament and common liberty of the subject; therefore I would to God the Lords and Commons would be pleased not to stand upon that. My heart, hand, and life shall stand for Parliaments, but for no ordinance only by Lords and Commons. If that were well understood, it would take away much mistaking.[6]

The establishment of civil war parties has been interpreted as the reluctant response of the localities to central events; it has thus been suggested that the prevailing mood in the counties in 1642 was one of 'fear and indecision', and that most men chose to delay choosing sides until they received a military commission from either the King or Parliament. This argument ignores the protracted build-up of partisan opinion which had taken place in 1640 and 1641 and which accelerated when the King left Whitehall. The King's commission of array did not arrive in Herefordshire until July 1642, while the rival parliamentarian militia ordinance was not executed for the county until the end of September. It is, of course, palpably true that the Civil War could not start until two opposing military organisations had been formed, but in Herefordshire the arrival of these two commissions did not create parties, for they were already in existence and had formed as the result of a gradual split in public opinion in the county, which had become obvious almost as early as the opening of the Long Parliament.

The months from the start of 1642 until the outbreak of hostilities in mid-July were the period of the so-called 'paper war', when both sides printed and circulated their own interpretations of the deepening crisis. It has been suggested that 'in general the content of the propaganda would serve to

[5] T. P. S. Woods, *Prelude to Civil War, 1642: Mr Justice Malet and the Kentish Petition* (Salisbury, 1980), 143; Husbands, *Exact Collection*, 91, 106, 113–14, 126, 139, 163–4, 175–6, 178, 181, 243, 250, 251, 254, 283, 297, 301, 302, 345, 363, 365, 373, 378, 379, 402, 443, 451.
[6] HMC, *Report on the Mss. of the Duke of Buccleuch and Queensberry K.G., K.T., Preserved at Montagu House, Whitehall.* III (1926), 414.

confuse. Both sides were aiming at the middle ground.'[7] Although such uncertainty may have characterised those who had not yet taken sides, for the committed this was certainly not the case and in Herefordshire the activists on both sides reacted with deep-felt principle to the propaganda and news which they received. The news which reached the county served therefore to exacerbate the growth of committed opinion as well as prompting some people to take a neutral or moderate course. Throughout the spring and summer imformation continued to be relayed fairly swiftly: thus on 12 March 1642 Lady Brilliana reported that 'many fears did arise in the country' because of the King's refusal at the start of the month to place the militia in the control of lords lieutenant nominated by Parliament. A week later she thanked Edward Harley for sending her a copy of the *Declaration* to the King from Parliament, which had been delivered to Charles at Newmarket ten days earlier, on 9 March. She already knew of this document and wrote: 'I did much long to receive the Declaration to the King. I thank you for it.' It embodied all of the central arguments which had persuaded parliamentarians that the King was not to be trusted, chief amongst these being the belief that the kingdom was in the grips of a catholic plot. The *Declaration* also added a new dimension to this fear by explicitly stating that the King intended to wage a civil war – 'the labouring to infuse into your Majesty's subjects an evil opinion of the Parliament through the whole kingdom, and other symptoms of a disposition of raising arms and dividing your people by a civil war'.[8]

The *Declaration* and other messages published by both the King and Parliament during the early months of 1642 also made constant reference to the 'fears and jealousies' felt by both sides. Underlying those fears were two very different perceptions of the nature of the crisis facing the nation. Despite the manifest desire of the gentry for accommodation, their differing beliefs only led them into further conflict. Leading county gentry and clergy were increasingly willing to enter public debate on issues of national importance and in Herefordshire the traditional relationships within the county community were placed under growing strain as rival parties gradually formed and local people came to realise that war was imminent. In this context it is illuminating to consider the contrast with which one particular piece of news was received in the county before the start of the war. Sir John Hotham's refusal to admit the King to Hull at the end of April was widely discussed throughout the kingdom and was eagerly seized upon by polemicists on both sides. Hull was both a major northern port and the site of the country's largest magazine, which had only recently been restocked for the Scottish wars, and

---

[7] Morrill, *Revolt of the Provinces*, 39, 35. The history of the two rival commissions in Herefordshire is discussed more fully in chapter 7, below.

[8] Lewis, *Letters of the Lady Brilliana Harley*, 150, 152; Husbands, *Exact Collection*, 99.

control of the town and its arsenal was strategically vital in the event of armed conflict.

Lady Brilliana regarded Hotham's action with approval and informed Edward Harley that 'we must all acknowledge God's great mercy that the plot for the taking of Hull was discovered'. In comparison, one of the royalist prebendaries at Hereford, Dr Henry Rogers, preached a sermon in the cathedral on 1 July 1642 in which he compared 'the taking away of the magazine at Hull . . . to a man robbing by the highway, pretending he did it to give the poor', and concluded that 'Sir John Hotham, for keeping the King out of Hull, was a traitor'. Using the familiar imagery of the body politic Rogers demonstrated that the two Houses did not constitute a Parliament in the absence of the King – 'as the limb of a man is not a man, or a body without a head, no more is the Parliament a Parliament without the King' he thundered.[9] His opinions were doubtless echoed from countless pulpits throughout the land.

Herefordshire, however, has been seen as an exception because 'local royalism does not seem to have existed before the actual declaration of war except in Herefordshire'.[10] This assessment ignores the evidence of royalism which has been detected in counties as far apart as Kent, Cornwall, Yorkshire, Somerset and Worcestershire, where opinion in favour of the King was being mobilised by local petitions in the spring or early summer. Furthermore, Lady Brilliana herself noted outbreaks of popular violence against parliamentarians in Ludlow during June 1642, which strongly suggest that Shropshire was experiencing the sort of divisions which led to public confrontations in Herefordshire in the same weeks.[11] Herefordshire was unique, not in the early emergence of royalism in the county, but in the strength and clarity with which its royalism was expressed and recorded.

The arrival of the commission of array thus gave military leadership to a number of Herefordshire gentlemen who had already identified themselves as principled supporters of the King. Their beliefs were set out in March and April 1642 in two lengthy and illuminating letters directed to Sir Robert Harley and his fellow knight of the shire, Humphrey Coningsby. Both of these letters were signed by Sir William Croft, Fitzwilliam Coningsby, Wallop Brabazon, Henry Lingen, Thomas Price, William Rudhall, William Small-man, Thomas Wigmore and John Scudamore (probably John Scudamore of

---

[9] Gardiner, *History of England, 1603–1642*, VIII, 367; Lewis, ed., *Letters of the Lady Brilliana Harley*, 166; John Wanklen to Harley, 1 July 1642, BL Loan 29/174 f.265r.

[10] Hutton, *Royalist War Effort*, 4.

[11] Everitt, *Community of Kent*, 95–107; D. Underdown, *Somerset in the Civil War and Interregnum* (Newton Abbot, 1973), 28–30; E. Green, 'On the Civil War in Somerset', *Somersetshire Archaeological and Natural History Society's Proceedings*, XIV (1867), 51–2; W. Cobbet, ed., *The Parliamentary History of England*, II (1807), 1366–7; J. T. Cliffe, *The Yorkshire Gentry from the Reformation to the Civil War* (1969), 331–5; R. H. Silcock,

Ballingham and not Viscount Scudamore). The majority of these men later formed the core of the royalist party in the county and, with the exception of Wigmore, they were all active commissioners of array in the early stages of the war.[12] The JPs' arguments in their two letters were based on their resistance to orders from Parliament which were not sanctioned by the King, combined with their conservative adherence to the established Church. Similar sentiments were expressed in the *Declaration or Resolution of the County of Hereford*, a major, but anonymous, statement of royalist thought, which was printed in London at the start of July.

Professor Fletcher's research indicates that the Herefordshire *Declaration* 'exhibited a lofty strain of royalist sentiment that had not at that stage been heard from any other county'. The House of Commons said much the same thing albeit in more colourful language, accounting this document to be 'the foulest and most scandalous pamphlet that was ever raised or published against the Parliament', and ordering immediate inquiry into its provenance. At least one commentator has suggested that the *Declaration* 'so clearly reflects the ideas associated with Hyde and Falkland that it is difficult not to discern the influence of at least one of them in its composition'. There is no concrete evidence to indicate that this document was a purely local paper or that it was penned by one of the King's advisors. Lady Brilliana, however, regarded it as a local effort and it was wholeheartedly accepted by the Herefordshire commissioners of array, who ordered its reading at the muster held at Hereford on 14 July. It was attested later in the same month by the grand jury at the Hereford quarter sessions.[13]

The gentry, however, were not alone in their willingness to take sides. As in other counties, the Herefordshire clergy were also drawn into the public debate. On the parliamentarian side the vicar of Leominster, John Tombes, quickly took the lead, actively organising the resubscription to the Protestation oath ordered by the Commons in January 1642 as a demonstration of support for Parliament against the King's attempt on the Five Members, and promoting a pro-parliamentary petition in March. His efforts were supported by Stanley Gower and by John Green, rector of Pencombe, both of whom would be chosen to represent Herefordshire on the Assembly of

'County Government in Worcestershire, 1603–1660' (University of London, Ph.D. Thesis, 1974), 230; Lewis, *Letters of the Lady Brilliana Harley*, 167, 172.

[12] Herefordshire JPs to Harley and Humphrey Coningsby, 5 March 1641/2 and 18 April 1642, BL Loan 29/173 ff.228r–229v, 239r–240r; Levy 'Thesis', 243–4.

[13] Fletcher, *Outbreak of the English Civil War*, 305; *CJ*, II, 661; R. Ashton, *The English Civil War; Conservatism and Revolution, 1603–1649* (1978), 162; Lewis, *Letters of the Lady Brilliana Harley*, 162; anonymous report of the muster held at Hereford, 14 July 1642, Lady Brilliana to Harley, 15 July 1642, BL Loan 29/174 ff.278v, 280r. The *Declaration* is printed in Webb, *Memorials*, II, 343–4.

Divines later in the year.[14] A number of royalist clergy were similarly involved in these months. At the January quarter sessions a pro-episcopacy petition was presented to the JPs by Mr Mason, vicar of Yazor and Mr Sherburn, rector of Pembridge, the latter minister having already been singled out by the local puritans in their 1641 survey as 'very pragmatical, preaching for ship money etc.'[15] Mason and Sherburn enthusiastically used their pulpits to preach the King's cause and their efforts were matched by those of Dr Rogers at the cathedral. In May Stanley Gower forwarded notes taken from their sermons to Sir Robert Harley and complained that

your worthy endeavours for the public, have in our county public opposers. The pulpit is made a stage, whereon to act their parts against the Parliament. Dr Rogers and Mr Mason of Hereford and Mr Sherburn of Pembridge are the Agonethi and leaders of the schism. I know not whether they have taught some of our gentry or these them, but they strive who shall outvie other in their railing rhetoric.

The cathedral clergy also set up a lecture in these months designed, according to one parliamentarian sympathiser, to 'work a hatred in the hearts of the people against the Parliament and all good ministers and people, calling them schismatic and other reproachful nicknames'.[16]

Support for the Parliament was increasingly seen by the Harley circle as a litmus test which would reveal the true ranks of the godly. In February, Lady Brilliana had informed her husband that the puritan JP Edward Broughton 'will tell you what they think at Hereford of the Parliament, but I trust the Lord will still keep your hearts upright in seeking His glory first'. Four months later Stanley Gower wrote to Harley and analysed the contentions between 'both sides' involved in the conflict at a national level, in which he clearly linked true religion with a desire for the 'liberty of subjects':

The wonders of God in this Parliament will never be forgotten. You are his most famous witness . . . I am the more confident of your safety and, in you, of the Church,
1. because both sides have appealed to God for judgement, whether you or they intend religion, law, liberty of subject and therefore God will give a perfect lot; the Achan shall be found.
2. because you go contrary ways; you by fasting and prayers, they by raging and blasphemy against the God of Heaven, and all his people, as they must, Revelation 16, so it's easy to judge on what side God is.
3. because you are of contrary spirits: you merciful, pitiful, slow (if not too slow) to justice, and study peace; they fierce, cruel, and thirst after blood, and therefore God will give them blood to drink for they are worthy.

[14] John Tombes to Harley, 5 March 1641/2, BL Loan 29/173 f.226r.
[15] Lady Brilliana to Harley, 15 January 1641/2, BL Loan 29/173 f.195v; Corpus Christi Mss., 206 f.6v.
[16] Stanley Gower to Harley, 8 May 1642, BL Loan 29/173 f.243r, John Wanklen to Harley, 1 July 1642, Loan 29/174 f.265r.

The good Lord keep you but close to the rule and fast to your ends, that you intend (come what will come) a thorough reformation, and the Lord is with you while you are with him.[17]

The Herefordshire royalists certainly did not oppose the institution of Parliament itself, but they did believe that pressing religious and constitutional problems had arisen by the beginning of 1642. The most immediate of these were the degree of religious reform necessary to restore harmony within the Church, and the exact legal status of a Parliament functioning without the King. These two issues were also to prove crucial in creating swelling support for the King in other regions and their influence has been traced by Anthony Fletcher in his major study of the outbreak of the Civil War, where he concludes that 'royalism emerged in many counties through conservative petitioning campaigns about the issues of episcopacy and liturgy . . . royalism as a coherent viewpoint, based consciously on dislike of and opposition to the Parliament's political policies and methods, took longer to crystallise'.[18] In Herefordshire, however, political opposition to Parliament emerged in parallel with the promotion of the pro-episcopacy petition at the quarter sessions of January 1642, when the county justices publicly confronted the constitutional problems raised by the spectre of Parliament acting tyrannically in opposition to the King.

The impeachment of Bishop Coke of Hereford and eleven other bishops by the Commons in December 1641 in an attempt to weaken the royalist party in the Lords was undoubtedly the catalyst which prompted the clerics Mason and Sherburn to canvass support for a pro-episcopacy petition from Herefordshire. Lady Brilliana informed Sir Robert about the petition on 15 January, when she noted that Viscount Scudamore had been the first to sign it and that his example was followed by all of the justices present at the Hereford quarter sessions, except for James Kyrle and Edward Broughton, both of whom had been instrumental in compiling information for the puritan survey of the Herefordshire ministry sent to Parliament at the beginning of 1641, and both of whom would be unequivocal in their support for Parliament once war had started.[19] Sir William Croft, on the other hand, noted Lady Brilliana, 'spoke much for' the pro-episcopacy petition, which had then been sent by Wallop Brabazon and Fitzwilliam Coningsby to the sheriff for circulation amongst the borough corporation of Leominster. There is no record in the printed *Journals* that the petition was presented to either House of Parliament, but it was printed in May 1642 by command of the

[17] Lady Brilliana to Harley, 26 February 1641/2, BL Loan 29/72, Stanley Gower to Harley, 20 June 1642, Loan 29/173 f.256r.

[18] Fletcher, *Outbreak of the English Civil War*, 283.

[19] Manning, *The English People*, 100–1; Lady Brilliana to Harley, 15 January 1641/2, Isaac Seward to Harley, 7 February 1641/2, BL Loan 29/173 ff.195v, 207r. For the subsequent parliamentarianism of Broughton and Kyrle see below, p. 152.

King in a collection of petitions on behalf of 'episcopacy, liturgies, and supportation of Church revenues, and suppression of schismatics', where it was claimed that 68 gentry, 8 doctors, 150 ministers and 3,600 freeholders and inhabitants of Herefordshire had subscribed.

In keeping with similar documents from other counties, the Herefordshire petition supported the prayer book and the Church hierarchy, but showed no sign of sympathy for Arminianism. It stated that a change in Church government would result in 'disturbances and disorders' and thus called for the retention of the established communion and episcopacy 'for the glory of God, preservation of order, peace and unity, the reformation and suppression of wickedness and vice, and the mature prevention of schisms, factions and seditions'.[20] The general lack of enthusiasm in the county for Laudian Church ceremony and ornamentation was confirmed in a letter from Lady Brilliana to Edward Harley, written a few weeks later on 17 February, in which she reported that 'in Hereford they have turned the table in the cathedral and taken away the copes and basins and all such things'. Very similar religious opinions were set out in the first letter from the nine JPs to the knights of the shire, in which the justices confirmed their support for episcopacy and for the prayer book, and at the same time explained their principled objections to Parliament functioning without the assent of the King. The nine also endorsed the 'purging' from Hereford cathedral of 'copes, candlesticks, basins, altars, with bowing and other reverences unto it' which had been introduced against the will of the cathedral clergy by 'a former Bishop ' (probably Lindsell or Wren), and expressed their hope that 'the present government of the Church (the abuses therein being reformed) and the uniformity of common prayer shall be so established as may preserve peace and unity amongst ourselves. The sectaries, separatists and all such recusants as have of late taken great liberty unto themselves being brought again under the obedience of the laws.' Similarly the *Resolution of the County of Hereford* firmly supported the established Church, complaining that the protestant religion had been 'assaulted in the in-works and skirts of it, the liturgy and decent ceremonies established by law; yea in the very body of the 39 articles. In what danger this Church of England has been to be over-run with Brownists and Anabaptism let all the world judge.'[21]

In Herefordshire the religious opposition to Parliament expressed in the pro-episcopacy petition appeared in tandem with the open resistance of a core of JPs to Parliament acting without the King. In mid-January the

---

[20] Fletcher, *Outbreak of the English Civil War*, 288. The pro-episcopacy petition is printed in Webb, *Memorials*, II, 337–8.

[21] Lewis, *Letters of the Lady Brilliana Harley*, 148; Herefordshire JPs to Harley and Humphrey Coningsby, 5 March 1641/2, BL Loan 29/173 ff.228r–229v; Webb, *Memorials*, II, 344.

Parliament had issued an order to all sheriffs to secure their county magazines with the assistance of the justices and the trained bands. This was a response to the news that armed supporters of the King led by Captain Thomas Lunsford and Lord Digby had gathered at Kingston, the site of the Surrey magazine, possibly intending to seize the county arms for the King. In Herefordshire the order provoked further public signs of an ideological split amongst the county JPs, which followed roughly the same lines as the split over the pro-episcopacy petition, and the sheriff, Isaac Seward, reported to Harley that the justices were 'cold' in performance of the order.[22] Both the King's advisors and the Parliament recognised the importance of securing public support and in January started to send propaganda to the counties setting out their own versions of the conflict. The newly appointed Secretary of State, Viscount Falkland, conducted a systematic campaign of circulating the King's declarations to the counties, despatching 50 copies to each sheriff.[23] Towards the end of January the House of Commons also ordered that the Protestation oath should be resubscribed in the counties and directed its members to send the oath to the sheriffs, accompanied by a letter from the Speaker and by a declaration of the House against the King's attempted coup earlier that month.[24]

Sir Robert sent the Parliament's documents to Isaac Seward, who replied that, since the order bore only the authority of the Commons, 'I fear I shall not give you so good an account of this'. He also informed Harley that he had already received some items from the King with the instructions to 'disperse them abroad'. Seward explained that he would obey both sets of instructions and desired 'to be found as ready to serve his Majesty and Parliament, as any other man'. The sheriff's response to the clear-cut split in political authority was the classic reaction of the neutral, assiduously carrying out the orders of both sides. Seward thus arranged to meet the county justices at Hereford in order to carry out the Commons' directions concerning the Protestation oath, but his apprehensions were justified, for only a few of the JPs attended the meeting and most half-heartedly suggested taking the oath when all the justices were assembled. There were, however, strong signs of a party split. Sir William Croft, who had spoken for the pro-episcopacy petition at the January quarter sessions, now took the lead in openly opposing the oath. He declared that he had already taken it the previous summer and the justices should neither resubscribe now, nor should they tender the oath to anyone else. Croft was opposed by James Kyrle and Edward Broughton, who had

[22] Husbands, *Exact Collection*, 51; Isaac Seward to Harley, 7 February 1641/2, BL. Loan 29/173 f.207r.

[23] J. Willis Bund, ed. *The Diary of Henry Townshend of Emley Lovett, 1640–1663*, II (1920), 48; G. L. T. Smith, 'Gentry Royalism in North Wales: The Sheriff's Letter Book of 1642' (University of Birmingham, MA Thesis, 1982), 27.

[24] *CJ*, II, 389.

earlier refused to sign the pro-episcopacy petition and who now took the oath in front of the sheriff.[25]

A month later, in the first of two letters addressed to the county MPs, the royalist justices formally stated their objections to obeying orders which had no royal warrant. They explained that they had all taken the oath the previous summer, when they had encouraged others to take it. Now, however, they objected to the contents of the Speaker's letter, which directed them to administer the oath on the sole authority of the House of Commons, 'which we know not how to do, but by our warrants to the inferior officers, and for that we . . . have no authority, and as little to tender the said Protestation to any'. The letter was imbued with the spirit of conciliation and the justices did not enter into any direct constitutional arguments; instead they insisted on their own ignorance concerning the 'power and privilege of Parliament', which had of late 'raised questions between His Majesty and both Houses, and between the Houses themselves'.[26] The manifest desire for conciliation expressed in this letter does not, however, imply that these men were not committed in their support for the King, as a second letter penned in April would soon reveal.

Sir Robert and the junior knight for Herefordshire, Humphrey Coningsby, replied swiftly to this initial overture from the justices. How much influence the youthful Coningsby had in framing the reply is doubtful, since the existing draft is in Harley's own hand. Harley started by declaring that the justices' letter was so open to exception that the MPs had not seen fit to deliver it to the Commons, since it might be considered a sign of 'disaffection' to Parliament. The draft then went straight to the constitutional points raised by the justices' refusal to obey the House of Commons and identified Parliament as the source of power within the constitution, reducing the status of the King to just one element within Parliament, with a burden of responsibility equal to that of the Lords and Commons:

the constitution of this kingdom . . . is resolved into the prudential power of Parliament, composed of the three estates, King, Lords and Commons . . . if either neglect his office or withhold his influence, symptoms of ruin will quickly appear and the crisis of this great body will extremely be endangered, if any such prognostics now show themselves, it will be all our wisdoms to study the means of cure.[27]

Medieval usage commonly described the three estates as representing the Lords spiritual, the Lords temporal and the Commons, but this was a fairly

---

[25] Isaac Seward to Harley, 7 February and 19 February 1641/2, BL Loan 29/173 ff.207r, 222v, John Tombes to Harley, 5 March 1641/2, Loan 29/173 f.226r.

[26] Nine Justices to Harley and Humphrey Coningsby, 5 March 1641/2, BL Loan 29/173 ff.228r–229v.

[27] Harley and Humphrey Coningsby to the Herefordshire JPs, 28 March 1642, BL Loan 29/124/63.

flexible conceit and the King was sometimes substituted for the Lords spiritual in some contexts, which might infer that the King's powers were on a par with those of the two Houses. Harley and Coningsby made no reference in their letter to the King's powers outside Parliament, a constitutional argument which was, however, central to the royalist programme. In his *Answer to the Nineteen Propositions* given on 18 June, King Charles emphasised the importance of the distinction between the role of the King in Parliament, which was to make laws, and the role of the King alone, which was to govern:

in this kingdom the laws are jointly made by a King, by a House of Peers, and by a House of Commons chosen by the people . . . The government, according to these laws, is trusted to the King.[28]

This was a distinction which the Herefordshire justices also emphasised. On receiving the reply to their first letter, the nine justices responded in a second letter dated 18 April in which they threw aside their pretended ignorance of the powers of Parliament and carefully analysed the arguments put forward by Harley and Coningsby. The justices stated that they were so 'cautious to preserve the liberty of the subject' that neither the fear of being sent for as delinquents, nor the threat of being removed from the commission of the peace would persuade them to 'yield obedience to any authority which is not derived from His Majesty'. The justices accepted that the King, Lords and Commons were the three estates, but remonstrated that the Commons were increasingly acting against the wishes of the other two estates. The JPs argued that the King, not the lower House, should have ultimate power over the other two estates:

you tell us truly that the constitution of this kingdom is composed of three estates, King, Lords and Commons. It is a triple cord, and it would be dangerous to untwist it. If we leave out either, it will not be so strong. We do not yield to any active obedience to His Majesty's commands, but such as are warranted by laws made by his authority and consent of both Houses. Nay we have seen the Lords more unanimously concurring with his Majesty then at present, and yet, the Commons thought themselves not tied to obey both those estates. Every one of the three has a negative voice and if any should have the power of binding it should rather be thought the King, than the Commons, for we find in the statute books those charters and other acts (which story tells us, cost our ancestors much blood) are yet there entered as proceeding from the free grace and favour of the Prince.

In order to stress the final authority of the King, the justices added the following telling point – 'He summons you to Parliament, and had always the

[28] Husbands, *Exact Collection*, 320; for a recent discussion of the use of the concept of the three estates in civil war propaganda see M. Mendle, *Dangerous Positions: Mixed Government, the Estates of the Realm, and the Answer to the xix Propositions* (Alabama, 1985).

power to dismiss you.' The justices then specifically denied that Parliament had the power to govern and insisted that it was purely a law-making body:

we send you, not with the authority to govern us or others (for who can give that to another that is not in himself), but with our consent for making or altering laws as to his Majesty, the Lords and Commons shall seem good.

Their letter ended by repeating the conciliatory sentiments of the first letter and argued that the King's confessions of his past errors and his resolution to govern 'by law for the future' should reconcile the King and his people. The justices insisted that although they were writing as private individuals, yet their opinion was grounded on 'information of our own and what we find to be the general desire of this shire'.[29]

The nine justices, as the traditional spokesmen of their county, were anxious that their MPs should convey their opinions to the House of Commons, but they were also well aware that they had no way of ensuring that they did so. In their first letter the JPs had reminded Harley and Coningsby of their duty to present the pro-episcopacy petition to the House, which they apparently never did. In that letter the JPs also demanded that their knights should propound 'to this Parliament some bill for the future more orderly and free election of knights and burgesses and to provide such means whereby they may be enjoined more diligently hereafter to attend that service, in discharge of the great trust reposed in them'. In their second letter the justices reproved the knights for not presenting the first letter to the House, but they were powerless in the face of Harley's refusal to act on their behalf.[30] This was to prove yet another element in arousing royalist sentiments in the county. The *Resolution of the County of Hereford* of July 1642 argued that Parliament had denied 'information by the humble way of petitions from the county, as that most excellent orthodox petition of our brethren of Kent, and rejecting information of letters to our knights and burgesses'. The fate of the Kentish petition had become a rallying point for the royalist party when the Commons had imprisoned two of its leading promoters, the poet Richard Lovelace and Sir William Boteler, at the end of the previous April.[31]

The Herefordshire royalists were not only eager to press their own opinions on the Parliament, they also attempted to discredit their opponents in the county. In their second letter, the nine JPs questioned the provenance of a pro-parliamentary petition which was then circulating in the county and they warned their knights not to present it to the House:

[29] Herefordshire JPs to Harley and Humphrey Coningsby, 18 April 1642, BL Loan 29/173 ff.239r–240r.

[30] Herefordshire JPs to Harley and Humphrey Coninsgby, 5 March 1641/2, 18 April 1642, BL Loan 29/173 ff.229r, 239r.

[31] Webb, *Memorials*, II, 343; Woods, *Prelude to Civil War*, 81–3.

if any should come from a corner of this county, which shall have none of our hands and few of those you know, it should not have credit enough with you to tender it to the House. There is one, or rather many (the copies varying) offered and recommended as by direction from Sir Robert Harley, which the relation of some of the solicitors to you Sir, would make us believe . . . and considering the composure and what kind of subscribers (we hear) it is tendered unto, to fill paper with names, we presume you are not acquainted with it.[32]

Harley had in fact first been told of the petition in early March 1642 by John Tombes, who wrote that it had been 'conceived' at a meeting held in his home attended by Stanley Gower and John Green, the rector of Pencombe, as well as some local laymen, including the sheriff, Seward, John Flackett the elder and Thomas Eaton. Lady Brilliana also wrote about this petition to her son Edward and she astutely identified the retaking of the Protestation oath and Tombes' petition as two flashpoints, which had further divided public opinion in the county. Her letters also reveal the emergence of Sir William Croft as one of the most influential royalists in the county. On 19 March Lady Brilliana told Edward that 'I hear the justices have sent up their answer, why they would not take the Protestation. Sir William Croft governs all of them . . . I hope shortly you will have the petition for this county, but Sir William Croft dissuaded it, as a thing unlawful to petition'. A week later she noted:

I much desire to hear how the Parliament took the answer of the justices of this country that sent word they knew not by what authority the Parliament did require the taking of the Protestation. Sir William Croft is much against the Parliament and utters his mind freely. He was much displeased that they would petition the Parliament; he told Mr Gower he was a mouther of sedition and my cosen Tomkins was very hot with him. They say the Parliament does their own business and not the country's . . . on Monday before Easter Mr Kyrle and some other gentlemen intend to set forward with the petition, which I hope will be well taken.[33]

Despite the efforts of Croft, the petition was delivered to the House of Commons by a group of 'divers gentlemen of the county of Hereford' at the start of May and was read out at once. The delegation of gentlemen who had delivered it were then called to the chamber and addressed by William Lenthall, the Speaker, who told them 'that this House finds their petition full of great expressions of duty to His Majesty and of love and respects to the House and the commonwealth (for which they give you thanks), and full of great concernment to the commonwealth'. Despite the approval of the Commons, the petition was derided in Herefordshire: a few days later Lady Brilliana wrote 'they have so mocked at our Herefordshire petition, that I

[32] Herefordshire JPs to Harley and Humphrey Coningsby, 18 April 1642, BL Loan 29/173 f.239r.

[33] John Tombes to Harley, 5 March 1641/2, BL Loan 29/173, f.226r; Lewis, *Letters of the Lady Brilliana Harley*, 152, 121 (see also p. xiv where Lewis explains this letter was misdated).

long to hear what they say to it at London'.[34] The favourable reception accorded to the petition by the Commons is hardly surprising since it contained a catalogue of praise for the policies pursued by Parliament, although couched in the conventional language of support for both King and Parliament, even when considering issues on which the two sides were completely opposed: 'we acknowledge . . . your prudent care in disposing the militia, the navy and places of importance to this kingdom, to such persons of trust, as may . . . give assurance of safety to the King's royal person and good subjects of all his Majesty's dominions'.

The petition also dwelt at large on religious matters, thanking the Commons for their:

zealous furthering of bleeding Ireland's relief; earnest desire of disarming papists and securing their persons . . . your zeal to provide a preaching ministry throughout the kingdom, whereof this country stands in great need, it now abounding with insufficient, idle, and scandalous ministers, whereby the people generally are continued in ignorance, superstition and profaneness, and are ready to become a prey to popish seducers, which idolatrous profession has of late years, with much boldness appeared in this county.

Tacked on to the end of these complaints was an attack on 'the excessive importation of Spanish wools', which had caused a decline in the price of Herefordshire wool, 'to our great impoverishing'.[35] This final point is strangely juxtaposed with the more obviously partisan comments which preceded it, but Leominster, where Tombes and his companions had drawn up the petition, was a wool town and the economic concerns of his parishioners thus found their way into the petition. Between December 1641 and August 1642 people in no less than 38 counties sent similar petitions of support to the Commons. The interpretation of their contents has been various and perhaps tells us more about the concerns of individual historians than of the petitioners themselves. Brian Manning deduces that 'their main and most insistent theme was the decay of trade and industry'. Anthony Fletcher, in a sympathetic and thorough analysis, believes that 'fear of popery was the most prominent theme running through the petitions'.[36] We can be certain that the economic clauses of the Herefordshire petition were unexceptionable; it was rather the petition's avowed support for the transfer of control of the militia from the King to Parliament and for the Commons' 'pious care to settle a government in the Church, according to the word of God' which had so angered Croft and his fellow JPs.[37] Furthermore, the

[34] *CJ*, II, 556; Lewis, *Letters of the Lady Brilliana Harley*, 159.
[35] The pro-parliamentary petition is printed in Webb, *Memorials*, II, 338–9.
[36] Manning, *The English People*, 118; Fletcher, *Outbreak of the English Civil War*, 200.
[37] Webb, *Memorials*, II, 338–9.

theme of anti-popery was, as we have seen, an integral element in the development of parliamentarianism amongst the Harley circle.

Many of the supporters of the Parliament were convinced that the King intended to convert the English to catholicism, by force if need be, and that he would not baulk at eliminating Parliament in the process. The accusation that the King was aiming at the destruction of Parliament drew upon fears for the survival of that institution which had been associated with the political policies of both James I and Charles I, and which had been reinforced by the experience of the 'Personal Rule', when Charles I had summoned no Parliaments for eleven years. The *Declaration* to the King from Parliament of March 1642 thus referred to the 'manifold advertisements, which we have had from Rome, Venice, Paris and other parts, that they still expect that your Majesty has some great design in hand, for the altering of religion, the breaking the neck of your Parliament'. The question of whether catholicism and the native catholic population presented a political and religious threat to the protestant nation was an issue which clearly divided royalists and parliamentarians in Herefordshire. In their first letter of March 1642, the nine royalist justices had dismissed the numbers of recusants of both kinds (catholic and protestant) in the county as being 'inconsiderable'.[38] In contrast the petition devised at Tombes' house in favour of Parliament insisted that catholicism was on the increase, and the spate of rumours which had followed on the outbreak of the Irish Rebellion continued to alarm the Harley circle in 1642. In mid-January Lady Brilliana informed her husband that she had heard that local catholics were arming. The sheriff, Seward, received similar information at the same time, which he also relayed to Sir Robert and it is quite possible that local catholics were afraid of reprisal attacks by protestants and were thus arming in self-defence.[39]

Fears that English catholics would attack their protestant neighbours were closely entwined with the belief that the King intended to employ foreign mercenaries to subjugate his own people. This belief had some basis, since both Charles and Henrietta Maria hoped to obtain aid from foreign states and once the war started the royalist army did include catholic troops from both Ireland and the continent. This was foreshadowed by Parliament's propaganda in the spring and summer of 1642; thus in March the *Declaration* to the King stated that the Pope had asked the Kings of Spain and France to supply 4,000 soldiers each 'to help maintain your royalty against the Parliament'. On 19 March the erroneous news reached Parliament that an army of 30–40,000 Danes would soon be landing at Hull and on the same day

---

[38] Husbands, *Exact Collection*, 100; Herefordshire JPs to Harley and Humphrey Coningsby, 5 March 1641/2, BL Loan 29/173 f.229r.
[39] Webb, *Memorials*, II, 338; Lady Brilliana to Harley, 15 March 1641/2, Isaac Seward to Harley, undated, BL Loan 29/173 ff.196r, 209r.

John Pym received an anonymous letter stating that French troops were to be sent to Ireland.[40] On 25 March, a week after she had received the *Declaration to the King*, Lady Brilliana wrote of these rumours:

I was never less satisfied in a week's intelligence than in this. Many rumours there are in the country and the King's going to York and they speak of foreign enemies, which made me exceeding long to hear the truth . . . send me word how things stand, for if there should be any stirs, Brampton, in respect of worldly help, is very weak.[41]

Lady Brilliana's response to this news was to increase the stock of arms held at Brampton and in April 1642 she received 'a box with match and 2 bandoliers', but she noted 'the box was open before it came to me'. She also asked Ned to purchase arms for the family doctor, which were not to be sent direct, but which should go first to Brampton. 'He desires', she wrote, 'you would do him the favour to buy him two muskets and rests and bandoliers, and 15 or 16 pound of powder in a barrel and he desires you would send them by Lemster carrier, and so directed them to Brampton and he will give order to have them sent to Hereford and will send you what they cost.' Lady Brilliana was openly alarmed by the rumours that were circulating and she took active measures to protect her home and her family; there was an enormous gulf, however, between her actions and the response of the royalists in the county. In the second of their letters to Harley and young Coningsby, the nine justices avowed that

we at distance only hear of foreign force, but God be thanked, nothing appears (as yet) from France or Denmark, and for plots of papists at home, they are still underground as formerly and with us they are so quiet as we have had no cause hitherunto to apprehend any danger from them. If it please God to protect the protestants in Ireland from the fury of the papists there, we shall little doubt anything here at home.[42]

The Herefordshire royalists were not alone in their assessment, for similar views appear in a set of royalist instructions framed in Kent in July 1642 for the MP Augustine Skinner, which roundly informed the House of Commons that 'we are persuaded your fears and jealousies of foreign forces, of French, or Danes, or of papists at home (an inconsiderable party, especially being

---

[40] Gardiner, *History of England, 1603–1642*, X, 55 n.2, 177; J. L. Malcolm, *Caesar's Due: Loyalty and King Charles, 1642–1646*, RHS Studies in History, XXXVIII (1983), 50–2, 94–5; Husbands, *Exact Collection*, 100; Gardiner, *History of England, 1603–1642*, X, 177.

[41] Lady Brilliana to Harley, 25 March 1641/2, BL Loan 29/173 ff.85r–86r (erroneously bound with documents dated 1641).

[42] Lewis, *Letters of the Lady Brilliana Harley*, 153–4; Herefordshire JPs to Harley and Humphrey Coningsby, 18 April 1642, BL Loan 29/173 f.239v. An inventory drawn up in 1623 shows that under normal circumstances the arms at Brampton were inconsiderable and consisted only of twenty-two halberds, three French pistols, four lances, one pike, three sets of horse armour and two sets of foot armour: see 'A schedule of the goods and chattels of Thomas Harley esq. at Brampton Castle . . . 6 May 1623', Brampton Bryan, Harley Mss., Bundle 83.

disarmed) are long since vanished'. Royalists were much more likely to be alarmed by the implications of radical protestantism, which they believed threatened both social and religious stability.[43] In a sermon delivered on 27 April 1642 Henry Rogers compared the flight of Charles I from London to King David's escape from Jerusalem and denounced the people of London, who had 'grown insolent against authority and irreverent in their carriages towards their sovereign'. Rogers depicted the supporters of Parliament as a combination of religious radicals and the lowest dregs of society, who would overthrow established order. This was a belief that was as common to the royalist cause as was the corresponding belief amongst the parliamentarians that the King was in the grip of a catholic plot. Rogers thus linked the presence of religious sects in the capital with the influence of the mob on Parliament:

there are sects of anabaptists, separatists and others. There are rents also in government. The base rabble rout assemble themselves and they will prescribe a way of government to the Parliament and make laws of their own. These are the causes of our King's flight.

Rogers instanced a number of historical examples of rebellion against Kings, including Richard II, and compared the present state of England to that of 'the low countries, where every man rules and does what he list'. Then he railed bitterly against the revival of what he termed 'old heresies':

the Arians against bishops, the Anabaptists and the old Priscillianists, who maintained lying and perjury, are sprung up again, and the Millianares, and I would there were not some such preachers too as John Drew and Wall, one of which chose this text — when Adam delved and Eve span, who was then the gentleman? And so he would have no man above another, but all men alike and to throw down all government, learning and religion.[44]

'When Adam delved . . .' was the text commonly believed to have been used by the priest, John Ball, at the outbreak of the Peasants' Revolt of 1381. Royal proclamations and other royalist statements issued during the summer of 1642 also drew on this historical allusion and identified Pym and his supporters with such celebrated rebels as Wat Tyler, Jack Cade and Robert Kett.[45]

The effect of all these arguments was to make people think very carefully about their own political and religious stance, and some took committed action long before war was seen as inevitable. As early as 17 May Lady Brilliana received news from her brother-in-law, Sir William Pelham of Brocklesby in Lincolnshire, that 'he has given up his lieutenancy and is going

---

[43] Woods, *Prelude to Civil War*, 154.
[44] Notes of Dr Roger's sermon, 27 April 1642, BL. Loan 29/173 ff.237r–238r.
[45] *DNB*, I, 994; Fletcher, *Outbreak of the English Civil War*, 296.

to York, to the King, being his servant, as he writes me word, and so bound by his oath . . . We hear that the King will summon all that will be for him to come to him.' On hearing this news Lady Brilliana immediately revived her plan for leaving Brampton Bryan, which she had first suggested to Harley in the aftermath of the Irish Rebellion. Then she had planned to go temporarily to a refuge such as Shrewsbury, but now she obviously expected to leave Brampton for a longer period and proposed to Harley that he should 'dispose' of his estate 'to your best advantage' so that she could join him in London, while Robin and Tom should continue their education at Oxford.[46]

Although Harley's reply is unknown he clearly advised her to remain at Brampton, just as he would repeatedly do in the months to come. At this stage he probably believed that his wife would be safe at their home and he would surely have been reluctant to advise her to leave, since this would have resulted in a loss of Harley influence in the county and would have increased the likelihood of his estate being plundered. Sir Robert's assumption that his family was safe in Herefordshire was doubtless reinforced by the fact that in some areas of county life the traditional loyalties of the 'gentry community' were still functioning normally. An example of this is the letter sent to Harley by the justices attending the April 1642 quarter sessions at Hereford, which demanded that he and Humphrey Coningsby should seek a reduction in the assessed contribution of the county for the prosecution of the Irish war. As had so often been the case in the past, taxation was an issue on which the county gentry could unite in a display of obstructive tactics. Men who were divided over national politics could thus find common ground on matters of local concern, and the parliamentarians Edward Broughton and James Kyrle placed their signatures on the letter along with royalists such as Croft, Brabazon and Fitzwilliam Coningsby. Harley penned a hurried reply in which he tartly assured the JPs that he had already pressed in the House for a reduction, to no avail, 'I hope you do not think that I was asleep when it was proposed, for I assure you I pressed earnestly to have our county eased,' he sniped. He also alluded to the urgent need for the money as a result of the 'cloudy and barbarous rebellion of the papists in Ireland, which . . . is like to endanger the peace of England'.[47]

Lady Brilliana similarly expected the relationships between the county gentry to remain unchanged and in May 1642 she suggested that Harley solicit the aid of Sir William Croft in promoting Edward Harley as a candidate in the coming by-election for Hereford. His mother was extremely eager that Ned should perform his 'first service for the commonwealth', and

---

[46] Lewis, *Letters of the Lady Brilliana Harley*, 161; Lady Brilliana to Harley, 17 May 1642, BL Loan 29/72.
[47] Herefordshire JPs to Harley and Humphrey Coningsby, April 1642 and Harley's draft reply, 3 May 1642, BL Loan 29/50/74.

had already supported an earlier unsuccessful plan to gain parliamentary representation for Wigmore, in the hope that Edward would be returned. Now Lady Brilliana ignored the religious and political tensions in the county as she canvassed the support of the local gentry. She explained to Edward that she had written to 'my cousin Elton, for his daughter has married Mr Weaver's son, and young Weaver has power over many voices. Doctor Wright persuaded me to write to my cousin Vaughan, who has interest in some of aldermen.' Lady Brilliana also sent a messenger to ask for the 'assistance' of Sir William Croft, who replied that 'he would not meddle in it; he would leave all men to themselves'. His refusal to involve himself in this election contrasts sharply with Croft's active support for Sir Robert Harley's return to the Short Parliament. While Croft's refusal to act either for or against the Harleys shows a reluctance to combine his stand on national politics with the election, it also reveals a subtle alteration in the relationship between the two families.[48]

The election itself did not become a focus for local party feelings because Lady Brilliana gracefully halted her own campaign on hearing that Viscount Scudamore's son was to stand. The Viscount had been chief steward of Hereford since 1631 and Lady Brilliana doubtless realised that he had superior links with the city. She thus informed Ned:

I sent to Hereford to let them know that I heard that my Lord Scudamore's son would stand for the burgeship, and then I did not further desire it for you; but gave them many thanks for their good will to you and desired if my Lord's son did not stand, that then they would give you their voices, which they then promised they would.[49]

Despite Sir William Croft's inaction Lady Brilliana had little reason to doubt that the friendship between the two families was still strong, and surprisingly at the beginning of June 1642 she tried, on Sir Robert Harley's instructions, to negotiate with Croft's mother about the purchase of arms from Croft Castle on behalf of the parliamentary commission for Irish affairs, of which Harley was a member. Sir William tactfully blocked the sale by telling Lady Brilliana that his mother had no authority to sell the arms at Croft Castle, but the Harleys clearly saw nothing incongruous in attempting to buy arms from one of the most royalist families in the county. Lady Brilliana doubtless believed she had nothing to fear from Croft at this date, despite his manifest opposition to the Parliament. He was not only a kinsman of the Harleys, but also a justice of the peace and Lady Brilliana could hardly have thought that he might be involved in any attack on Brampton. Instead her thoughts were running on the likelihood of a popular insurrection. In the same letter which

---

[48] Lewis, *Letters of the Lady Brilliana Harley*, 162, 105–7, 163–4; Hereford and Worcester County RO, Croft Mss., S33/8.
[49] PRO C115/M23/7687, M21/7638, 7639; Lewis, *Letters of the Lady Brilliana Harley*, 166.

describes Croft's refusal to part with the arms, Lady Brilliana informed her husband, 'the country grows very insolent and if there should be any rising I think I am in a very unsafe place . . . in my opinion it were much better for me to be at London, there is nobody in the country that loves you or me'.[50]

It would, however, be an error to regard Lady Brilliana's request for Croft's aid, in both the election campaign and in buying arms for Parliament, as evidence that the relationships between the major gentry had been unaffected by the course of national politics. It must not be overlooked that on both occasions Croft refused to help the Harleys. Although Sir William was polite and reserved in these instances, many people were not so restrained in showing their dislike of the local parliamentarians. On the same day that she informed Harley of the dangers of a rising, Lady Brilliana also wrote to her son Edward and for the first time she reported the existence of popular hatred directed against parliamentarians in the area around Brampton, including Ludlow and Sir William Croft's home:

at Ludlow they set up a maypole, and a thing like a head upon it, and so they did at Croft, and gathered a great many about it and shot at it in derision of Roundheads. At Ludlow they abused Mr Bauges [*sic*] son very much and are so insolent that they durst not leave their homes to come to the fast. I acknowledge that I do not think myself safe where I am.[51]

This is the earliest reference amongst the Harley papers to the use of the party label 'Roundhead'. Clarendon and Rushworth both dated its origin to the last days of 1641, when the crowds calling for the exclusion of the bishops and catholic peers from the House of Lords were nicknamed 'Roundheads' and the army officers supporting the King were tagged 'Cavaliers'. In his *History of the Rebellion*, Clarendon described the conflicts between the two groups and the first use of these terms:

and from these officers, warm with indignation at the insolence of that vile rabble which every day passed by the court, first words of great contempt, and then . . . blows, were fastened upon some of the most pragmatical of the crew . . . and from those contestations the two terms of 'Roundhead' and 'Cavalier' grew to be received in discourse, and were afterwards continued, for the most succinct distinctions of affection throughout the quarrel; they who were looked upon as servants to the King

---

[50] Lady Brilliana to Harley, 4 June 1642, BL Loan 29/173 f.252r; on 20 May 1642 the minute book of the commission for Irish affairs records that the commissioners had been 'advertised that the Lady Croft hath a good number [of arms] in the county of Hereford, which she may be willing to sell'. Harley was asked to 'write unto some trusty person in those parts to view them', in order to ascertain whether the commission should buy them, Snow and Young, *The Private Journals of the Long Parliament, 7 March to 1 June 1642*, 457.

[51] Lewis, *Letters of the Lady Brilliana Harley*, 167.

being then called 'Cavaliers' and the other of the rabble contemned and despised under the names of 'Roundheads'.[52]

From January 1642 onwards a number of pamphlets were published in London satirising the two parties, but there was an obvious gap between the adoption of these terms in the capital and their acceptance as party labels in the provinces. The term 'Roundhead' was exported to York with the arrival there of the King and his entourage in mid-March. At the end of that month a group of twenty Lincolnshire gentlemen who had travelled to York in order to petition for the King's return to London were set upon as 'Roundheads' by a mob egged on by Cavalier supporters of the King.[53] Although there is no evidence amongst the Harley papers that the term 'Cavalier' was being used in Herefordshire in the summer of 1642, Lady Brilliana's reports of the local employment of the term 'Roundhead' were confirmed by John Tombes at the end of June. Leominster, where Tombes was rector, was already religiously divided and he now wrote to Stanley Gower 'that there are a number of persons that do quarrel with Lemster headsmen under the appellation of Roundheads, that they can scarce safely walk the streets or be in houses in Hereford'.[54]

In mid-July Lady Brilliana dramatically recounted to her husband the type of abuse which she had experienced within the grounds of Brampton itself, when people from Ludlow cursed the Harleys as they passed Brampton each Thursday, probably *en route* to a market in Radnorshire. Brampton Castle lay close to the main road running from Ludlow to Knighton, and this proximity gave the travellers an easy opportunity to jeer at its owners:

they are grown exceeding rude in these parts. Every Thursday some of Ludlow, as they go through the town [Brampton] wish all the puritans of Brampton hanged and as I was walking one day in the garden, Mr Longly and one of the maids being with me, they looked upon me and wished all the puritans and Roundheads at Brampton hanged, and when they were gone a little further they cursed you and all your children and thus they say they do every week as they go through the town.

In the same letter Lady Brilliana described events at the annual fair held at Brampton on 11 June, when 'an unruly fellow' was taken before Edward Broughton, who was acting in his capacity as a JP, to maintain the peace. The

---

[52] Macray, *History of the Rebellion and Civil Wars in England*, I, 456; Rushworth attributed the coining of the term 'Roundhead' to David Hide, 'a reformado in the late army against the Scots, and now appointed to go in some command into Ireland', who 'began to bustle and said he would cut the throats of those Round-headed dogs that bawled against Bishops (which passionate expressions of his, as far as I could ever learn, was the first miniting of that term or compellation of Round-heads, which afterwards grew so general)': J. Rushworth, ed., *Historical Collections of Private Passages of State*, IV (1721), 463–4.

[53] See, for example, *The Resolution of the Roundheads* (Jan. 1641/2), TT E132 (39) and *The Answer to the Rattle-heads concerning their fictionate resolution of the Roundheads* (Jan. 1641/2), TT E132 (30); Fletcher, *Outbreak of the English Civil War*, 280–1.

[54] John Tombes to Stanley Gower, 24 June 1642, BL Loan 29/121.

fellow 'abused Mr Broughton exceedingly', who sent him to the stocks, 'but he so resisted that they were fain to take the halberds and to watch the stocks a long time and the next morning he ran away. All night he swore against the Roundheads and one came to and bid him be quiet for there would come a day would pay for all and then they would say remember this.'[55] Whether the two men involved in this incident would actively support the King once the war had started is, of course, open to question, but this episode vividly illustrates the tensions which were apparent in Herefordshire more than two months before the declaration of war.

Later that month Lady Brilliana described the near riot in Hereford which occurred when John Yates, the Harleys' rector at Leintwardine, had tried to preach in one of the city churches. Before Yates could start his sermon he was challenged by two men, who wanted to know why he had not prayed for the King. Yates retorted that he was at liberty to pray for the King and Church after the sermon, but the men then rang the church bells and a number of the congregation left the church and assembled in the churchyard crying 'Roundheads', some even threatening to stone Yates. In the afternoon he once again tried to preach, but this time was thwarted by the churchwardens, who refused to let him set foot in the pulpit because he could not show them his licence to preach. Lady Brilliana noted that throughout the time Yates was in Hereford he 'could not look out, but he was called Roundhead'. This incident served to reinforce Lady Brilliana's poor opinion of episcopacy, as she informed Sir Robert: 'in my opinion this reflects upon the bishop that they refused a minister in this manner that he had licensed and I think a more barbarous thing in a civil commonwealth is not done. The godly there were very grieved.'[56] Just across the county border in Shropshire another confrontation outside a church led to blows, but here it was the parliamentarian who was dishing out the punishment, as Lady Brilliana reported to Ned:

Mr William Littleton being at Ludlow last week, as he came out of the church, a man came to him and looked him in the face and cried 'Roundhead'; he gave the fellow a good box of the ear and step to one that had a chugell [cudgel] and took it from him and beat him soundly. They say, they are now more quiet in Ludlow.[57]

During June Lady Brilliana was also preoccupied with arrangements for the despatch of horses and valuables to London for the parliamentarian war effort. On 3 June Sir Robert had been named to a Commons committee which

[55] Lady Brilliana to Harley, undated, BL Loan 29/72. Internal evidence indicates that this letter was written after 11 June and before 24 June 1642: see Lewis, *Letters of the Lady Brilliana Harley*, 168–9, 172.
[56] Lewis, *Letters of the Lady Brilliana Harley*, 170–1 (this letter concerns a Mr Davies, which is an apparent error in transcription and should read Yates); Lady Brilliana to Harley, 24 June 1642, BL Loan 29/174 ff.3v–4v (erroneously bound with material from 1643); John Wanklen to Harley, 1 July 1642, BL Loan 29/174 f.265r.
[57] Lewis, *Letters of the Lady Brilliana Harley*, 172.

was to treat with anyone willing to lend money to the Parliament. A week later the two Houses drew up propositions for raising money, plate and horses for the 'defence of the King and both Houses of Parliament', in which they accused the King of intending 'to make war against his Parliament'.[58] Harley was amongst those MPs who rose in the House to pledge their support to the contribution, and he wrote at once to his wife requesting that she despatch both horses and the family plate to London. Lady Brilliana informed Ned that she would send the horses, but thought that it would be better to borrow money rather than part with the family silver and asked Ned to give her message to his father.

I purpose, and please God [she wrote] to send Martin with the horses your father sent for on Monday next. I doubt not but that your father will give to his utmost for the raising these horses, and in my opinion it were better to borrow money if your father will give any, than to give his plate; for we do not know what straits we may be put to, and therefore, I think it is better to borrow whilst one may and keep the plate for a time of need.

Sir Robert was adamant that the plate be sent to London and on 9 July his wife forwarded a voider, knife, 18 plates and a salt by the Leominster carrier, intending to send a second assortment a week later. She avoided sending everything at once in case its weight betrayed the contents of the hamper. The value of the Harleys' donation was considerable and by 19 September 1642 was worth £350; on that day Sir Robert also pledged a further £150 worth of plate and two more horses.[59]

By mid-June, when Lady Brilliana was making the first preparations for sending the horses and plate to London, she must have been aware that a civil war was imminent. The King's commission of array arrived in the county at the beginning of the following month and by then there could have been no doubt in her mind about the likelihood of war. On 5 July she sent Sir Robert a list of some of the twenty men who had been chosen to call out the county militia for the King. Her belief that this was a religious quarrel is reflected in her opinion that 'this does much appal the godly in this country', and three days later she reminded Harley that it would be safer if she left Herefordshire, 'for I account myself amongst my enemies'. On 13 July she made one last appeal to Sir Robert to allow his family to leave Brampton before it was too late:

Dear Sir, let me earnestly desire you to consider well whether it is safe for me and my children to be at Brampton. I hear the King will have [. . .] army to cut off all that are

[58] *CJ*, II, 589; Husbands, *Exact Collection*, 339–42.
[59] BL Harl. Mss., 163 f.545r; Lewis, *Letters of the Lady Brilliana Harley*, 169; Lady Brilliana to Harley, 9 July, 8 July 1642, BL Loan 29/174 ff.272r, 270r–v; *CJ*, II, 772.

for the Parliament. Many in this country say within this 6 weeks all the Puritans shall be rid out of the country.[60]

At this juncture Sir Robert could have predicted neither the length of the coming conflict nor the course that hostilities would take in his home county, and he again advised his wife to stay on the family estate. Perhaps he also felt that the journey to London would be perilous for his wife and children, for they would have to pass through areas where they were unknown and where there might be considerable dangers from troops raised by either side. Lady Brilliana herself was quite aware of the depth of hostility in the county against the parliamentarians and in the event her fears were to prove justified. For the moment, however, she resolved to obey her husband's wishes and on 15 July, the day after the commissioners of array had mustered the trained bands at Hereford, replied that she would place her trust in God and remain: 'since you think Brampton a safe place for me, I will think so too and I would not for anything do that which might make the world believe our hopes did begin to fail in our God'.

A few days later she wrote in similar vein to her son Edward in London:

My dear Ned, I thank God I am not afraid. It is the Lord's cause that we have stood for, and I trust, though our iniquities testify against us, yet the Lord will work for His own name sake, and that He will now show the men of this world that it is hard fighting against heaven. And for our comforts, I think never any laid plots to rout out all God's children at once, but that the Lord did shew Himself mightly in saving His servants, as He did Pharoah, when he thought to destroy all Israel, and so Haman. Now the intention is to rout out all that fear God and surely the Lord will arise to help us; and in your God let your confidence be and I am assured it is so.[61]

The letters which Lady Brilliana had written during the first six months of 1642, and the letters which Sir Robert had received from other people in Herefordshire at the same time, demonstrate that the growth of royalist and parliamentarian parties in the county was a long drawn out process, which was already under way well before the arrival of the first military commission in the county. Within Herefordshire existing religious divisions had widened, as the leading puritans continued their tenacious support of Parliament in an increasingly royalist environment. By the summer of 1642 the Harleys were openly stigmatised by local folk as both puritans and Roundheads, and the isolation which Lady Brilliana felt at that time served to reinforce her conviction that the supporters of Parliament were suffering for the cause of God and the true religion. Her belief in the righteousness of the godly

---

[60] Lady Brilliana to Harley, 5 July, 8 July and 13 July, BL Loan 29/174 ff.268v, 271r, 277r.
[61] Lady Brilliana to Harley, 15 July 1642, BL Loan 29/174 f.279r; Lewis, *Letters of the Lady Brilliana Harley*, 180–1.

community would prove to be the force which sustained Lady Brilliana throughout the harrowing outbreak and early months of civil war preceding her death in October 1643.

The outbreak of the Civil War and the siege of Brampton Bryan

The first bloodshed of the Civil War took place at Manchester on 15 July 1642, when Lord Strange commanded a band of troopers to attack townsmen engaged in executing the militia ordinance. A number were wounded and one died a few days later from the injuries he had sustained. The effects and course of the war varied from county to county according to the prevailing local allegiances. While the gentry in counties such as Herefordshire, Shropshire and Worcestershire swiftly declared for the King, elsewhere parliamentarian sentiment was so strong that royalism made hardly any impact. Thus, in Essex, 'no coherent royalist party ever emerged . . . because its potential leaders were isolated and neutralised at the outset'. Yet other regions were less clearly partisan: in Leicestershire, Nottinghamshire, Cheshire, Lancashire and Yorkshire the two sides were well matched and neither was able to achieve dominance over the other in the winter of 1642–3. Elsewhere neutralism played a dominant role, as in Staffordshire where a neutralist group tried to raise an alternative force to keep the two warring sides at bay, and neutralist sentiment was strongly evident in Derbyshire, Cumberland and Westmorland.[1] As the pace of war escalated, however, the local effects of conflict heightened the enmities between the opposing parties. Private houses were searched; private property seized or destroyed; civilians were imprisoned, injured or killed. Such actions violated the conventions of peaceful society and led people into increasingly hostile behaviour as they attempted to extract redress or vengeance for themselves and their dependants.

Yet neither parliamentarians nor royalists were intent on waging war: on both sides people hoped for accommodation and for peace. On 23 April 1642 Lady Brilliana had written to Edward Harley: 'I see the distance is still kept

[1] Gardiner, *History of England, 1603–1642*, X, 214; Morrill, *Revolt of the Provinces*, 36–45; W. Hunt, *The Puritan Moment: The Coming of Revolution to an English County*, Harvard Historical Studies, CII (Cambridge, Mass., 1983), 295; A. J. Fletcher, 'The Coming of War', in Morrill, *Reactions to the English Civil War*, 29–38.

between the King and Parliament. The Lord in mercy make them one and in His good time incline the King to be fully assured in the faithful counsel of his Parliament.' Four months later, on 20 August, Sir William Croft suggested a peace formula to Sir Robert, advising that 'the forces already raised for a civil war might presently be diverted for the relief of the protestants and King's good subjects in Ireland'. Such calls for unity cannot, however, be interpreted purely as proof of moderate opinion or of a lack of ideological commitment. It would be difficult to find a more committed supporter of Parliament than Lady Brilliana in 1642, or a more committed royalist than Sir William, who was to die in 1645 in a skirmish for control of Stokesay Castle in Shropshire. The desire for peace was real enough, but on both sides people wanted peace on their own terms, and they were unable to compromise. Thus, far from being able to rely on traditional gentry loyalties to protect her, Lady Brilliana fully expected that local royalist gentlemen would attack Brampton from the earliest stage of the war, for the estate was isolated in the centre of royalist terrain. To the north and to the east of the county, Shropshire and Worcestershire were staunchly royalist; to the west and to the south the Welsh counties of Radnorshire, Monmouthshire and Brecknockshire were dominated by royalists. Only Gloucestershire, to the south-east, was controlled by parliamentarians in this opening phase of the war. The parliamentarian garrison at Gloucester, under the command of Colonel Edward Massey, drove a wedge through royalist communications between the King's headquarters in Oxford and the royalist hinterland of Wales. Massey's chaplain, John Corbet, in an account published in 1645, described this stronghold as

the block-house to the river of Severn, and a bar to all passages between Worcester, Bristol and the sea; the stop of intercourse between Oxford and Wales; the key to open the passage upon the Welsh and their frontiers, and the lock and bar to keep out their incursions; the only refuge and safety for the Parliament party and their friends in this part of the kingdom; and the enemy's sole hindrance from the command of the whole west.

Gloucester was the nearest major parliamentarian garrison to Brampton, and Lady Brilliana was in regular communication with Massey, although he was unable to give her much practical aid.[2]

Despite Brampton's formidable encirclement by royalist sympathisers, the castle was not besieged until 26 July 1643. The restraint shown by the local royalist gentry in postponing any direct attack on Brampton for so long stemmed in part from their personal regard for Lady Brilliana, although military considerations also played their part. Lady Brilliana's rank as a

[2] Lewis, *Letters of the Lady Brilliana Harley*, 154; Sir William Croft to Harley, 20 August 1642, BL Loan 29/174 ff.33r–34r; Webb, *Memorials*, II, 193–6; Hutton, *Royalist War Effort*, 10–17; J. Corbet, *An Historical Relation of the Military Government of Gloucester* (1645), 138–9.

gentlewoman and her status as a kinswoman of some of her opponents undoubtedly helped stave off the moment when royalist troops finally surrounded the castle, but the letters which Lady Brilliana wrote between July 1642 and her death in October 1643 do reveal the gradual collapse of many of the traditional loyalties of county society. In these sixteen months the Harley's relationships with the local royalist gentry were increasingly strained by the demands of the Civil War. The Harley's authority with other social ranks was also impaired and Lady Brilliana was to discover that the influence which the family had customarily exercised in the county was becoming increasingly worthless. Nevertheless, she was determined to face the breakdown of familiar social ties, and the threat of royalist violence, with her characteristic deference to the judgement of her husband allied with her faith in God. Even the eventual ordeal of the siege of Brampton did not weaken Lady Brilliana's resolve to preserve the Harley estates in the county, nor did it lessen her trust in God and her profound belief that she was furthering the cause of the godly and of true religion.

As the loyalties of the local gentry community deteriorated, the loyalties of the supporters of Parliament were simultaneously strengthened by their perceptions of the war as a religious struggle. Writing of the local royalists in August 1642, Lady Brilliana informed Sir Robert that 'they say they maintain the true religion, but they shamefully use all that profess it'. By February 1643 she explained to her husband that only the truly religious would now associate themselves with those living in the castle, 'my God being so merciful to me, in that he has offered me and mine his word, to be shut up with us and many of his dear servants, so that we take company of those that fear him, for indeed not anyone else will come near us'.[3] Her analysis was shared by parliamentarians in other counties. In the biography of her husband, Lucy Hutchinson described the outbreak of the war in Nottinghamshire, which had much in common with Herefordshire, since the royalists were in the ascendancy in both counties in the summer of 1642:

before the flame of the war broke out in the top of the chimneys, the smoke ascended in every county; the king had sent forth commissions of array, and the parliament had given out commissions for their militia, and sent off their members into all counties to put them into execution. Between these, in many places, there were fierce contests and disputes, almost to blood, even at the first; for in the progress every county had the Civil War, more or less, within itself. Some counties were in the beginning so wholly for Parliament, that the King's interest appeared not in them; some so wholly for the King, that the godly, for those generally were the Parliament's friends, were forced to forsake their habitations, and seek other shelters: of this sort was Nottinghamshire.[4]

---

[3] HMC, *Manuscripts of the Marquess of Bath*, I, 1; Lady Brilliana to Harley, 3 August 1642 and 26 February 1642/3, BL Loan 29/174 ff.301r, 13r.
[4] Sutherland, *Lucy Hutchinson's Memoirs*, 60–1.

In Herefordshire leading parliamentarian clergy and gentry also fled to safer strongholds. John Tombes was one of the first to leave, in August 1642, finding the 'barbarous rage and impetuous violence of people so increased, that I could have no safety in my proper station, but was enforced to remove myself, wife and children, and since have suffered the spoiling of my goods, of my dwelling house, with many other injuries'. At the end of February 1643 William Lowe, curate of Aston, and John Yates, vicar of Leintwardine, where Sir Robert was patron, quit Herefordshire for London. They were joined later in the year by Stanley Gower and John Green, who had been chosen as the Herefordshire representatives on the Assembly of Divines. Tombes and Lowe were certainly not native to Herefordshire and none of these five ministers seems to have been bound by the considerations of estate and family ties which affected the gentry.[5] Despite the more complex nature of their ties within the county, a number of gentry also left: James Kyrle had settled at the parliamentarian garrison at Gloucester by the start of 1643. After a period of imprisonment Edward Broughton also went to Gloucester, where he and Kyrle were active members of the parliamentarian 'grand committee' in 1644. Lady Brilliana's eldest sons Edward and Robert joined William Waller's forces in June 1643, for the most committed parliamentarian gentry such as the Harleys saw the successful prosecution of the war as more important than the peace of the county. The removal of committed parliamentarians from the county left Lady Brilliana in an increasingly weakened and isolated position, unable to exercise traditional Harley influence in the county. In May 1643 she noted that her attempts to lend the parsonage at Leintwardine to Francis Boughey, vicar of Stokesay, had been resisted by 'some of the parish' who 'would not let him be there'. Instead they allowed a cleric whom Lady Brilliana described as 'a popish minister' to supply Yates' place.[6]

Lady Brilliana's letters also contained a great deal of local information which was invaluable to Sir Robert at Westminster, where he served on numerous administrative committees directly concerned with the prosecution of the war. In August 1642, for example, Harley, along with three other

---

[5] John Tombes to Harley, 5 August 1642, BL Loan 29/121; J. Tombes, *Fermentum Pharisaeorum, or, The Leaven of Pharisaicall Wil-Worship: Declared in a Sermon on Matthew 15.9. November 24 1641 at Lemster Herefordshire* (1643), sig., A2v; Lewis, *Letters of the Lady Brilliana Harley*, 190; Lady Brilliana to Harley, 3 July 1643, BL Loan 29/72; *CJ*, II, 251; R. S. Paul, *The Assembly of the Lord: Politics and Religion in the Westminster Assembly and the 'Grand Debate'* (Edinburgh, 1985), 549; A. G. Matthews, *Calamy Revised: Being a Revision of Edmund Calamy's Account of the Ministers and Others Ejected and Silenced 1660–1662* (Oxford, 1932), 487, 329.

[6] James Kyrle to Harley, 24 January 1642/3, BL Loan 29/120; PRO SP28/228 part 3, no.545; part 4, nos.771, 773; part 5, nos.854, 865, 921; Lewis, *Letters of the Lady Brilliana Harley*, 204–5; Lady Brilliana to Harley, 9 May 1643, BL Loan 29/173 f.247v (erroneously bound with material dated 1642), Lady Brilliana to Harley, 24 September 1643, Loan 29/72.

MPs, was appointed to receive papers concerning Shropshire, Herefordshire, Worcestershire, Lancashire, Cheshire, Monmouthshire and North Wales, to 'solicit the affairs of these counties for their defence'. This was the first step in the creation of a military association of adjacent counties, which was to be successful in East Anglia with the formation of the Eastern Association in December 1642. Other associations, such as those under the command of Lord Grey in the Midlands, and Waller in the south-east, proved to be failures for a variety of reasons. The initial association of Herefordshire and the surrounding counties had little hope of success, however, because of the military domination by royalists in those areas. Nevertheless Lady Brilliana's letters undoubtedly helped Harley to keep abreast of developments within his home county and the surrounding regions. In practice, however, there was very little that he could do to influence events inside the county.

Control of Herefordshire passed from the royalists to the parliamentarians and back again according to the movements of the main field armies. The county administration was firmly in the hands of royalist gentry from July 1642 until the arrival of parliamentarian troops under the command of the Earl of Stamford, who entered Hereford unopposed on 1 October 1642. Stamford was only able to occupy the city for two months and after the battle of Edgehill on 23 October he was in a strategically weak position, caught between the King's forces at Oxford and royalist troops in Wales. In November his position was further weakened when the parliamentarian garrison at Worcester withdrew and was replaced by a local royalist administration. Almost completely surrounded by opposing forces, Stamford decided to withdraw to Gloucester in December and, as at Worcester, the local royalists re-established their control of Hereford instantly. In the following April Sir William Waller held Hereford for Parliament for a month, but left in order to oppose Sir Ralph Hopton's advances in the west. The county then remained under a royalist administration until Hereford was once again taken by parliamentarian forces commanded by Colonel Birch in December 1645.[7]

The permanence of parliamentarian influence in Herefordshire after December 1645 raises questions about the real strength of royalist feeling in the county during the earlier stages of the war. Clearly the disintegration of the King's forces following the defeat at Naseby in 1645 and the fall of Oxford in 1646 explains why Parliament retained military control in Herefordshire. Yet civilians were found who replaced the royalist administrators in the county and it is hard to believe that these new men could have carried out their task if Herefordshire had been entirely royalist in its sympathies. War weariness undoubtedly accounts in part for this, but also, the prompt execution of the commission of array and the lack of any parliamentarian initiative in the county in July 1642 combined to give a false impression of the strength of royalism in Herefordshire and obscures the fact that there were many shades of commitment in the county at that date. In Herefordshire, where the royalists had taken control, committed parliamentarians are easy to find, but on the other side it is not easy to distinguish between committed royalists and those who went along with the ruling party through fear or inertia. There is an obvious parallel with events in Essex, where parliamentarian hegemony masked the existence of 'a significant body of neutralist, even royalist, opinion in the county'.

During June, July and August of 1642 the House of Commons sent MPs into a number of counties, including Shropshire and Gloucestershire, in order to oversee the execution of the militia ordinance, but in Herefordshire no action was taken. Lady Brilliana was well aware that the delay in executing the ordinance was a tactical mistake and twice in July she urged that some MPs should be sent to the county for that purpose. The House of Commons had named Lord Dacre as lord lieutenant for Herefordshire, ignoring Harley's plea that Lord Saye should serve for the county. Dacre proved to be a neutral and was formally replaced on 8 August by the Earl of Essex. As Commander-in-Chief of the parliamentarian forces Essex was clearly under considerable pressure, and it was not until 30 September at Worcester that he named his deputies in Herefordshire and on the same day despatched Stamford to take Hereford.[8]

In contrast, the commission of array had reached Herefordshire three months earlier, at the beginning of July, and was put into prompt execution. On 5 July Lady Brilliana informed Sir Robert of the names of ten commissioners. In all some twenty local gentlemen had been named, including obvious neutrals such as the sheriff, Seward, and moderate royalists such as Viscount Scudamore. The commission also included staunch royalists such as Sir William Croft, Fitzwilliam Coningsby and Henry Lingen, who had already identified themselves as opponents of the policies of Parliament. Dr Hutton's research into the royalist war effort in Wales and the West Midlands has revealed that the commissioners 'were on the whole accurately chosen'. Although up to a third of the commissioners in each county proved either hostile or indifferent, 'the remainder always included men who became the

---

[8] Hunt, *The Puritan Moment*, 295; Aylmer, 'Who was Ruling in Herefordshire from 1645 to 1661?', 376; Fletcher, *Outbreak of the English Civil War*, 351-3; *CJ*, II, 685, 686, 719; Lewis, *Letters of the Lady Brilliana Harley*, 176, 179; *CJ*, II, 424; Coates, Young and Snow, *The Private Journals of the Long Parliament: 3 January to 5 March 1642*, 342; Fletcher, *A County Community in Peace and War*, 285; *CJ*, II 709; list of deputy lieutenants for Herefordshire, 30 September 1642, BL Loan 29/174 f.326r; PRO SP16/492/32.

royalist leaders of their counties'. This suggests that the King and his advisors were well informed about the loyalties of the local gentry, which was certainly the case in Herefordshire. In June a group of Herefordshire gentry had sent a letter to the King at York, which, according to Lady Brilliana, 'let him know that they would serve him with their lives and estates'. The signatures on this letter would have provided some guidance in the choice of commissioners. The two letters sent by the nine JPs to their MPs earlier in the year were also known outside Herefordshire and provided similar information.[9]

On 14 July 1642 the commissioners, led by Sir William Croft and Fitzwilliam Coningsby, mustered the trained bands at Hereford. Sir Robert Harley, being absent in London, was removed from his capacity of a band of foot and replaced by Coningsby. Lady Brilliana had sent one of her servants to observe the muster and she reported to Harley that

> when the soldiers were all gathered together and your company was called, your name was first called and then a great many cried out and wished you were there that they might tear you in pieces . . . he heard everyone rail at you and the Parliament. He dared not take upon him whose man he was and the people were so rude.

Lady Brilliana noted that there were pockets of dissent and even opposition to the commissioners outside her immediate circle, but this did not add up to full-scale resistance to the royalists. On 8 July, writing of the imminent muster, she noted: 'many are troubled what they shall do, if they be required to find arms, for they are resolved not to do it'. This reluctance to obey the commissioners may have stemmed from doubts about the authority of the commission itself, which were raised in a declaration by Parliament on 1 July stating the illegality of the commission. At least one JP, Ambrose Elton senior, refused to attend the Hereford assizes at the end of July because he thought the commission was 'unlawful'. Lady Brilliana, however, persuaded him to change his mind and attend the assizes, undoubtedly hoping that Elton would help to counteract the influence of the royalists. At Hereford, however, Sir William Croft and Wallop Brabazon were able to influence the assize judge in the choice of grand jurors and a number of parliamentarian JPs, including James Kyrle and Edward Broughton, boycotted the proceedings in protest.[10]

---

[9] Lady Brilliana to Harley, 5 July 1642, BL Loan 29/174 f.269r; Northamptonshire RO, Finch Hatton Mss., 133 unfoliated (I am grateful to Dr Richard Cust for this reference); Hutton, *Royalist War Effort*, 5–6; Lewis, *Letters of the Lady Brilliana Harley*, 170; Fletcher, *Outbreak of the English Civil War*, 306; for the two letters from Herefordshire JPs see above, pp. 133–6. The Commission of Array was reissued for Herefordshire on 7 January 1643 when party lines had become more clearly apparent: see PRO C115 I.26/6511.

[10] Anonymous report of the muster at Hereford, 14 July 1642, and Lady Brilliana to Harley 15 July 1642, BL Loan 29/174 ff.278r–v, 279v–280r; HMC, *Manuscripts of His Grace the Duke of Portland*, III, 92; unfortunately the original letter from Lady Brilliana to Harley, dated 17 July 1642 (BL Loan 29/174 ff.281r) is in too damaged a condition to be used here;

Other men may have taken a lead from their social superiors in their resistance to the commissioners. For example, nearly half of Sir Robert's band of foot defaulted at the Hereford muster. Many of these men were Harley dependants and may have defaulted through a sense of personal loyalty to Sir Robert, but, given the Harley's propensity for choosing servants and tenants with a godly disposition, the defaulters may have combined that loyalty with a genuine desire to oppose the royalists based on religious and political conviction. In this context it is interesting to note that, while the remaining three bands of foot appeared in almost full strength, the greatest number of defaults were to be found in the troop of horse commanded by Viscount Scudamore, only a third of whom appeared in the field. The Viscount was at best a moderate royalist and may well have been absent from the muster himself. The unusually large number of defaults suggests that some at least of Scudamore's men shared his reservations about committing themselves to the royalist cause. Lady Brilliana's letters make very little reference to Scudamore as a commissioner and he appears to have been very lukewarm in his commitment to the King. Following the fall of Hereford to Waller in 1643, Fitzwilliam Coningsby complained of Scudamore's 'coldness and slow appearance', which had 'damped the country's zeal'. Scudamore was taken prisoner at this engagement and was sent to London, where he appealed for leniency to the parliamentarian MP Sir Robert Pye in terms which confirmed his lack of energy, 'for this action of Hereford, wherein I was but a volunteer, and had no command, and being here casually and a sworn citizen and steward of the town, I knew not in honour how to run away from it, just when a force appeared before it'.[11]

Some of the other commissioners were also reluctant to carry out their duties. In July 1642 Lady Brilliana noted that Sir Richard Hopton, Sir John Kyrle and John Scudamore of Kentchurch did not appear with the other commissioners. These three were subsequently named as deputy lieutenants by the Earl of Essex, which neatly illustrates the dangers of using the bare data of names of commissioners or committee men as a guide to allegiance. Hopton and Kyrle probably had moderate leanings towards Parliament, but they were insufficiently committed to attempt to raise any organised opposition to the county's royalists. Scudamore of Kentchurch appears to have been a neutral, offering no support to either side. In contrast, one of the most zealous commissioners of array in 1642, Wallop Brabazon, later tried to

Lady Brilliana to Harley, 8 July 1642, BL Loan 29/174 f.271v; Husbands, *Exact Collection*, 386–95; Lady Brilliana to Harley, 27 July and 30 July 1642 BL Loan 29/174 ff.293v, 300r.
[11] Anonymous report of the muster at Hereford, 14 July 1642, BL Loan 29/174 ff.278r–v; Bodleian Library, Tanner Mss. 303 f.113r; Webb, *Memorials*, I, 265.

conceal his true involvement in an attempt to save his lands from sequestration by the parliamentarian committee for compounding. The Harley papers reveal a very different story. Not only was Brabazon present at the muster of trained bands at Hereford, he was also one of the commissioners who signed a warrant for the arrest of Priam Davies, a parliamentarian captain and kinsman of the Harleys.[12] Brabazon also tried to use his powers as a commissioner in order to intimidate his old enemy, John Tombes of Leominster, although his efforts proved in vain.

On 31 July 1642 Brabazon entered the parish church at Leominster accompanied by some of the county's royalist volunteers. Brabazon carried with him a copy of a pamphlet from the King, which he intended to force Tombes to read from the pulpit. Tombes, however, was not present and Matthew Clarke, rector of Bitterly in Shropshire, was conducting the service. As Clarke rose to enter the pulpit Brabazon pressed him to read the pamphlet, but Clarke quick-wittedly refused on the grounds that 'it is to be read in every church by the parson, vicar or curate of the same . . . and I am a stranger here entreated to preach and no curate here'. In the exchange which followed Brabazon failed to control the tempers of the volunteers, thirteen of whom crowded around Clarke calling him 'Roundhead' and threatening to cudgel him to the ground. One of the congregation then appealed to Brabazon's sense of duty as a justice, asking whether he would 'see a gentleman to be murdered among us'. With some effort Brabazon reasserted his authority and allowed Clarke to preach without further hindrance. The entire incident is reminiscent of the scenes which took place in Rugby in the county of Warwickshire at the same time, possibly even on the same day, when a group of armed men tried to force the minister, James Nalton, to read *The King's Answer to the Parliament's Petition*. It was probably this printed pamphlet which Brabazon had tried to force Clarke to read, since it contained the specific demand that it should be 'read in all churches and chapels within the Kingdom of England and Dominion of Wales by the parsons, vicars or curates of the same'. Doubtless similar scenes were enacted in parishes elsewhere, and Lady Brilliana was certainly worried that the royalists might try to force Stanley Gower to read the same pamphlet.[13]

At Leominster Brabazon had probably expected to find John Tombes conducting the service, but Tombes was in Worcester five days later, on 5

---

[12] Lewis, *Letters of the Lady Brilliana Harley*, 182; Lady Brilliana to Harley, 27 July 1642 and list of deputy lieutenants, 30 September 1630, BL Loan 29/174 ff.293v, 326r; Levy, 'Thesis', 285–6; CCC, 1478; Lady Brilliana to Harley, 25 July 1642, BL Loan 29/174 f.291r; CJ, II, 775.

[13] Relation of Matthew Clarke, 31 July 1642, BL Loan 29/121; A. Hughes, 'Politics, Society and Civil War in Warwickshire, 1625–1661' (University of Liverpool, Ph.D. Thesis, 1979), 243; Husbands, *Exact Collection*, 466–73; Lady Brilliana to Harley, 3 August 1642, BL Loan 29/174 f.301r.

August, and may already have left the county. The antagonism between these two men dated back at least to the mid-1630s and was firmly based on the clash between their different religious outlooks. Brabazon was an enthusiastic supporter of Laudian innovation and had been instrumental in repositioning the communion table at Leominster 'altar-wise'. Prompted by the deliberations of the House of Commons in December 1640, Tombes had turned the table 'with the two sides north and south, and began to disuse the surplice, and the cross at baptising', which had provoked Brabazon to further 'reviling speeches'. In May 1641 Tombes begged Harley for help to abate Brabazon's power, 'which we see is wholly bent to blast any beginnings of godliness, or good design for promoting of godliness'.[14]

The actions of these commissioners illustrate some of the many shades of allegiance which existed and which were modified by the prevailing local conditions. Lady Brilliana recognised that there were degrees of commitment on the part of the royalists and she advised Harley to have some of the moderates named as deputy lieutenants under the terms of the militia ordinance: 'if you do not take some of the other side, you will mightily incense them and some are much more moderate than others. I am persuaded a letter from you to my cousin Rudhall would do much with him.'

Her hopes that the moderates could be persuaded to switch allegiance were not unreasonable and a month later she was able to record an early example of a commissioner changing sides. Lady Brilliana wrote to Harley about John Nanfan, a Worcestershire commissioner, who later supported Parliament. In September he visited Brampton and explained that 'he was of the commission of array, but now declines it and here enclosed has sent you the relation how far he went in it and desires your advice'.[15]

Between July and September 1642 Lady Brilliana was convinced that Brampton would be attacked, either by royalist forces from outside the county, or by the county commissioners using the pretext that they were searching for arms. She accordingly took further measures to protect the house and on 15 July reported that she had received twenty bandoliers, but still awaited the delivery of muskets and rests, which were probably being sent to her on the instructions of either Sir Robert or Ned Harley. She subsequently received a consignment of powder and match and also asked the plumber to send to Worcester for '50 weight of shot'. On 4 August Ned returned home to strengthen the numbers at Brampton and in the same month his mother took a number of men into the house and paid them 3d a day plus meat and drink, which corresponded exactly with the wage rates for

---

[14] John Tombes to Harley, 5 August 1642, BL Loan 29/121, petition of the borough of Leominster, undated, Loan 29/50/73, John Tombes to Harley, 12 December 1640, Loan 29/172 f.344r, *idem* to Harley 3 May 1641, Loan 29/173 f.99r.

[15] Lady Brilliana to Harley, undated and 16 September 1642, BL Loan 29/174 ff.307r, 315r.

day labourers set out by the county magistrates in 1632. A few months later Lady Brilliana dismissed them on the grounds that they had killed a man and plundered the sheriff of Radnorshire. Her own attitude towards such actions was summed up in a letter to Ned in the summer of 1643: 'I am confident you will hate all plundering and unmercifulness'. Yet within weeks Lady Brilliana herself was enforced to order the plundering of her opponents near Brampton in order to ensure the survival of the garrison after the first siege had been lifted.[16]

Despite Lady Brilliana's precautions, no force was in fact used against Brampton in the first summer of the war. Lower down the social scale, however, those with parliamentarian sympathies were at greater risk. A Mr Herring was driven from his home and the home of Edward Dalley, the Harleys' tenant, was searched and his arms seized. A messenger sent from the parliamentarian garrison at Gloucester with a letter for Lady Brilliana was imprisoned at Hereford for taking the letter to the home of a traitor; while the Harleys' own gardener was arrested on suspicion of being a spy in royalist Ludlow, where he had offended town officials by openly declaring Ludlow to be 'so bad it would shortly be as bad as Sodom'. Brampton itself obviously provided a tempting target. A centre of parliamentarian sympathy in the midst of royalist heartland could not fail to attract the hostility of the King's sympathisers, and Lady Brilliana told Sir Robert that the son of one of the commissioners, Price of Westerton, swears 'bitterly what he would do to you if you were in the country and that Brampton must be his'. Yet during these early months of war Lady Brilliana remained unharmed because the leading royalist gentry were unwilling to transgress traditional modes of social behaviour. At the beginning of August Sir William Croft, one of the most active commissioners, visited Brampton and reconfirmed his personal attachment to the Harleys, but warned Lady Brilliana that he could show her no favour in executing his public duty, claiming that 'in his private affection he was to you [Harley] as he has been, but in the way of the public he would favour none'.[17]

Croft thus made an explicit distinction between his private and his public affections, with the clear assertion that his public duty would prevail. He was, however, eager to heal the breach between himself and the Harleys and later

---

[16] Lewis, *Letters of the Lady Brilliana Harley*, 178, 181–2, 183; Lady Brilliana to Harley, 5 August 1642, and undated, BL Loan 29/174 ff.303r, 306v, rates for wages for servants and labourers, 10 April 1632, Loan 29/172 f.56r; HMC, *Manuscripts of the Marquess of Bath*, I 9–10; Lewis, *Letters of the Lady Brilliana Harley*, 206; HMC, *Manuscripts of the Marquess of Bath*, I, 26–7.

[17] Lady Brilliana to Harley, 17 July 1642, BL Loan 29/174 f.281v, extracts from a letter from Lady Brilliana to Harley in Harley's hand, 29 August 1642, Loan 29/27 part 1, Lady Brilliana to Harley, 22 September 1642, Stanley Gower to Harley, 23 September 1642, the examination of John Aston, 3 September 1642, Lady Brilliana to Harley, 30 July and *idem* to Harley 11 August 1642, BL Loan 29/174 ff.322r, 323r, 312v, 299r, 305r.

in the month wrote to Sir Robert urging him to return his allegiance to the King. Croft called upon the amity between their families and the loss of prestige which Harley had suffered both locally and nationally as grounds for conciliation:

> we are grown so jealous of one another as your Lady cannot be confident of me while we are thus divided in our ways. I wish this happy accommodation might move from you and that you would earnestly profess it to the regaining that esteem I wish you might have in your country and the whole kingdom.

Croft's letter is a further illustration of his clear understanding of the constitutional implications of the conflict between King and Parliament. His letter presents the King and his adherents as moderates, striving to maintain the status quo in the face of the Parliament encroaching on the King's powers by use of ordinances, but he stressed that in time of war the King could legally exercise wide emergency powers;

> we are for the old way, our forefathers finding Parliaments useful, though subject to Kings and never attempted the gaining a power above them . . .
> . . . study moderation and comply with the King and greatest part of the kingdom, since the King has done and promises so much for our satisfaction and with such protestations and execrations, as he is better to be believed than those that tell you he is not to be trusted in his promise of governing us according to law. The instance of the commission of array is no contradiction of that . . . for, I know what the opinions have been in former Parliaments and of the King's power for the militia, but grant it may not stand with other laws in time of peace, that now, for the defence of himself and all his subjects that adhere to him, he may better justify more than that commission requires, than you, what you have done by virtue of your ordinances.

Finally Croft explained that should the King lose the war then his supporters would remain passively obedient to him and would not give their active obedience to any new regime. Croft ended by offering to petition the King for 'an act of oblivion and setting you right in his Majesty's opinion' if Harley so wished. Croft's appeal to his kinsman Harley to 'lay aside our unnatural quarrel' could be interpreted as the plea of a moderate, concerned to see the continued unity of the local community. Taken out of context Croft's letter could be interpreted as evidence that the bonds uniting the Harleys and the local gentry were still intact; within context his words are revealed as a desperate attempt to avert the effects of war and it must be stressed that in this he failed. Croft's call for peace was genuine enough, but his letter cannot be regarded as a moderate statement, or as evidence of uncommitted opinion. He wanted peace on the King's terms and had made his opposition to the Parliament known in the county since the start of the year. A few days before he wrote this letter, Croft had drilled fifty volunteers at Croft Castle and had arranged that they should return weekly for military training. Before taking down the men's names he had asked each one of them 'if they would go with him, if there should be occasion, for the King's service any way'. Croft was realistic enough to know that his letter would have little effect on a man as committed to Parliament as was Sir Robert and prefaced his remarks with the words 'I think the much I have written to you is of little purpose.'[18]

Nevertheless, before the effects of warfare were felt in the county, the local gentry had not completely abandoned their assumptions about the ways in which local society should function. Lady Brilliana was keenly aware that the traditional social habits of the county gentry were not yet in total eclipse. In the letter in which she advised Sir Robert to choose some moderate royalists as deputy lieutenants she also commented:

if you choose men of little estates and those that are of little value it will make them odious to the country, as it did Mr Broughton in making him a justice of peace. Dear Sir, I beseach the Lord to direct you in this great business, for if it be not so carried that they may see there is a respect paid to the gentry it will extremely inflame them.

Her letter also points to the fact that few of the leading gentry in the county openly supported the Parliament, a social pattern which was repeated elsewhere, as county studies of Yorkshire, Cheshire, Shropshire and Warwickshire have suggested.[19]

Despite the apparent ascendancy of the royalists in Herefordshire, the parliamentarians there did not give up their hopes of reversing the balance of power. At the end of September 1642 'a company of knights, gentlemen and yeomen of the county of Hereford' consulted with the Earl of Essex at Worcester and asked for military aid to be sent to the county. Probably amongst the company were Sir Richard Hopton, Henry Vaughan, Edward Broughton, James Kyrle and John Flackett, all of whom signed an agreement in Worcester a week later for the military association of the four English marcher counties, 'for the withstanding and expelling of the . . . forces . . . raised without consent of Parliament that shall come into or be in any of the

---

[18] Sir William Croft to Harley, 20 August 1642, BL Loan 29/174 ff.33r–34r, John Coulbourne to Richard Sankey, 15 August 1642, BL Loan 29/119.

[19] Lady Brilliana to Harley, undated, BL Loan 29/174 f.307r; Cliffe, *Yorkshire Gentry*, 358; Wanklyn, 'Thesis', Abstract; Hughes, *Politics, Society and Civil War*, 179–80. The judgement of these studies are at odds with Professor Everitt's findings in Kent, where he concludes that the gentry did not divide along lines either of class or wealth. Kent seems to have been exceptional, since the gentry were not divided by religion or abstract political principle either: Everitt, *Community of Kent*, 116. Two older studies of the members of the Long Parliament similarly suggest that there was no distinction between royalist and parliamentarian MPs in terms of economic or social status: see Keeler, *Long Parliament*, 27, n.134, and D. Brunton and D. H. Pennington, *Members of the Long Parliament* (1954), 4. What was true of MPs would not necessarily hold for the wider population in the counties, however. Furthermore, the methodology of Brunton and Pennington has been rightly criticised by Christopher Hill in his 'Recent Interpretations of the Civil War', *History*, XLI (1956), 75–80.

said counties'. Essex had already responded to their pleas by despatching 900 foot and three troops of horse commanded by Stamford, who had taken Hereford on 1 October. During the parliamentarian occupation of the city, Sir Robert Harley took advantage of the change in military control of the county to return to his home. On 3 October the Commons resolved that Harley should attend the Earl of Essex with instructions from Parliament and five days later Sir Robert had reached Worcester, for on that day he joined with the other Herefordshire gentry in signing the agreement of association. From there Sir Robert probably went to Brampton, since Lady Brilliana's last letter to Sir Robert in 1642 is dated 22 September and her correspondence with him resumes again on 17 January 1643. There is a similar gap in Lady Brilliana's letters to her son Edward, since he returned home to Brampton on 4 August 1642 and stayed in Herefordshire until mid-December of that year.[20]

The presence of both Sir Robert and Ned Harley in Herefordshire unfortunately presents us with a gap in Lady Brilliana's letters directed to them, but in compensation they are mentioned in a number of official documents. In his despatches to Parliament Stamford commended Edward for the capture of some royalist troops and for showing 'much courage and vigilancy since my coming into these parts and very much affection to the Parliament'. Sir Robert was also able to use his local knowledge to aid Stamford, who remarked: 'I have found Sir Robert Harley a mightly operator in any good that hath happened to me since I had the honour to command this place.' Sir Robert was also clearly active in processing parliamentary business while he was in Herefordshire and on 22 November he and Sir Robert Cooke, MP for Tewksbury, wrote from Hereford to Parliament to recommend that Stamford's powers be enlarged to give him overall military command in the four marcher counties. This advice was formally put into action on 13 December, but the next day Stamford was forced through lack of money, ammunition and provisions to withdraw to Gloucester. It was doubtless this reversal which prompted Ned Harley to return to London. His father was already in Gloucester and from there Sir Robert probably returned directly to London where he became increasingly important to the parliamentarian leadership. In January and February 1643 Harley helped to steer the discussions for the peace treaty at Oxford through the two Houses and in July he was asked to oversee the making of a great seal to be used by Parliament in opposition to that of the King. Harley's connections with the engravers at the

---

[20] PRO SP16/492/32; agreement of association, 8 October 1642, BL Loan 29/174 f.327r; *CJ*, II, 791; Lady Brilliana to Harley, 22 September 1642, 17 January 1642/3, BL Loan 29/174 321v, 322r, 1r–2v. For Edward Harley's arrival at Brampton see Lady Brilliana to Harley, 5 August 1642, BL Loan 29/174 f.303r. Lady Brilliana's letters to Edward stop in July 1642 and resume on 13 December 1642: see Lewis, *The Letters of the Lady Brilliana Harley*, 183, 186.

Mint, where he had been restored as Master and Worker in the previous May, made him the obvious person to execute this task.[21]

After Stamford's retreat from Hereford, the city was occupied by royalist troops under the command of Colonel Lawdey, who was joined by the Marquess of Hertford with a force of 2,000 Welsh recruits *en route* to join the King at Oxford. Hertford appointed the sheriff, Fitzwilliam Coningsby, as governor of Hereford before continuing his march. The arrival of the King's soldiers in the county and the resumption of the authority of the local royalist gentry meant a renewal of Lady Brilliana's fears. On Christmas Day she wrote to Edward to tell him how the royalists 'revenge all that was done upon me, so that I shall fear any more Parliament forces coming into this country'. Two of her servants had been carried off to Hereford whilst trying to collect rents and one of her tenants had been imprisoned on the grounds that he was Lady Brilliana's bullet maker, which she denied. In an attempt to free her dependants Lady Brilliana appealed to Viscount Scudamore for help. She disingenuously claimed that she could not understand why the gentlemen of the county should break the bonds which existed between them and the Harleys. Her letter is a classic description of the ways in which local gentry were tied to one another through kinship, friendship and respect, and she carefully highlights her own position as a 'stranger' brought into this network through her marriage to Sir Robert:

> my thoughts are in a labyrinth to find out the reason why they should be thus to me. When I look upon myself I can see nothing but love and respect arising out of my heart to them, and when I look upon the many bonds by which most of the gentlemen in this country are tied to Sir Robert Harley, that of blood and some with alliance and all with his long professed and real friendship and for myself that of common courtesy, as to a stranger brought into their country, I know not how all those I believed to be so good should break all these obligations.[22]

The sentiments expressed in this letter were genuine, which could suggest that Lady Brilliana was simply being very naive if she could not understand why she was being treated as an outcast. Such an explanation is obviously inadequate, since it contradicts everything that we know about Lady Brilliana's character. She was an observant and spirited woman, and far from being naive was shrewd enough to know that Scudamore was a moderate, who might be more sympathetic to her plight than the more committed royalists in the county. Her letter also emphasises the fact that the desire for local unity and a deep commitment to Parliament could exist side by side.

[21] *LJ*, V, 426, 444; Harley and Sir Robert Cooke to the Committee for the Safety of the Kingdom, 22 November 1642, f.334r; *CJ*, II, 865, 886; Lewis, *Letters of the Lady Brilliana Harley*, 186; Harley to Viscount Scudamore, 2 February 1642/3, BL Loan 29/121; *CJ*, II, 928, 935, 978, 998, 999; III, 26, 27, 155, 69, 72, 73.

[22] Webb, *Memorials*, I, 206–11; BL Harl. Mss., 6851 f.243r; Lewis, *Letters of the Lady Brilliana Harley*, 186; PRO C115/N2/8521.

Such appeals to the traditional bonds of the county gentry community were heartfelt, but this letter once again illustrates that they cannot be construed simply as evidence of moderation. Lady Brilliana also wrote to Sir William Croft concerning the arms stored at Brampton. An undated draft of the letter survives, which shows that in approaching Croft, whom she knew to be an implacable royalist, she made a more muted reference to county loyalties, possibly because she felt that this was an argument that would have made little impact with him. Instead she concentrated on the legal basis of her right to keep arms, a line of argument which she would use repeatedly with the local royalist authorities. She reminded Croft that he had 'made that Protestation to maintain the laws of the land, of which I think this is a part', and continued, 'Sir, it is a mystery to me that the arms I have, which are not the hundred part so many as those you have at Croft, should be looked at with an ill eye and yours to be there of right and mine not. I understand it not.'[23]

Lady Brilliana's efforts proved to be in vain. Scudamore was himself suffering from the effects of the war by the time that he received her letter and he did not respond in a conciliatory manner. In the middle of January 1643 he wrote to Sir Robert Harley, James Kyrle and Henry Vaughan, accusing them of making Lady Scudamore 'a prisoner and hostage for the security of Sir Robert Harley's lady'. He complained of the 'felonies and barbarous plundering acted upon Llanthony', his Gloucestershire estate, and threatened that if any trees were cut down there, then 'axes should be laid to the roots of the trees which stand about Brampton Castle', while Kyrle's estate at Walford and Vaughan's estate at Moccas would suffer the same fate. Kyrle, who was at Gloucester, contacted Harley and commented: 'by these you may perceive the continuance of the malice of our kindred in Herefordshire towards your family'.[24]

In his reply to Scudamore, Harley confessed ignorance of these charges and stated that he would rather all the trees and his home at Brampton should be laid waste than he should have been guilty of the offences committed against Scudamore. Kyrle also replied to Scudamore, but he countercharged with the accusation that 'my corn, cattle and household stuff at Walford is prised and commanded from me', nevertheless 'assure yourself that it shall be far from me to offer the least violence unto any of yours or any other bodies, however I am dealt withal'. In his letter Kyrle carefully insisted that he had no hand in either 'the taking of any of your goods from Llanthony, or any thought of felling one tree of yours'. This, however, left him with quite a degree of latitude, for Lady Scudamore later complained that Kyrle had seized rents due from her Gloucestershire estates in retaliation for the sequestrations at

---

[23] Lady Brilliana to Sir William Croft, undated, BL Loan 29/72.

[24] Viscount Scudamore to Harley *et al.*, 13 January 1642/3, BL Loan 29/121; James Kyrle to Harley, 24 January 1642/3, BL Loan 29/120.

Walford, 'his estate being seized upon by the Governor of Hereford and others, for supposed delinquency, he professes to do the same to my tenants, as he has already begun on James Collins and Richard Meek'.[25]

This exchange of letters exemplifies the gradual breakdown of friendly relations between the two warring parties at gentry level, as their property, rents and estates were increasingly vulnerable to plunder and sequestration. In turn this helps to explain why Brampton was finally threatened in earnest from the start of 1643. In January the King ordered Fitzwilliam Coningsby to prepare for an assault on the castle, and at the beginning of February the royalist commander, Lord Herbert, called a council of war where it was decided to use the trained bands of Radnorshire with some Herefordshire soldiers to take Brampton. The plan collapsed, partly because the trained bands refused to cross into Herefordshire and partly because Herbert's forces were diverted to attack the parliamentarian garrison at Gloucester and suffered a crippling defeat at the battle of Highnam at the end of March. Coningsby, however, sent a token force of eleven men to Brampton, bearing a summons to Lady Brilliana and her supporters 'to deliver up to his Majesty's use the fort and castle of Brampton Bryan, with all arms, munitions, and all other warlike provisions about or in the said fort and castle under the pain to be taken and proceeded against both by law and martial force as persons guilty of high treason'. Lady Brilliana phrased a firm and careful reply to the summons, using the crown's own propaganda as the basis for her arguments:

to the demand of my house and arms (which are no more than to defend my house), this is my answer. Our gracious King, having many times promised that he will maintain the laws and liberties of the kingdom, by which I have as good right to what is mine as anyone, maintains me these, and I know not upon what ground the refusal of giving you what is mine (by the laws of the land), will prove me, or anyone that is with me, traitors.[26]

The Marquess of Hertford, commander of the royalist forces in the west, replied to this letter and assured Lady Brilliana that she, her family, servants and possessions would be unharmed if she were to surrender. Lady Brilliana clearly placed little faith in such offers. Four days after receiving the summons from Coningsby she heard that Herbert had appointed 600 men and two cannon to be sent to reduce Brampton and she once again asked her husband if she should leave the estate for a place of safety. The royalists were in fact unable to spare the force to attack Brampton and the planned assault was postponed until the end of July. Nevertheless, in the intervening months Lady

---

[25] Harley to Viscount Scudamore, 2 February 1642/3, BL Loan 29/121; PRO C115/12/5614; Folger Library, Scudamore Mss., Vb2(13).

[26] King Charles to Fitzwilliam Coningsby (copy), 26 January 1642/3, BL Loan 29/122/3; Lady Brilliana to Harley, 14 February 1642/3, BL Loan 29/174 f.8r–v; Hutton, *Royalist War Effort*, 54–5; Fitzwilliam Coningsby to Lady Brilliana and her reply, 4 March 1642/3, BL Loan 29/174 f.15r.

Brilliana's situation was becoming increasingly untenable, since Brampton was effectively isolated in an area that was largely under royalist control. The nearest parliamentarian stronghold was at Gloucester and although Lady Brilliana was in contact with its governor, Colonel Massey, it was too far away to offer practical protection to Brampton. Although the local royalists were not in a position to attack Brampton during the first half of 1643, nevertheless they did their best to intimidate the inhabitants into submission. The restraint which the royalist gentry had apparently exercised in relation to Lady Brilliana in the summer of 1642 had clearly been weakened by their experience of parliamentarian rule in the county and the surrounding areas. The King's decision in January 1643 that Brampton should be reduced also played its part in increasing royalist hostility towards the parliamentarian enclave there.[27]

In January 1643 Lady Brilliana informed her husband that 'none that belongs to me dare go to Hereford, nor dare they go far from my house'. The physical dangers for the parliamentarians were very real. In the same month a messenger from Sir Robert was arrested at Richards Castle and Lady Brilliana revealed that a number of local men were languishing in royalist gaols, including Sir Robert's drummer, who 'is almost starved'. Lady Brilliana told Edward that she was being treated

with all the malice that can be. Mr Wigmore will not let the fowler bring me any fowl, nor will he suffer any of my servants pass. They have forbid my rents to be paid. They draw away the young horses at Wigmore and none of my servants dare go scarce as far as the town. And dear Ned, if God were not merciful to me I should be in a very miserable condition. I am threatened every day to be beset with soldiers. My hope is the Lord will not deliver me nor mine into their hands; for surely they would use all cruelty towards me, for I am told that they desire not to leave your father neither root nor branch.

Later some royalist troops entered the park at Brampton, took four oxen, beat the workmen and opened fire, shooting Edward Morgan twice in the chest: he was dead from his wounds 'within half an hour'.[28]

The plunder of her horses and cattle, and the threats to Lady Brilliana's dependants, form a constant backdrop to her letters in these months, and were accompanied by the problems which she faced in collecting rents. Lady Brilliana had noted that tenants had started to refuse to pay their rents as early as April 1641, and though initially such refusals had economic origins, rent strikes were to become increasingly common throughout the country in 1642 and were encouraged by the political situation. In February 1643

---

[27] The Marquess of Hertford to Lady Brilliana, undated, BL Loan 29/174 between ff.18 and 19, Lady Brilliana to Harley, 8 March 1642/3, BL Loan 29/174 f.17r; Lewis, *Letters of the Lady Brilliana Harley*, 202.

[28] Lady Brilliana to Harley, 28 January 1642/3, BL Loan 29/72; Lewis, *Letters of the Lady Brilliana Harley*, 187; Lady Brilliana to Harley, 23 April 1643, BL Loan 29/72.

Fitzwilliam Coningsby, acting in his capacity as sheriff and as governor of Hereford, ordered the Harleys' tenants to pay their rents directly to him. The continued need for funds for the royalist war effort was quite sufficient to explain Coningsby's order, but Lady Brilliana believed it to be a move aimed specifically at her own safety, for 'their aim is to enforce me to let those men I have go, that then they might seize upon my house and cut our throats by a few rogues and then say they knew not who did it'.[29]

It was clear that traditional Harley influence, which had been so strong in the north-west of the county, was gradually being eroded. In May the Harleys' steward at Kingsland turned his own cattle onto the tenants' land and claimed it as his own. The tenants there had already refused to pay their rents on the grounds that the Harleys were behind in their payments of the chief rent to the crown. Harley may well have been paying the money to receivers acting on behalf of Parliament, but he was also in arrears as early as April 1642. In April 1643 Lady Brilliana informed Harley that some local landowners were being forced to abate rents at the rate of 4 shillings in the pound and suggested that he take a similar course. If Harley did accept this advice then it appears to have had little effect, since in June and July Lady Brilliana complained that she was unable to collect rents at all and she was forced to borrow, although the sums involved were 'not much money'. Some of the tenants may have paid their rents to the royalist administration, others may have taken advantage of the confusion to pay nothing, yet others turned the lands back to the Harleys since they were unable to farm the land profitably themselves. Throughout the country landlords were facing similar problems: in Kent Henry Oxinden noted that rents were abated at the rate of 'one part of three'; on the Warwickshire and Gloucestershire estates of the Earl of Middlesex his agents despaired of collecting the full sums and took whatever men would pay.[30]

Lady Brilliana's problems were eased by the brief occupation of Hereford by parliamentarian troops under the command of Sir William Waller at the end of April 1643, although the effects of this were shortlived. In March Waller had left Bristol and marched against the royalist forces besieging Gloucester, taking Malmesbury on the way. At Gloucester he had taken the royalists by surprise and had captured about 1,600 men. In early April his army moved from Gloucester through the southern marches and into

[29] Lady Brilliana to Harley, 2 April 1641, BL Loan 29/173 f.93r; Manning, *The English People*, 212–15; Lady Brilliana to Harley, 14 February 1642/3, BL Loan 29/174 f.8v; Lewis, *Letters of the Lady Brilliana Harley*, 188–9.

[30] Lady Brilliana to Harley, 28 May 1643, BL Loan 29/72; Nathaniel Tomkins to Harley, 8 April 1642, BL Loan 29/173 f.235r, Lady Brilliana to Harley, 1 April 1642, Loan 29/72; Lewis, *Letters of the Lady Brilliana Harley*, 205; Manning, *The English People*, 213–14; see also J. T. Cliffe, *Puritans in Conflict: The Puritan Gentry During and After the Civil Wars* (1988), 88–90.

Herefordshire, where they successfully besieged Hereford and entered the city on 25 April. Some of the county's leading royalists were now taken prisoner: Viscount Scudamore was conducted to London, and the Coningsbys, Sir Walter Pye, and Sir William Croft were all sent to Bristol. Waller, however, retreated to Gloucester at the start of May without securing Hereford with a garrison and the royalists reasserted their control in Herefordshire, where Henry Lingen took over as sheriff from Fitzwilliam Coningsby. At the end of June Lady Brilliana described the renewed efforts of the county's royalists:

in this country they begin to raise new troops, and they have set the country at £1,200 a month. My Lord Herbert and Colonel Vavasour, who is to be governor of Hereford, is gone up into Montgomeryshire to raise soldiers. All of them are returned into Herefordshire; Sir Walter Pye, Mr Brabazon, Mr Smallman, Mr Wigmore, Mr Lingen, and Mr Stiles and Gardnas, who has quartered soldiers in Kingsland.[31]

In spite of her fears that Brampton would be attacked, Lady Brilliana resolutely refused to take a neutral stand and she allowed Brampton to become a centre of refuge for parliamentarians. She sent some of these men to join her son's troops, furnishing one with a horse costing £8. Lady Brilliana also promised to 'see whether any will contribute to buy a horse', and sent money to Edward towards a horse for his regiment. Lady Brilliana also organised an efficient intelligence service, which operated even at the height of the siege of her home. Her information was sent both to Sir Robert at Westminster and to Colonel Massey at Gloucester in the hopes that they could take measures to counter the movements of the local royalists. In June she thus despatched Priam Davies to Massey to ask for two troops of horse to attack Lord Molyneux, camped with 200 horse outside Leominster. In the light of these activities it is not surprising that the royalist plans to attack Brampton were eventually revived, but it was only after the defeat of Waller's army and the fall of Bristol in July 1643 that the siege of Brampton finally became feasible. Waller's forces had moved south-west in June to counter the advance of Sir Ralph Hopton's Cornish army, and after an indecisive engagement at Lansdown, near Bath, Waller cornered Hopton in Devizes, but his own forces were destroyed in mid-July at the battle of Roundway Down and the remainder limped back to Bristol and thence to London.[32]

At Lansdown Edward Harley's horse was killed during a furious charge and in a letter to his father he described the 'miserable rout' of the Parliament's forces at Roundway, which he philosophically accepted as 'the hand of God mightily against us, for 'twas he only that made us fly. We had

[31] *DNB*, XX, 588; Webb, *Memorials*, I, 299–300; Lewis, *Letters of the Lady Brilliana Harley*, 205.
[32] Lewis, *Letters of the Lady Brilliana Harley*, 196, 199, 201, 206, 207; Priam Davies to Edward Harley, 3 July 1643, BL Loan 29/174 f.33r; *DNB*, XX, 588–9.

very much self confidence and I trust the Lord has only brought this upon us to make us look more to him, who I am confident, when we are weakest, will show Himself a glorious God over the enemies of His truth.' Almost immediately after Waller had left Bristol the city was stormed and taken by Prince Rupert on 25 July. This was the signal for the commencement of the siege of Brampton Bryan, and the very next day the newly appointed governor of Hereford, Sir William Vavasour, had Brampton surrounded by a 700-strong force of horse and foot. The siege was to last nearly seven weeks, until the royalists were called away to reinforce the regiments surrounding Gloucester, which, after the fall of Bristol, was highly exposed as the principal parliamentarian garrison between Oxford and the royalist counties of Wales and the Marches. The strategic importance of Gloucester is reflected in the fact that the King himself commanded the forces which besieged the town on 10 August.[33]

The final decision to move against Brampton was taken by Vavasour, who was acutely aware that the continued existence of a parliamentarian haven in the midst of territory under royalist control could only reflect badly on his own command. As an outsider Vavasour may also have found it easier to make this decisive move against the Harleys. On 26 July 1643 Vavasour wrote to Prince Rupert justifying his action on the grounds that 'I found that I had been lost in the opinion of these counties, neither should I get half the contribution promised me, unless I made an attempt upon Brampton Castle, Sir Robert Harley's house, which I ventured upon, it is a strong place, but I am lodged very near it, three pikes length from the port.' The approach to the castle was protected by the gatehouse, an early fourteenth-century structure flanked by two round towers and protected by a fully working double portcullis. A passage led from the gatehouse into the inner courtyard, where the hall, also originating in the fourteenth century, was situated on the north. The inmates of the castle reckoned that they were surrounded by two or three troops of horse, plus two or three hundred foot, in all about seven hundred men. Inside the castle were fifty musketeers and another fifty civilians – men, women and children. Lady Brilliana was accompanied by her three youngest children, Thomas, Dorothy and Margaret, and by a number of friends including Dorothy, Lady Coleburn, the family doctor Nathaniel Wright, his wife and his apothecary, and Samuel More, son of Richard More, the MP for Bishop's Castle.[34]

---

[33] Edward Harley to Harley, 15 July 1643, BL Loan 29/174 f. 38r; Webb, *Memorials*, I, 291–313, 328.
[34] Webb, *Memorials*, I, 318; Pevsner, *Herefordshire*, 82; HMC, *Manuscripts of the Marquess of Bath*, I, 23, 1, 3, 22, 33; Lewis, *Letters of the Lady Brilliana Harley*, 208; Lady Brilliana to Harley, 6 August 1642, BL Loan 29/174 between ff.303 and 304; *DNB*, XIII, 874–5.

Inside Brampton conditions were extremely uncomfortable and dangerous. The siege lasted for just over six weeks, during which time the cattle, sheep and horses were plundered; the mills, town houses and barns were all burnt to the ground and the castle was extensively damaged by continual bombardment with cannon and small shot. Casualties were surprisingly slight – the cook was killed after being hit by a bullet and Mrs Wright and Lady Coleburn were both wounded.[35] The inhabitants of the castle accepted the assault with great courage and Lady Brilliana's own fortitude strengthened the resolve of those around her. Priam Davies, a captain who was present throughout the siege, later recalled: 'all our bread was ground with a hand mill, our provisions very scarce, the roof of the castle so battered that there was not one dry room in it: our substance without plundered and all our friends fled, yet this noble lady bore all with admirable patience'. Davies declared with great bravado that they were more disturbed by the swearing of the royalists than by their military endeavours:

the enemy continued this battery, cursing the Roundheads, calling us Essex's bastards, Waller's bastards, Harley's bastards, rogues, thieves, traitors, and all to reduce us to the obedience of the King and protestant religion . . .

Upon the 22nd day the enemy made their approach nearest to us, cast up breast works in our gardens and walks, where their rotten and poisoned language annoyed us more than their poisoned bullets.

Lady Brilliana's own conviction that she was engaged in a religious battle is evident in her letters to Vavasour written during the siege. She informed him that

if it has pleased the Lord to appoint that your cruelties and wrongs to me and mine, and some of the inhabitants of this town, must help fill up the measure of all the cruelties now used against those that desire to keep faith in a good conscience, I shall not be displeased; for when the measure of cruelties is full, the day of deliverance will soon appear to the Church of God, which is now afflicted.

Throughout the siege Lady Brilliana was in continual negotiation with either local royalist gentlemen or with Vavasour. Initially Lady Brilliana was sent a summons signed by three commissioners, Henry Lingen, Sir Walter Pye and William Smallman, who subtly reminded Lady Brilliana that because of their relationship with her they would like to help her, but Sir William Vavasour was in command. If she resisted they would be unable to protect her and she was likely to be treated particularly harshly in revenge for the handling of Lady Aubigny, who had been forced to appear before a parliamentarian court martial for her alleged part in Waller's plot:

our relations to your ladyship make us careful to prevent if we can any further inconvenience to you, and therefore to that end we think fit to acquaint you that Sir

[35] HMC, *Manuscripts of the Marquess of Bath*, I, 1–33.

William Vavasour by His Majesty's command hath drawn his forces before your castle, with resolution to reduce it before he stirs from thence, your ladyship may do well to take into your consideration the posture you are in. Bristol is taken by Prince Rupert and [he] is now before Gloucester. His Majesty's forces are successful everywhere, so that your ladyship cannot hope for any relief, and upon these terms if your ladyship should be obstinate we cannot promise and expect those conditions for you that are fit for your quality, especially my Lady Aubigny having been so ill treated by the Parliament, neither any quarter for those that are with you, who further must look for all extremity upon their families and substance forthwith.[36]

Drawing once again upon the language of the crown's own statements, Lady Brilliana replied that since the King had promised to maintain the laws and liberties of the kingdom, she could not believe that the King 'would give a command to take away anything from his loyal subjects, and much less to take away my house. If Sir William Vavasour will do so I must endeavour to keep what is mine as well as I can, in which I have the law of nature, of reason, and of the land on my side, and you none to take it from me.' Vavasour himself responded to this by reinforcing the commissioners' threats:

truly madam I must deal plainly with you . . . for we will never suffer the King's power to be affronted by so small a part of the country . . . I am your servant and to one so noble and virtuous am desirous to keep off all insolencies that the liberty of the soldiers, provoked to it by your obstinacies, may throw upon you; yet if you remain still wilful, what you may suffer is brought upon you by yourself.

Lady Brilliana continued to maintain that she and her family were 'the King's most faithful subjects' and that Vavasour should withdraw his troops. She scorned his suggestion that he should place guards inside Brampton, since 'I would become a prisoner in my own house'. Taking full advantage of her position as a woman she argued that she could only act on Sir Robert's instructions and since she did not know if he would approve this plan, she could not take the decision herself because 'I never will voluntarily betray the trust my husband reposes in me'. Lady Brilliana's chief strategy was to draw out the negotiations in the hope that help could be sent to her, and she asked for permission to send a message to her brother-in-law, Sir William Pelham, 'who is with the King, that by his means I may obtain a pass, by which I may go safely to some other place of more safety than my own house'. Pelham, however, was not with the King, who instead despatched Sir John Scudamore of Ballingham to offer Brilliana a full pardon if she would surrender to Vavasour. Lady Brilliana now insisted on addressing a petition to the King, assuring him 'your poor subject did never offend your Majesty, or ever take up arms against your Majesty, or any man of mine, or any by my appointment was in actual rebellion against your sacred Majesty'. She begged that the besieging forces be removed 'and restore to me my goods', but failing that,

[36] *Ibid.*, 26, 24–5, 12–13, 8.

'my humble desire is that you will in your clemency allow unto me some maintenance for me and mine and fit time to remove myself and family by your protection to pass to some other place where we may find subsistence, that we perish not'.[37]

Lady Brilliana's protests were not strictly true; she had certainly harboured parliamentarians and had helped volunteers to join the army by providing both horses and money. Nevertheless, on 1 September she received a letter from Secretary Falkland, offering 'unto the petitioner and also the persons with her, full pardon and free licence to depart out of the castle whither and with what arms and ammunition – ordnance only excepted – they shall please themselves, and to assure them of a convoy accordingly'. Despite such assurances Lady Brilliana had no inclination to turn her home over to men whom she regarded as 'spoilers'. Furthermore, the inhabitants of the castle were convinced they would be ill-treated if they surrendered, so they chose instead to hold out and were encouraged in this by the news that Sir William Brereton 'would send a party to our release'. Outside events did eventually save the garrison at Brampton, for on 9 September the royalist forces were diverted to counter Essex's army marching to the relief of Gloucester. Inside the castle the news was received with jubilation:

this night we had secret intelligence that the Lord General was with a very great army near Gloucester, that the Cavaliers had raised their siege to give him battle, and that all the King's forces were called together for that purpose from Exeter, from Shrewsbury etc.; that Sir William Waller came out of London upon Monday last and that the Cavaliers about us would be gone. This indeed was the day of our deliverance, a day to be remembered and never to be forgotten throughout our generations.[38]

Sir Robert Harley now wrote to his wife advising her to leave Brampton. In her reply Lady Brilliana bravely stated that she was not afraid to die in preserving the Harley estates and true religion in the county. She asked for Edward Harley to come home to 'do his country service and himself good in helping to keep what I hope shall be his, and in maintaining the gospel in this place'. Writing to her children at the same time, Lady Brilliana revealed her self-doubts more plainly by asking Edward 'whether I had best stay or remove' and telling her daughter, Brilliana, that she longed to leave Brampton, adding realistically that 'there is no stirring without a convoy'. Sir Robert may have had problems in arranging safe passage for his family, for in her last extant letter to her husband, dated 16 October 1643, Lady Brilliana wrote: 'I very much long to hear from you and whether you would have me come from Brampton and how I should come.' Although Lady Brilliana had decided to leave Brampton, she was also convinced that she was not safe from

[37] *Ibid.*, 8–9, 10, 12, 17.
[38] *Ibid.*, 17–18; Lady Brilliana to Harley, 24 September 1643, BL Loan 29/72; HMC, *Manuscripts of the Marquess of Bath*, I, 25, 26, 7.

further attack and took measures to secure the castle and its inmates. She ordered the levelling of the enemy's earthworks and the castle was restocked with provisions, which had to be plundered from her most active opponents, as Priam Davies recorded:

the noble lady instead of revenging herself upon the inhabitants of that country who were active against her to the utmost of their might and power, yea none more forward and false than her own tenants and servants, in a courteous and winning way gently entreated the part adjacent to come in to level those works which they pretended the enemy had compelled them to raise against her promising to protect them, and that none of her soldiers should plunder them, all which they barbarously refused, whereupon we took out a party and compelled them in, but by her special command that none should take a pennyworth from any of them, which was as truly observed, I dare appeal to their own consciences, until their malice broke forth again. Many that had not paid their rents of some years before refused; yea they would not let us have any provisions nor any of the conveniences of life which they could hinder from us.
Our necessities and resolutions would no longer brook such barbarism; we then daily sent our parties only against those that had been most active against us; whereby our necessities were in a short time supplied. Also we sent and burnt those engines of war which the enemy had prepared to undermine us. They termed them 'hoggs', which are used in approaches in war.[39]

Despite both her own appeals to the law of the land and her manifest dislike of plundering, necessity had forced Lady Brilliana to contribute to the general collapse of the laws. Lady Brilliana now went a step further and ordered an attack on royalist troops quartered just over the border in Radnorshire. In his description of this foray Priam Davies emphasises that Lady Brilliana was a commander in every sense of the word:

this noble lady, who commanded in chief, I may truly say with such a masculine bravery, both for religion, resolution, wisdom, and warlike policy, that her equal I never yet saw, commanded that a party of about forty should go and beat up their quarters in Knighton, a market town in Radnorshire, four miles off, where Colonel Lingen's troops, her late antagonist, was quartered. This was so performed that we brought some prisoners, arms and horses without the loss of one man.[40]

Despite these hostile actions Lady Brilliana continued to insist that she was doing no more than protecting her own property, for which she claimed the laws gave her sufficient warrant. In a letter written to her brother, the second Viscount Conway, she declared: 'I never desired any more than to live upon my own, in my own house and never anything that in the least kind might provoke or occasion an army to come against me.' Lady Brilliana maintained that she had kept muskets in readiness, 'to keep me from the plundering of

---

[39] Lady Brilliana to Harley, 24 September 1643, BL Loan 29/72; Lewis, *Letters of the Lady Brilliana Harley*, 208; Lady Brilliana to Brilliana Harley, 7 October 1643, BL Loan 29/174 between ff.55 and 59, *idem* to Harley, 16 October 1643, Loan 29/174 f.61r; HMC, *Manuscripts of the Marquess of Bath*, I, 26–7.
[40] HMC, *Manuscripts of the Marquess of Bath*, I, 27.

soldiers', and she resisted Vavasour's demands because 'I thought it was a poor thing to give away my own, with my own will, and I thought it was worse to be contented to receive a guard into my house by which I become a prisoner and so speak myself guilty.' Her fears that she would be ill-treated by the royalists formed the backdrop to her arguments and she added: 'what you mean by resisting with all extremity I know not . . . I believe if I fall into their hands I should suffer much'.[41]

In the summer of 1642 Lady Brilliana could have accounted herself innocent of any direct involvement in the conflict, other than sending the family plate to London for the war effort, but in the intervening months she had become increasingly entangled in the prosecution of the war, and by mid-October 1643 her protestations of innocence no longer ring true. Lady Brilliana, however, sincerely believed that she had been driven to act purely in the spirit of self-defence. At the same time that she wrote to her brother she also received a warning from Vavasour that he would renew the siege, but before he could act Lady Brilliana fell fatally ill, her final sickness and death being both sudden and unexpected. On 29 October 1643 Samuel More wrote to London warning Sir Robert's servant Sankey that his mistress was ill. She had suffered a fit of the stone, from which she apparently recovered, but was then afflicted with a cough, had fallen into a fit and been seized with apoplexy, lethargy and convulsions. More knew Lady Brilliana was near death and advised that should 'the Lord take this sweet lady' it was necessary that someone should govern the family and suggested that Edward Harley 'had best come'.[42]

Lady Brilliana died two days later on the sabbath, her final days fortified by her deep religious faith, as Priam Davies testified:

this honourable lady, of whom the world was not worthy, as she was a setting forward the work of God, suddenly and unexpectedly fell sick of an apoplexy, with a defluxion of the lungs. Three days she continued in great extremity with admirable patience. Never was a holy life consummated and concluded with a more heavenly and happy end. Myself and many others of quality being both ear and eye witnesses, to our great admiration. The last period of her mortal abode in this vale of tears drawing on apace, she with an undaunted faith and resolution looked death in the face without dread, and the Lord Jesus with joy and comfort, to whom she resigned her soul. From whom she has received an immortal, an incorruptible inheritance and crown, which none of her enemies can reach to rob or despoil her of.[43]

[41] PRO SP16/498/9.
[42] Lady Brilliana to Harley, 16 October 1643, BL Loan 29/174 f.61r, Samuel More to Richard Sankey, 29 October 1643, Loan 29/174 two copies between ff.63 and 64.
[43] HMC, *Manuscripts of the Marquess of Bath*, I, 27. For the genre of the 'godly life' see P. Collinson, 'A "Magazine of Religious Patterns": An Erasmian Topic Transposed in English Protestantism', in Baker, *Renaissance and Renewal*, 223–49; and P. G. Lake, 'Feminine Piety and Personal Potency: The "Emancipation" of Mrs Jane Ratcliffe', *The Seventeenth Century*, II (1987).

Although this account is clearly derivative of the 'godly life', a popular genre of religious literature which typically, but not inevitably, stressed the peaceful death-bed scenes of the elect, it should be remembered that Davies was not writing a biography of Lady Brilliana. He was primarily concerned with recording the events of the two sieges of Brampton, and although he followed the conventions of puritan literature his words were also a sincere tribute to the woman who had bravely refused to surrender to enemy forces. On learning of his wife's death, Sir Robert wrote at once to Brampton, appointing More and Wright guardians of his estate and family:

having received the sad news that the Lord has taken from me my dear wife, to whose wise hand of providence I desire with a heart of resignation humbly to submit. Beseeching him in mercy to sanctify it unto me and my poor children, and that he will be pleased to make up this . . . breach with . . . consolations of his holy spirit . . .
    Entreating you both to manage the affairs of my poor estate, to receive my rents etc. keep my house for the King and Parliament against all opposers and the Lord in mercy by the bulwark with you. I would have my children and my nephew Smith guided by your counsels.[44]

Dr Wright now received a commission from Parliament appointing him commander of the castle, and he raised a troop of horse and victualled the castle with food sufficient for a year, 'all which was gained by the sword', wrote Davies. The siege was not resumed until Lent the next year and lasted three weeks, ending in surrender to Sir Michael Woodhouse, Sir William Vavasour and Sir William Croft. An outpost set up by Samuel More at Hopton Castle had fallen a little earlier and, according to the accounts of both More and Davies, twenty-five of the men at Hopton were slaughtered after they had surrendered. The prisoners at Brampton were treated more leniently, having secured the promise of quarter, although their fates hung in the balance after the arrival of an order from Prince Rupert 'to put us all to the sword, especially Doctor Wright our Lieutenant-Colonel'. A council of war was held at which Sir William Vavasour insisted that the offer of quarter should hold good, 'by whose means, through God's mercy, we were preserved'. Amongst those taken prisoner were Thomas, Dorothy and Margaret Harley, Edward Smith, Nathaniel Wright and his two captains Priam Davies and John Hackluit, and two ministers, William Stephenson of Wigmore and Francis Boughey of Stokesay. They were taken first to Ludlow, 'thence to Shrewsbury, some of us to Chester Castle. The inhabitants of Ludlow baited us like bears and demanded where our God was.'[45]
    At Shrewsbury they were visited by Edward Symmons, chaplain to Sir Michael Woodhouse, who debated their disloyalty with them and later

---

[44] Harley to Nathaniel Wright and Samuel More, 4 November 1643, BL Loan 29/174 f.64r.
[45] HMC, *Manuscripts of the Marquess of Bath*, I, 28, 29–33, 36–40, 32–3; Longleat, Portland Mss., vol. 23 ff.199r–203r; HMC, *Manuscripts of the Marquess of Bath*, I, 33.

incorporated their replies into a tract aimed against the parliamentarian divine, Stephen Marshall. The prisoners were justifying their actions to an opponent and their arguments are thus a very clear statement of the beliefs of the people who had supported Lady Brilliana's resistance to the royalists, in particular the conviction that the supporters of episcopacy were sympathetic to catholicism and the profound belief that all the godly would be moved to act in unison against the threat posed to them by popery. It would be difficult to find a more clear-cut statement of the sympathies of the godly community in action. They told Symmons 'they took up arms against Antichrist and Popery', and gave him a detailed account of the religious nature of the war arguing that their stand was legally warranted by the command of Parliament alone:

all the true godly divines in England (amongst whom they named in special M. Marshal) were of their opinion, that Antichrist was here in England as well as in Rome, and that the bishops were Antichrist, and that all that did endeavour to support them were popishly affected, Babilonish and Antichristian too, yea many professed papists were in our armies, who (they said) did fight against Christ and protestant religion, and therefore they thought, they were bound in conscience to fight against them, and us that took part with them, and in so doing they did but help God against his enemies. I urged them to shew by what call or warrant they had to do so, being not authorised by the King, they seemed to infer a threefold call or warrant. 1. The command of Parliament. 2. The example of all godly and powerful ministers, leading, encouraging, and stirring them thereunto and 3. The motion of God's spirit in all God's people, provoking them all with one mind, to undertake the same business.[46]

Catholic participation in the war was in fact considerable, as a number of recent studies have shown, and Lady Brilliana had also been convinced that her enemies were reinforced by catholics. After the first siege had been lifted she wrote to her daughter in London and told her: 'all the papists from many parts were gathered against me when I was besieged'. The impact of such beliefs should not be underestimated. For Lady Brilliana and her supporters in Herefordshire religious belief provided both a motivating and a sustaining force in their resistance to the crown. Sir Robert was similarly motivated; in 1650 he stated that when he first gave his support to Parliament he believed he was involved in a religious struggle:

I found the Lord's good providence in my sufferings in my estate . . . to have been very great, which may be computed to little less than £20,000 for the cause of the Parliament, into which when I first engaged in Parliament, I understood it on conscientious deliberation to be the cause of God.[47]

---

[46] E. Symmons, *Scripture Vindicated* (Oxford, 1644), Preface to the Readers.

[47] Although Dr Lindley's work on the subject suggested that the majority of catholics tried to remain neutral, more recent studies suggest that catholic participation on the side of the King was considerable: see K. J. Lindley, 'The Part Played by Catholics', in B. S. Manning ed., *Politics, Religion and the English Civil War* (London, 1973), 126–76; P. R. Newman, 'Catholic Royalists of Northern England, 1642–1645', *Northern History*, XV (1979), 88–

Her letters to the Marquess of Hertford and to Sir William Vavasour in particular reveal that Lady Brilliana was quite capable of discussing her situation in terms of allegiance to the crown and her faith in the laws of the land, but her private letters to her family reveal the true depth of her perception of the Civil War as a struggle by the godly few against the enemies of true religion. Despite her obvious concern for the unity of the county gentry, which surfaces, for example, in her letter to Viscount Scudamore, it was not a sense of county community or even of gentry community which claimed Lady Brilliana's ultimate loyalties, it was her belief in the community of the godly. When Sir Robert did finally agree that his family should leave Brampton at the end of the first siege, his wife bravely assured him that she was prepared to accept the providence of God. Lady Brilliana's reply to Sir Robert illustrates her desire to preserve both her home and the profession of true religion in the county, even at the risk of her own life. The extent to which Lady Brilliana perceived her duty to her family and to the county in religious terms, rather than in terms of the welfare of the local community, is strikingly phrased:

Dear Sir, hitherto God has made me (though an unworthy one) an instrument to keep possession of your house, that it has not fallen into the hands of spoilers, and to keep together a handful of such as feared the Lord . . . so that His word has still an abiding in these parts, which if the Lord remove Herefordshire is miserable. In this work I have not thought my life dear, neither shall I.[48]

95; and Malcolm, *Caesar's Due*, 50–2, 94–5; Lady Brilliana to Brilliana Harley, 7 October 1643, BL Loan 29/174 between ff.55 and 59, Harley to Humphrey Mackworth, 29 April 1650, Loan 29/176 f.177r. In July 1646 Sir Robert's steward, Samuel Shilton, estimated that his master's losses since the start of the war amounted to £12,990, Lewis, *Letters of the Lady Brilliana Harley*, 230.

[48] Lady Brilliana to Harley, 24 September 1643, BL Loan 29/72.

8

Conclusion

The siege of Brampton and the death of Lady Brilliana did nothing to shake Sir Robert Harley's firm support for the policies pursued by the parliamentary leadership at Westminster. This group, headed by Pym until his death in December 1643 and thereafter by Oliver St John, were ready to negotiate with the King, but believed that only a vigorous war policy would persuade Charles to accept peace on their terms. In 1643 they continued to adhere to the limited political and religious objectives which had been outlined in the course of 1641 and 1642, and which had been enshrined in the Grand Remonstrance and the Nineteen Propositions. This grouping consisted of men with clear political aims and a sufficient grasp of parliamentary tactics to pursue a middle course between those who wanted immediate peace on the one side and those who favoured a ruthless war and a dictated peace on the other.[1]

Harley's commitment to waging an effective war was illustrated on 7 August 1643, when he acted as a teller in a crucial vote on whether the House of Commons should consider the peace proposals to the King drawn up by the Lords. The military situation of Parliament was at its weakest since the start of the war; Fairfax had been defeated at Adwalton at the end of June and Waller's losses at Lansdown and Roundway had been the prelude to the fall of Bristol. Pym and his supporters opposed the resumption of peace negotiations and hoped instead that a military alliance could be forged with the Scots to counter the royalist successes. On 5 August Denzil Holles and Sir John Evelyn had secured a vote in the House to consider the Lords' overtures for peace, despite Pym's passionate plea to the contrary. Two days later, after stormy debate, the question was put once again. Holles, who was emerging as the leader of the peace party, and Sir John Holland were the tellers for the ayes

[1] The classic study of the middle group until the time of Pym's death is contained in J. Hexter, *The Reign of King Pym*, Harvard Historical Studies, XLVIII (Cambridge, Mass., 1941). Hexter's thesis that the middle group disintegrated on the death of Pym has, however, been modified by Professor Valerie Pearl, who demonstrates the survival of the middle group under the leadership of Oliver St John: V. Pearl, 'Oliver St John and the "middle group" in the Long Parliament: August 1643 – May 1644', *English Historical Review*, XXXI (1966), 490–519.

and counted 81. Harley and Sir Thomas Barrington were the tellers for the noes and D'Ewes records that Sir Robert, 'being in years and missing nine of their own number in telling gave the noes to be but 79, whereas in truth they were 88'. There was a recount and the noes were established as the winners, thus ending, as D'Ewes noted, 'all our hopes of peace and tranquillity for the present'.[2]

D'Ewes' suggestion that Harley had miscounted because of a decline in his mental powers takes no account of the fact that by the day of the vote Brampton had been under siege for nearly two weeks. By then Harley would certainly have heard news of the assault on his home and his lack of concentration is quite explicable for that reason alone. Nor is D'Ewes' comment convincing in the light of Sir Robert's subsequent active parliamentary career. Throughout the next five years, except when he withdrew from the House in the wake of the army crisis in the summer of 1647, Harley was frequently employed on committees and on other parliamentary business, as the *Commons Journals* reveal. Most notably he chaired both the committee for the destruction of superstitious and idolatrous monuments, set up in April 1643, and the committee for elections (sometimes known as the committee for privileges), the work of which was dramatically increased after 1645 by the 'recruiter elections', held to replace members who had died or who had been dismissed from the House as royalists. Harley's work on these and other committees demonstrates that he continued to be held in high regard by the parliamentary leadership.[3]

As the war progressed the cohesion of the middle group became increasingly fragmented, however. The arrival of the Scottish troops in England in January 1644 and the re-organisation of the army leadership in the winter of 1644–5 under the command of Lord Fairfax (resulting in the creation of the New Model Army), were issues which strongly divided opinions between the peace and war parties in Parliament and made it increasingly difficult for the middle-group leaders to direct policy. The help of the Scots was initially enlisted by the middle group with the aid of Vane and other war enthusiasts, but the course of 1644 was to see a surprising *volte face* as Vane and St John drew away from the Scots, fearing that they would try to impose a rigid presbyterian church settlement on England by concluding their own peace

---

[2] *CJ*, III, 197; Gardiner, *Civil War*, I, 162, 174, 179; P. Crawford, *Denzil Holles, 1598–1680: A Study of his Political Career*, Royal Historical Society Studies in History, XVI (1979), 93–5; BL Harl. Ms. 165 ff.148r.

[3] The siege of Brampton had started on 26 July 1643: see HMC, *Manuscripts of the Marquess of Bath*, I, 1; R. Culmer, *Cathedral News from Canterbury Showing the Canterburian Cathedral to be in an Abbey-Like Corrupt and Rotten Condition, which calls for a Speedy Reformation, or Dissolution* (1644), 6; for Harley's work on the committee for elections see *CJ*, III, 311, 319, 337, 352, 683; IV, 260, 283, 432; V, 30, 258. Sir Robert's notes from the committee for elections for 1646 and 1647 survive in BL Add. Mss., 28716 and BL Loan 29/50 respectively; for Harley's involvement with the peace treaties see *CJ*, II,

terms with the King. Holles, on the other hand, was increasingly attracted to the Scots and was known to be working with them by the spring of 1645. Rather misleadingly from 1645 contemporaries dubbed Denzil Holles and his supporters as 'Presbyterians', and Vane and his followers as 'Independents'. These religious labels in fact had very little to do with the political stance taken by members of Parliament and they mask the true complexity of the cross-currents between politics and religion at Westminster in the years from 1645 until the purge of the Commons in December 1648, when alliances in the House were highly fluid.[4]

Sir Robert's sympathy for the Scots and his religious presbyterianism meant that from 1645 he was increasingly drawn into alliance with Holles' group, and he was frequently employed by the House to liaise with the Scots commissioners in London, who described Harley in August 1645 as 'a worthy and religious gentleman, to whose affection and constant assistance in the House of Commons in all affairs which concern our nation we are singularly obliged'. Sir Robert's close relations with the Scots was later underlined in 1647 when he chose a Scottish cleric, Alexander Clogie, to serve as rector of Wigmore.[5] Four years earlier, on 25 September 1643, Harley had also been among the majority of MPs who took the Solemn League and Covenant in St Margaret's church next to the Palace of Westminster, which sealed the military alliance between Parliament and the Scots. The Covenant committed its adherents to establishing religious uniformity in the Churches of England, Ireland and Scotland. To the Scots this meant one thing, the spread of the presbyterian system to the other two kingdoms. Inside England the Covenant was interpreted more widely and was taken by religious independents such as Vane and Cromwell, who believed that the oath was sufficiently vaguely worded not to compromise their religious principles.[6]

Sir Robert clearly favoured a centralised system, as opposed to the independency of the sects, but it is unlikely that he supported the introduction of the clerically dominated system envisaged by the Scots. It is hard to believe that a man such as Harley, who was used to introducing his own nominees

---

928, 935, 978, 999; III, 26, 27, 428, 478; IV, 232, 613; for the committee of South Wales, see *CJ*, IV, 678; for finance committees see, for example, *CJ*, III, 391, 487, 592, 601; IV, 202, 472–3, 663, 666.

[4] Pearl, 'Oliver St John and the "middle group" in the Long Parliament', 502–16; V. Rowe, *Sir Henry Vane the Younger: A Study in Political and Administrative History*, University of London Historical Studies, XXVIII (1970), 73–5; J. Hexter, 'The Problem of the Presbyterian Independents', *American History Review*, XLIV (1938–9), 29–49; Underdown, *Pride's Purge*, 16–23.

[5] *CJ*, III, 387; IV, 68, 273, 422, 675; H. W. Meikle, ed., *Correspondence of the Scots Commissioners in London 1644–46* (1917), 102; Harley to Edward Harley, 18 September 1647, Bl. Loan 29/175 f.75r; Clogie held the living of Wigmore until his death in 1698: see *DNB*, IV, 576–7.

[6] Rushworth, *Historical Collections of Private Passages of State*, V (1721), 480; the Solemn League and Covenant is printed in Gardiner, *Constitutional Documents*, 267–71.

into the livings under his control would relish handing total control of the Church to the clergy. Harley was, of course, closely associated with measures against the bishops and with the introduction of presbyterianism, but, as has already been noted, the 'root and branch' bill of 1641 was perhaps rather more Erastian in tone than the Scottish model of presbyterianism would allow.[7] That bill was allowed to rest in committee after the summer recess of 1641, at which date it would have failed in the Lords in any case because of the votes and influence that the bishops wielded there, but at the end of that December the imprisonment of the twelve bishops severely weakened the episcopal party in the Lords; and in February 1642 the bill disabling 'all persons in holy orders to exercise any temporal jurisdiction' was accepted by the King. It removed the bishops from the House of Lords and prevented the clergy from holding the commission of the peace. Sir Robert carried this measure to the upper chamber on 7 February and four days later Lady Brilliana wrote: 'I thank God that you were employed in that great work'.[8] The way was now cleared for action against the episcopal government of the Church, although it was not until November 1642 that the Commons appointed a committee to draw up legislation to abolish the episcopate and all inferior Church officers. Sir Robert once again carried the bill to this effect to the Lords in January 1643, where it was passed three days later. Although his acceptance of the bill was presented to Charles as one of Parliament's conditions for peace at the treaty of Oxford, the King never gave his formal assent to the bill. There the matter rested until the end of the First Civil War, but the abolition of episcopacy consistently remained a central part of any demands put forward by Parliament for peace. The parliamentary leadership may well have believed that the unilateral abolition of episcopacy without the King's consent would have given renewed impetus to the royalist cause. Furthermore, the promise of abolition was always a useful bargaining factor in negotiations with the Scots and it was not until the First Civil War was safely at an end that a parliamentary ordinance was passed, in October 1646, to abolish the Church hierarchy. A presbyterian system of sorts was gradually introduced into some areas of England between 1645 and 1648, but it comprised greater lay participation than the Scots Kirk.[9]

[7] For Harley's involvement with the 'root and branch' bill see above, pp. 110–13.
[8] W. A. Shaw, *A History of the English Church During the Civil Wars and under the Commonwealth 1640–1660*(London 1900), I, 99; J. Morrill, 'The Attack on the Church of England in the Long Parliament', in D. Beales and G. Best, eds., *History, Society and the Churches: Essays in Honour of Owen Chadwick* (Cambridge 1985), 110; Shaw, *History of the English Church*, I, 119; Lady Brilliana to Harley, 11 February 1641/2, BL Loan 29/173, between ff.211 and 212.
[9] Shaw, *History of the English Church*, I, 120–1; *CJ*, II, 938; *LJ*, V, 572; Shaw, *History of the English Church*, I, 121 n.2; C. H. Firth and R. S. Rait, eds., *Acts and Ordinances of the Interregnum*, I (1911), 879–83; J. Morrill, 'The Church in England, 1642–9', in Morrill, *Reactions to the English Civil War, 1642–1649*, 97.

Although the majority of the Westminster divines leant towards a centralised presbyterian form of Church government, the debates in the Assembly were protracted and often heated. It was not until November 1644 that the divines presented the Commons with their directory for public worship, which gave guidelines for the conduct of public worship to replace the set forms of the prayer book, and which also contained the procedure for baptism, marriage, burials, fasting and public thanksgiving. Sir Robert took a prominent part in securing the passage of the ordinance establishing the directory in place of the Book of Common Prayer, and was later involved in supervising orders for the publishing and dispersal of the directory. There was, however, a strong attachment in many parishes to the traditional forms of worship and there is little evidence that the directory was widely distributed.[10]

Sir Robert's personal stamp can also be seen in his work as chairman of the committee for the destruction of monuments of superstition and idolatry, which had been set up in April 1643. Originally the committee was empowered to remove images from Westminster Abbey and from 'any church or chapel in or about London', but its powers were enlarged to include the demolition of such monuments 'as they shall find in any public or open place in or about the cities of London and Westminster'.[11] Under Sir Robert's chairmanship the committee was responsible for the destruction of stained glass in the abbey, in St Margaret's church, and in the royal chapels at the palaces of Whitehall, Greenwich and Hampton Court. In the abbey the high altar in the Henry VII Chapel was ripped out and statues of the saints were pulled down. The royalist newsbook, *Mercurius Aulicus*, reported that Harley had carried out the work of destruction with his own hands. The account was laced throughout with the accusation that the iconoclasm was not merely aimed at the removal of religious symbols, but at the removal of symbols of royalty and the destruction of monarchy itself:

Sir Robert Harlow, who sits in the chair of reformation, having already so reformed the church of Westminster (by breaking down all the carved work thereof with axes and hammers, and spoiling even the necessary utensils which the law requires) that it was made unfit for the service of God; betook himself to the reforming of his Majesty's palace of Whitehall, and made it as unfit for the use of the King. For calling for the keys of the house with as much authority, as if he were Lord Steward and Lord Chamberlain both, his first care was to get a ladder (though commonly a ladder is the end of such reformations) which having procured, he caused it to be set up against the east window in the chapel, which he reformed of all the glass, because all was painted;

---

[10] For debates in the Assembly see J. R. Pitman, ed., *The Whole Works of the Rev. John Lightfoot*, XIII (1824), and A. F. Mitchell and J. Struthers, eds., *Minutes of the Sessions of the Westminster Assembly of Divines* (Edinburgh, 1874); *CJ*, III, 705, 722; IV, 9, 11; Firth and Rait, *Acts and Ordinances*, I, 582–607; Morrill, 'The Church in England', in Morrill, *Reactions to the English Civil War*, 93.

[11] *CJ*, III, 57, 63.

and afterwards proceeded to the reforming of the rest of the windows. Which done, he broke in pieces the communion table (because some good old christians called it by the name of an altar) pulled up the rails (for they allow of rails in no place but their own two houses, where they rail every day against their sovereign) and cast the broken fragments on the maddest [sic] of the pavement. Thence he proceeded in his visitation to his Majesty's gallery, which he reformed of all such pictures as displeased his eye, under pretence that they did favour too much of superstitious vanities (for Kings and Queens, as well as apostles, fathers, martyrs, confessors, are counted monuments of vanity and superstition) and so went on, according to the principles of reformation, till there was nothing left which was rich or glorious. What pity 'tis Sir Robert did not live in those blessed times, when there was neither King in Israel, nor any place to worship God in, but the groves and wildernesses?

The propaganda value in depicting Harley as a crazed religious fanatic is obvious, but this description is largely a fabrication designed to alarm those who did not sympathise with Parliament. The destruction undoubtedly took place and Harley may well have led the way in defacing or breaking some of the images that he found in Westminster and Whitehall. The earlier accounts that survive of his attacks on images in 1639 and 1641 reveal that he had destroyed religious icons himself, but his private papers also show that in 1643 much of the work of the committee was carried out by workmen such as Peter Petley, who charged 10 shillings for taking down the high altar in Henry VII's chapel, and Thomas Stevens, who charged £1 17s 6d for defacing pictures in the chapel at Whitehall and plastering over them. At Whitehall the east window was reglazed with 241 feet of new white glass at the cost of £7.[12]

This iconoclasm was supplemented by two ordinances drawn up by Harley's committee and passed by Parliament in August 1643 and May 1644. The first was directed at the destruction of altars, rails, candles, crucifixes and images of the Trinity or the saints. This was in effect a final assault on the church furnishings introduced during the Laudian period. The second ordinance called for the removal and defacement of copes, surplices, roods, fonts and church organs and demanded the use of plain church plate. The response to the ordinances was probably limited, for a little over a year after the second was passed the House of Commons ordered the committee to take care that the ordinances be put into execution. A large proportion of the damage inflicted on religious images from 1642 onwards was the work of the parliamentarian troops, and the cathedrals in particular suffered greatly at their hands. There are also instances of individual iconoclasts who responded

---

[12] *Mercurius Aulicus* (16–22 June 1644), 1040; Receipts dated 19 April 1644 to 26 January 1645/6, BL Loan 29/175 ff.107r–135r; Brilliana Harley to Edward Harley, 14 January and 8 February 1638/9, BL Loan 29/172 ff.207r, 213r; for earlier evidence of Harley as an iconoclast see above, pp. 47, 115.

enthusiastically to the ordinances, such as the cleric Richard Culmer in Canterbury, and William Dowsing, who kept journals recording the damage he wrought in Cambridge and in numerous churches in Suffolk, especially around Ipswich, but they seem to have been exceptional and in general there appears to be little evidence of spontaneous response to these central directives.[13]

The importance which Harley attached to the defacing or demolition of images so that they could not be stored and reused was underlined in April 1645, when the House of Commons considered the sale of the Duke of Buckingham's art collection at York House in order to raise revenue to pay for Scottish troops in Ireland. Harley headed the committee sent to view the paintings and subsequently insisted that the superstitious pictures be burnt, arguing that to sell the pictures was nothing less than an encouragement to idolatry. Harley believed that by preserving the pictures the House was doing the 'papists' work for them' and he argued that the sale would draw the scorn of the reformed churches and would lead 'the godly of the land that fight for you and supply you' to forsake the Parliament. Harley's arguments seem to have carried some weight, and after he had made his report the House ordered that any pictures of the persons of the Trinity or of the Virgin should be burnt. In fact this order seems not to have been carried out; part of the collection was later auctioned at Antwerp in 1648 and part remained in England, where it was broken up between various collectors, including the parliamentarian Earl of Northumberland.[14]

Between the time of the loss of Brampton and the end of 1645 Sir Robert was primarily concerned with such religious and political matters of national importance, largely because Herefordshire remained under royalist control until the end of 1645. Hereford was one of a string of royalist garrisons which capitulated after the parliamentarian victory at Naseby in June 1645. By the winter all that remained was a mopping-up operation, and in April 1646 Fairfax's troops closed on Oxford, prompting the King to abandon his headquarters in disguise with only two companions. He gave himself up to the Scots army investing Newark and a few days later ordered Oxford to

[13] Firth and Rait, *Acts and Ordinances*, I, 265–6, 425–6; *CJ*, IV, 246; Morrill, 'The Church in England', in Morrill, *Reactions to the English Civil War, 1642–1649*, 95; Culmer, *Cathedral News from Canterbury*; E. H. Evelyn-White, ed., *The Journal of William Dowsing* (Ipswich, 1885); *DNB*, V, 1311–2. For the background to the iconoclasm of the 1640s see M. Aston, *England's Iconoclasts: Laws Against Images* (Oxford, 1988).

[14] BL Add. Mss., 31116 f.206v; *CJ*, IV, 121; Sir Robert Harley's holograph notes endorsed 'April 23 1645 at York House', Brampton Bryan, Harley Mss., Bundle 10 and Sir Robert Harley's holograph notes on idolatry, Bundle 29; *CJ*, IV, 216. For a description of the York House collection and its subsequent sale, see Lita-Rose Betcherman, 'The York House Collection and its Keeper', *Apollo*, 92 (October, 1970) (I am grateful to Roger Lockyer for this reference).

surrender.[15] The royal cause was lost, but Charles refused to come to terms and never gave up hope of defeating Parliament through any means available. His intransigence would lead directly to the renewal of civil war in 1648 and to his own trial and execution in January the following year.

In 1646, however, the end of the war brought numerous new problems to the fore. The most pressing from Parliament's point of view was what should be done with its own army, whose leaders refused to disband until arrears of pay and other grievances had been met. The New Model Army itself was seen as a hotbed of sectarianism, and Holles and his supporters were intent on disbanding the army even before terms had been concluded with the King. Vane's supporters, on the other hand, saw their links with the army as a means of consolidating their own demands and wanted to keep it intact until Charles has accepted their terms; but in the counties local people resented the continued presence of troops in their midst once the war was over. They also objected to the methods of the parliamentary committees set up during the war to replace traditional local government by JPs and deputy lieutenants, and often staffed by men who would not normally have been admitted to the county elite. The committees, unable to provide back pay, were often in dispute with the local soldiery, who in turn were becoming contemptuous of the authority of the committee men.[16] In Herefordshire the Harleys championed the county committee against the local garrison and increasingly identified themselves as opponents of the army leadership both locally and in Parliament.

In December 1645 Hereford was taken for Parliament by Colonel John Birch and the Harleys were once again drawn into the arena of county politics. Sincs 1643 Sir Robert and Edward Harley had been named to the various parliamentary committees to govern Herefordshire, but these had largely been a dead letter while the royalists controlled the county. Unable to take any part in local politics, Edward Harley had remained in the army and in 1644 was made governor of Monmouth, which was briefly held by Parliament. In August 1645 he became governor of Canon Frome, a garrison near Hereford, and was appointed general of horse in the counties of Hereford and Radnor at the start of 1646. In November that year he was returned to Parliament in the recruiter elections as junior knight for Herefordshire, despite a vigorous campaign waged by Birch, who offered himself as an alternative candidate. Sir Robert's own local influence was increased at the end of 1646 when he was elected to the stewardship of Hereford, a post that had previously been held by Lord Scudamore, and in the new year

---

[15] C. V. Wedgewood, *The King's War* (1958), 485–557.
[16] Crawford, *Denzil Holles*, 112–20, 130–1; Ashton, *The English Civil War*, 264–7, 284–7, 291–8; Hughes, *Politics, Society and Civil War*, 179–80; Cliffe, *Yorkshire Gentry*, 358.

Harley's son, Robert, was elected to Parliament as the burgess for New Radnor.[17]

Edward Harley used his position on the county committee in order to counter the growing influence of the newcomer Birch, who came from a Lancashire family and who had made his fortune as a merchant in Bristol. After his capture of Hereford Birch was appointed its governor and he tried to develop his own power base by opposing Edward Harley as parliamentary candidate for the county. The Harleys efficiently mobilised their interests in the county and paid £402 12s 6d on 577 suppers and 2,898 dinners in order to woo the voters (more than double the sum spent on Sir Robert's election to the Long Parliament in October 1640).[18] During the course of his campaign, Birch attempted the desperate ploy of trying to move the county court to his own stronghold of Hereford from Leominster, which was closer to the centre of Harley influence in the north-west of the county, but the sheriff, a Harley supporter, refused to comply. Birch was eventually returned as burgess for Leominster, but his unwelcome electoral ambitions coincided with growing friction between local people and his troops garrisoned in Hereford Castle, who had been demanding arrears of pay since February 1646, and the Harleys took advantage of this in their attempts to undermine Birch's local position. In September 1646 the county committee wrote to the Speaker of the Commons urging the reduction and disbanding of the troops in the county and Edward Harley backed this with a charge against one of Birch's captains, who had slighted the authority of the committee.[19] In October Harley presented a petition from the Herefordshire grand jury to the Commons asking for the reduction of the numbers of troops in the county, and that no writs for the Herefordshire election should be issued until the soldiers had disbanded. He simultaneously charged Birch with various misdemeanours, undertaking to prove the validity of the accusations. The attempt to hold off the election reveals the obvious fear that Birch would use his troopers to coerce the voters, and Sir Robert had already tried to reduce the numbers in the garrison at Hereford by suggesting that a regiment of foot under the command of Birch could be spared to serve in Ireland and offered a month's pay from the county for the men.[20]

[17] Firth and Rait, *Acts and Ordinances*, I, 92, 113, 148, 170, 231, 428; *LJ*, VII, 24, 27; *CJ*, IV, 225, 228, 401; Thomas Harley to Edward Harley, 24 November 1646, BL Loan 29/175 f.78r; letter addressed to Harley as steward of the city of Hereford from the Mayor, BL Loan 29/175 ff.83r, 84v; *Return of the Names of Every Member*, I, 498.

[18] *DNB*, II, 524–6; Election disbursements dated 14 November 1646, BL Loan 29/175 f.71r–74v.

[19] Letter from Ambrose Elton to Edward Harley, 10 October 1646, County committee to Lenthall, 21 September 1646, Edward Harley to Lenthall, 22 September 1646 and charges against Captain Thomas Millward, undated, BL Loan 29/175 ff.61r, 46r, 49r, 51r.

[20] *CJ*, IV, 696, 703, 708; petition to the House of Commons, 6 October 1646, BL Loan 29/175 f.59r–v; Cambridge University Library, Add. Mss., 89 f.82r.

In 1646 the continued presence in England of both the Scottish forces and the English Army was seen by the political presbyterians in Parliament as the main obstacle to a settlement with the King. As a foreign invasion force, the Scots were becoming more and more unpopular and this feeling was extended to their English allies, who were seen as the main agents in keeping them on English soil. After lengthy negotiations in the autumn of 1646, the Scots were promised payment of £400,000 by Parliament and marched out of Newcastle at the end of January 1647, leaving the King in the hands of English troops led by Major-General Philip Skippon, who moved him to Holmby House in Northamptonshire.[21]

Although the Scots had left peaceably, the problems posed by the English troops were to prove intractable. In February 1647 the House voted to disband the infantry and retain 6,600 cavalry and dragoons. In response the army addressed a petition to their Commander-in-Chief, Lord Fairfax, embodying the soldiers' demands for indemnity, arrears of pay and adequate pensions. The petition was promoted by a group of officers including Edward Harley's own Lieutenant-Colonel, Thomas Pride, who had persuaded the men of Harley's regiment to subscribe to it. Edward Harley presented an anonymous letter addressed to himself to the Commons, which alleged that the soldiers 'do intend to enslave the kingdom', and that Pride had threatened that anyone who would not sign the army petition would be cashiered.[22] In delivering this letter to Parliament Edward Harley clearly marked himself as an opponent of the increasingly politicised army leadership.

The Commons had already ordered Fairfax to halt subscriptions to the petition. Denied the right to address Parliament, the army elected representatives – agitators – to present their grievances to their Council of War and to the army officers such as Cromwell, Fairfax and Skippon, who also served in Parliament. Distrust between Parliament and the army escalated during the next few weeks. On 4 June the King was seized at Holmby by Cornet Joyce and taken to Newmarket in an attempt to prevent his capture by the army's political opponents. The next day the General Council of the Army was set up at Newmarket as part of the *Solemn Engagement of the Army,* by which the soldiers undertook not to disband until their grievances were met.[23] On 14 June the army indicted eleven of their leading opponents in Parliament, including Edward Harley, Denzil Holles, Sir Philip Stapleton and Major General Massey, and accused them of plotting to restore the King with

---

[21] Crawford, *Denzil Holles,* 127–32; Wedgewood, *King's War,* 611–12; Gardiner, *Civil War,* III, 212.

[22] Crawford, *Denzil Holles,* 130, 139–40; Gardiner, *Civil War,* III, 223–7; *CJ,* V, 130–1; *LJ,* IX, 115.

[23] Crawford, *Denzil Holles,* 142; M. A. Kishlansky, *The Rise of the New Model Army* (Cambridge, 1979), 204–24; Crawford, *Denzil Holles,* 146; Gardiner, *Civil War,* III, 269–98.

Scottish help and raising an armed force in order to plunge the country into another civil war. Charges were prepared against a group of another thirty or so members and a committee was set up under the chairmanship of Miles Corbet to consider these cases. The eleven members withdrew from the House and the political Independents temporarily held sway over proceedings. Meanwhile, in the army the agitators were pressing for a march on London to purge Parliament and suppress any show of military opposition from the City.[24]

As the crisis quickened Sir Robert drafted a letter on 22 June to the divine Stephen Marshall, suggesting a compromise between the Parliament and the military. He addressed Marshall because of his links with the army; Marshall was chaplain to Skippon, who had accepted overall command of the troops to be sent to Ireland, and both Marshall and Skippon tried to mediate between Parliament, the army and the City. In his letter Harley proposed that the soldiers should receive their pay and disband and then reform. A core of some 10–12,000 men should remain in England and the rest should go into Ireland with their own officers. By this means, he argued, 'I conceive the honour of the army will be well kept up, and the honour of Parliament entire by the army's obedience.' If Marshall concurred, Harley intended to 'use my best endeavours how it may be presented to the House with most advantage'. Harley was also at pains to avoid any suspicion that he was acting as a stooge of the Scots, whom many believed might invade England in order to achieve their own terms with the King. Harley thus insisted that he acted 'as a native of England bewailing the distractions we are under and apprehending the imminent miseries we may justly fear from the distance between the Parliament and the army'.[25]

Westminster now became the scene of a desperate power struggle between those who opposed the army and its supporters. At the end of July, fifty-eight members, including Speaker Lenthall, fled to the army for protection and a few days later the City opened its gates to the army without resistance. Lenthall and his companions returned to Westminster and the eleven members went into exile.[26] Edward Harley retired to Hill Hall in Essex, the home of his royalist cousin Edward Smith, while Sir Robert remained at his house in Westminster but did not attend the Commons for some months. On 8 September the House ordered that Sir Robert should attend in three weeks' time to answer matters 'objected against' him and was under investigation by

[24] *A Charge Delivered in the Name of the Army* (1647), 3. TT E393(5); *Articles of Impeachment Agreed Upon by the Army* (1647), 1–6, TT E393(12); Underdown, *Pride's Purge*, 82–3.

[25] Draft letter from Harley addressed 'to M.M.', 22 June 1647, BL Loan 29/122; Crawford, *Denzil Holles*, 158; DNB, XVIII, 355; Kishlansky, *Rise of the New Model Army*, 237.

[26] Underdown, *Pride's Purge*, 83; Crawford, *Denzil Holles*, 156–7; CJ, V, 260, 265; Gardiner, *Civil War*, III, 345–9.

Corbet's committee. He was anonymously accused of having 'deserted the godly party' and of soliciting 'divers delinquents . . . and papists for their voices' in the election campaigns of his sons and other MPs returned for Welsh and marcher constituencies in the recruiter elections. The anonymous charges also blamed the Harleys with packing the county committee with 'their own creatures' in order to embezzle public funds. The suggestions of fiscal corruption were particularly damaging, given Sir Robert's position as Master of the Mint and the fact that both he and Edward were handling sums of money on behalf of the county committee, but there is no evidence that the Harleys were guilty of the charge. Sir Robert's chairmanship of the committee for elections also meant that he was vulnerable to accusation of electoral misdemeanours, and David Underdown's research on the recruiter elections shows that the Harleys had used royalist connections in their campaigns in 1646 and 1647. However, this does not prove any lack of affection for the parliamentary cause on Sir Robert's part, since he was experienced enough a politician to realise that all votes in the elections would have to be canvassed regardless of the political or religious stance of the voters. Lady Brilliana had similarly made use of traditional gentry contacts in approaching the local royalists in May 1642, when she had proposed that Edward Harley be returned in the Hereford by-election.[27]

It is not surprising to find that the former alliances between the gentry, although considerably weakened and altered by the experience of civil war, were still in evidence during the recruiter elections. The enduring strength of the links between the gentry are emphasised most clearly in the conciliatory attitudes adopted by the Harleys towards their own relatives who were under suspicion for dealing with the royalists. Most notable are the cases of Viscount Conway and the nonagenarian Viscount Tracy. Conway, Lady Brilliana's eldest brother, had been briefly imprisoned for his part in Waller's plot in 1643 and had then deserted to the King at Oxford. Sir Robert was diligent in securing his brother-in-law's goods, which were stored in the Tower of London, and Conway later returned to Parliament and compounded for his former delinquency.[28] Both Sir Robert and Edward Harley

---

[27] Harley to Edward Harley at Hill Hall, 18, 21 and 27 September 1647, BL Loan 29/175 ff.75r, 77r, 79r; *CJ*, V, 296; C. H. Firth, ed., *The Clarke Papers*, Camden Society, New Series, LIV, vol. II (1894), 157–9; for the monies handled by the Harleys, see for example BL Loan 29/15 *passim*; D. Underdown, 'Party Management in the Recruiter Elections, 1645–1648', *English Historical Review*, 83 (1968), 242, 245, 258–60; For the 1642 election see above, pp. 141–3.

[28] I. Roy 'The Libraries of Edward 2nd Viscount Conway and Others: An Inventory and Valuation of 1643', *BIHR*, XLI (1968), 35–46; order from the House of Lords, 16 June 1643, Harley to Francis Edgock, 17 June 1643, Edward Conway to Sir Robert, 20 January 1643/4, Viscountess Conway to Harley, 5 June 1644, BL Loan 29/174 ff.29r, 31r, 1r–v, 36r; Gilbert Garrard to Harley, 30 June 1643, BL Loan 29/119; lists of Conway's goods, 11 March 1643/4, 11 June 1644, BL Loan 29/122/20a and 20b.

were sympathetic to Lady Brilliana's uncle, Viscount Tracy, who, 'being unfortunately and unremoveably seated within the King's quarters', had signed a warrant for contribution to the King's army, 'for the which single and (as he thought) harmless act' Tracy too was threatened with sequestration.[29]

Following the charges against him, Sir Robert did not return to the House until the spring of 1648, but during his absence he had not allowed his influence over local affairs to wane. A series of letters written by Sir Robert to Edward Harley in September 1647 show that in that month alone he took pains to confer with William Crowther, the recruiter member for Weobley, over the choice of a sheriff for the county and a few days later he accompanied a group of citizens from Hereford at a meeting with Speaker Lenthall. He also remained in contact with members of the Westminster Assembly, and informed Edward that he had dined with a number of divines that month, including Stephen Marshall, 'by whose ministry my weak heart hath been so often cheered'.[30]

With the absence of the eleven members and their close sympathisers, such as Sir Robert Harley, affairs in the House were now dominated by a group which included Cromwell, Ireton, Vane, St John, Nathaniel Fiennes, Sir John Evelyn and William Pierrepont, who were still able to restrain the more radical members such as the republicans Henry Marten and Edmund Ludlow. The King, however, continued to hope for military aid from the Scots and refused to accept overtures from Parliament and from the army alike. In response the Commons passed the Vote of No Addresses at the beginning of January 1648, which called a halt to negotiations with the King, although it was not until 25 April that Parliament received definite news that the Scots were raising an army for the King. This news ruptured the alliance between the middle group, who wanted a settlement, and the political Independents, who were openly suggesting that the King should be tried; and Sir Robert chose this moment to resume his attendance in the chamber. On 27 April he was named to a committee for the first time since the previous August. In yet another dramatic shift of alignments the middle group threw their support behind the political presbyterians, and after long debate on 28 April the House asserted that it would not alter the 'fundamental government of the kingdom by King, Lords and Commons', and voted to suspend the

[29] Petition of Sir John Tracy, BL Loan 29/50/73; Viscount Tracy to Edward Harley, 12 August, 14 August 1644, Thomas Tracy to Edward Harley, 24 August, September 1644, Viscount Tracy to Harley, 9 September 1644, BL Loan 29/174 ff.52r, 56r, 60r, 70r, 68r; Viscount Tracy to Harley, 24 November 1645, and 21 January 1646/7, BL Loan 29/121.

[30] *CJ*, V, 543, 546; Sir Robert to Edward Harley, 18 and 27 September 1647, BL Loan 29/175 ff.75r, 79r; draft letter from Harley addressed 'to M.M.', 22 June 1647, BL Loan 29/122.

Vote of No Addresses and reopen negotiations with the King. At the beginning of June the impeachments of the eleven members were reversed and they were free to resume their seats. Sir Robert carried the votes to this effect to the House of Lords.[31]

Parliament was now faced by the outbreak of the Second Civil War. Sporadic risings in England and Wales were suppressed in May and June and the invading Scots army under Hamilton was defeated by Cromwell at Preston in August 1648. In the counties demands were growing for the disbandment of the army and a final treaty with the King, and the House of Commons responded by setting up a joint committee with the Lords to consider terms to be offered to the King, which was dominated by political presbyterians and middle groupers including Sir Robert Harley. At the same time the House began to debate a new militia ordinance designed to return the militia to the control of the local gentry rather than the county committees. The ordinance was debated in a committee of the whole House chaired by a succession of men with middle-group connections. The original chairman, John Bulkeley, withdrew through illness and was replaced briefly by John Boys and then by Sir Robert, who steered the ordinance through the committee stage from mid-June until it was sent to the Lords in October. It was finally passed on 2 December, four days before Pride's Purge.[32]

The Purge itself followed on the heels of the failure of the parliamentary commissioners to conclude terms with the King at Newport on the Isle of Wight. The commissioners were largely middle groupers such as Saye, Northumberland, Pierrepont, Bulkeley, Crewe and Browne, accompanied by old peace-party men such as Holles and Mr Harbottle Grimston. They wanted the King to surrender the militia for an agreed term of years, to submit his choice of ministers to Parliament for approval and to abolish episcopacy and establish the presbyterian Church settlement for a minimum of three years. They arrived at Newport on 15 September and by 9 October the King had agreed to relinquish the militia for twenty years. At the same time he refused to countenance the abolition of episcopacy and on 21 October suggested that the jurisdiction of the bishops should be approved by Parliament. Harbottle Grimston wrote to Harley telling him that the commissioners were 'almost fully satisfied in all other matters' and that not one of them thought it was worth 'endangering the kingdom' in order to hold out for further religious concessions. He urged Harley to 'desire all our friends to

---

[31] Underdown, Pride's Purge, 85; Gardiner, Civil War, III, 354; IV, 17–19, 31–41; CJ, V, 415–16, 546; Underdown, Pride's Purge, 96–7; CJ, V, 584, 587.
[32] Ashton, The English Civil War, 320–5; Underdown, Pride's Purge, 99–101; CJ, V, 597, 623, 632, 634, 660, 663, 664, 665, 668, 671, 683, VI, 1, 6, 33, 42; Firth and Rait, Acts and Ordinances, I, 1233–51.

attend the House diligently and let not a ship richly laden after a long voyage full of hazards, be cast away within sight of land'.[33]

As the negotiations at Newport progressed, discontent amongst the military mounted and by the end of November the army was once again marching on London amid demands for a purge of Parliament and the trial of the King. On 2 December Fairfax's men reached Westminster and were quartered throughout the capital. Despite this provocation, the House continued to debate the King's recent concessions, and on Monday 4 December the moderates in the House tried to persuade their fellows to accept the King's answer to the commissioners at Newport as sufficient to 'proceed upon to a settling of the kingdom'. According to *Mercurius Pragmaticus*, 'it was maintained very bravely in the affirmative by the ancient men of the House, as Sir Robert Harlow, Sir Ben Rudyerd, Sir Simonds D'Ewes, Mr Edward Stephens, Sir [*sic*] Harbottle Grimston, Mr Walker and many others'.[34] The debate carried on far into the night and on Tuesday morning the motion was finally accepted, but those who voted in favour were marked out by the army leaders as their avowed opponents, who must be removed. As the House rose, a group of army officers and their friends amongst the MPs met at Whitehall Palace and debated whether to proceed with a purge of the Parliament or whether to force a dissolution and new elections. They agreed that any member who had voted to proceed to a settlement with the King, or who had voted to repeal the Vote of No Addresses, or who had opposed an earlier notion that those who assisted the Scottish invaders were rebels and traitors, should be excluded by armed force from the chamber the next morning.

On 6 December, Colonel Pride and a number of armed troopers stood at the entrance to Westminster Hall and prevented certain members from entering the House. A group of forty-five, including Sir Robert and Edward Harley, were imprisoned at a tavern called Hell, where they kept their spirits up by spending their first night of captivity reading, singing psalms, talking and walking about. According to both contemporary sources and to a later account penned by Edward Harley, Sir Robert and five other older MPs were told they could go home on the second night if they agreed to return the next morning. Harley was also asked to 'give his word not to oppose the present actings and proceedings of the House or Army ... at which Sir Robert desired time to advise with his fellow prisoners, being a matter which equally concerned them'. The offer was refused, once more underlining Harley's sense of public duty, for, as Edward recorded, 'he refused that favour that it

---

[33] Underdown, *Pride's Purge*, 104–15; Gardiner, *Civil War*, IV, 220–2; Harbottle Grimston to Harley, 21 October 1648, BL Loan 29/176 f.47r.

[34] Gardiner, *Civil War*, IV, 233–47; Underdown, *Pride's Purge*, 123–36; Sir Robert only avoided having troops billeted in his house by paying for them to lodge elsewhere: see orders from Fairfax, 4 December 1648, BL Loan 29/176 f.48r; *Mercurius Pragmaticus*, no.36–7 (5–12 December 1648).

might not prejudice his public trust'.[35] Sir Robert was set free on 31 January 1649, the day after the execution of the King at Whitehall, and Edward Harley was released nearly two weeks later. During the trial of the King, Edward had drafted a letter to Lord Fairfax urging him to act on the King's behalf. Although he was one of the judges, Fairfax was known to oppose the trial and had attended only the first session, but he had not spoken out in public nor had he taken any open action against the regicides.

Edward may also have hoped that their mutual family connections with the Veres would give him licence to address the general so directly. He exhorted Fairfax to remember

that in your condition neither God nor man can be satisfied with any passive dislikes of what is done amiss by your army. Their evils for want of your prohibition will become your guilt, which I beseech your excellency seriously to consider. I hope God hath given your excellency this command for such a time as this. But if you altogether hold your peace – and a General's words cannot be other than commands – at this time, then shall there enlargement and deliverance arise from another place.

Edward assured Fairfax that

no respect to our particular advantage, nor envy, or revenge against your army, but the powerful ties of the greatest trust from men, and solemn covenant to God have caused myself and other my fellow sufferers to oppose your army in their late and present actions, by which I must take leave to say they are hastily digging a miserable sepulchre for all the beauty and strength of our native kingdom, if God be not pleased wonderfully to deliver.

Fairfax failed to act on the advice in Edward's letter and did not appear in Westminster Hall during the judicial proceedings against the King.[36]

The death of King Charles marked an end to the Harleys' political influence both at Westminster and in the county for a period of about five years. Initially they refused to recognise the republic and refused to take the Engagement to the Commonwealth. In May 1649 Sir Robert resigned his office as Master of the Mint and his sons were all briefly imprisoned in the autumn of 1650 on the grounds of their 'disaffection to this present government'. The family was removed from local office until 1654, when Sir Robert and Edward Harley were named to the commission for the ejection of scandalous ministers. This paved the way for Edward's resumption of local power. In the following year he regained his place on the Herefordshire bench of justices and in 1656 was returned to Parliament as one of the four

---

[35] Underdown, *Pride's Purge*, 134–48, 211–12; *A True and Full Relation of the Officers' and Armies' Forcible Seizing of Divers Eminent Members of the Commons House, December 6 and 7 1648* (1648), 3–11. TT E476(14); *The Parliament under the Power of the Sword* (1648), 3–4. *TT* E476(1); Sir Edward Harley's notes on the character of his father, undated, BL Loan 29/88/73.

[36] Warrants from Fairfax, 31 January and 12 February 1648/9, copy of a letter from Edward Harley to Fairfax, 23 January 1648/9, BL Loan 29/176 ff.66r, 67r, 64r–v; *DNB*, V1, 1010.

representatives of Herefordshire, but was once again secluded from the chamber.[37]

Sir Robert, however, did not pursue an active local career and never returned to the national political arena. He died at the age of 76 on 6 November 1656 at his home in Ludlow and was buried at Brampton four days later. In the sermon delivered at the funeral, Thomas Froysell, the minister of Clun, described how Sir Robert had been confined to his chamber for 'some years' through the disease of 'stone and Palsie', which caused him sharp 'pains and torments'. Froysell, who had known Sir Robert for many years, described him as an outstandingly godly individual, a pattern and leader both for those who knew him and for later generations:

If other saints are candles, he was a torch. If others are stars, he was a star of greater magnitude. He made his outward greatness but a servant to the exercise of his graces. He was a copy for all great men to transcribe in all descending ages. He was a man of desires: a saint in great letters: famous (I think) throughout the land, one where or other, for his graces. To my knowledge eminent ministers did most prize him. Sir Robert Harley was a sweet name upon their lips. When they spake of him, they would speak with honour and delight in him . . .

He was the first that brought the gospel into these parts. This country lay under a veil of darkness till he began to shine. He set his first choice upon that transcendant holy man, Mr Peacock, in Oxford, but God took him to Heaven, which prevented him coming to Brampton. Then providence led him to the knowledge that now blessed servant of God, Mr Pierson, whose exemplary graces and ministry shed a rich influence abroad the country.

And as God removed godly ministers by death, he continued still a succession of them to you. Not only Brampton, but ye of Wigmore, and ye of Leintwardine, owe your very souls to Sir Robert Harley, who maintained your ministers upon his own cost, that they might feed you with the gospel of Jesus Christ.

He was the pillar of religion among us. How would he countenance godliness? His greatness professing Christ brought profession into credit and cast a lustre on it. Profession began to grow and spread itself under his shade.

His planting of godly ministers, and then backing them with his authority, made religion famous in this little corner of the world. Oh! What comfortable times had we (through God's mercy) before the wars! How did our public meetings shine with his exemplary presence in the midst of them . . .

He was (I know not how oft) chosen by his country to the High Senate and court of Parliament, and there (that I may speak within my knowledge) he was a bright and glorious star in that shining constellation; as some stars are more excellent than others, so was he there. He was a man of fixed principles: religion and solid reformation was all the white [sic] he shot at. He appeared all along for a settled ministry, and the liberal maintenance thereof. He procured the ordinance for settling the ministers at Hereford; his compass, without trepidation or variation, stood

<hr>

[37] Thomas Harley to Sir Robert, 7 February 1648/9, Colonel Mackworth to Harley, 8 May 1650, BL Loan 29/176 ff.137r, 179r; *CJ*, VI, 210; Major Winthrop to Edward and Robert Harley, 3 August 1650, BL Loan 29/176 f.185r; McParlin, 'Thesis', Appendices VIII, XVII; Firth and Rait, *Acts and Ordinances*, II, 971; *DNB*, VIII, 1276.

constantly right to that pole, the good of his country and gospel, which he kept ever in his eye.[38]

Froysell saw religious zeal wedded to public duty as the key to Sir Robert's public and private actions. The religious outlook of the Harleys has indeed been emphasised throughout this study as a guiding principle which moulded their beliefs and actions, but it should also be acknowledged that the Harleys were influenced by a strong sense of public duty, which they shared with their fellow gentry. Both Lady Brilliana and Sir Robert came from families which had traditionally taken office as local governors and as court officials. Court office could reap rich rewards, but the county governors were unpaid for their labours and undertook hours of work with little obvious compensation, other than social prestige and the confirmation of their standing in local society. The men who took local office used such positions as staging posts in their own careers, but many were also, like the Harleys, motivated by a real sense of duty to their communities and to the country.

The Harleys were certainly integrated into the official and social life of the 'gentry community' in Herefordshire before the wars. Lady Brilliana's letters to her family are strongly imbued with her belief that the Harleys had a natural role as leaders of county society and there is nothing in her letters written before 1640 to suggest that the Harleys' puritanism might exclude them from that role. Even after the assembly of the Long Parliament, when the Harleys gradually became isolated from the opinions of the most influential county gentry in Herefordshire, Lady Brilliana continued to believe that her family would sustain their influence in county affairs. This belief is particularly clear in her letters to Edward Harley, which were in part intended to prepare him for the future assumption of office. Thus, in 1642, when Lady Brilliana orchestrated the unsuccessful campaign for Edward's election as burgess for Hereford, she wrote to him: ' I should be very glad that you might act your first service for the commonwealth.'

Lady Brilliana also understood that public duty necessarily entailed personal sacrifice, which she was fully prepared to undertake. In 1626, when Sir Robert was attending Parliament, Lady Brilliana gave birth to their second son, Robert. She wrote to tell Harley how much she longed to see him, but she acknowledged that the affairs of Parliament took precedence over her personal desires: 'in this I must yield to the will of the Lord; and as the public good is to be preferred before private ends, so at this time I must show that indeed I love that better than my own good and I pray God enable you for that work you are now called to'.[39] In her letter, Lady Brilliana linked Harley's

---

[38] Copy of inscription on Sir Robert's coffin, BL Loan 29/177 f.90r; Froysell, *The Beloved Disciple*, 98–109.

[39] Lewis, *Letters of the Lady Brilliana Harley*, 163; Lady Brilliana to Harley, 21 April 1626, BL Loan 29/202 f.204r.

public duty to the will of God and the Harleys consistently related every aspect of their lives to religion and the correct religious behaviour expected of the elect. The religious commitment of the Harleys was not in itself exceptional, and intense religious belief was by no means the sole preserve of the puritans. During the siege of Lathom House, for example, the royalist Countess of Derby was careful to maintain religious observance amongst the garrison. A contemporary account of the siege described her 'first care' as 'the service of God, which in sermons and solemn prayers she saw duly performed. Four times a day she was commonly present at public prayer.'[40]

The Harleys' puritanism did, however, involve them in a distinct set of religious perceptions, which were not necessarily shared with non-puritans. It certainly should not be argued that these perceptions led irrevocably to war in 1642. The Harleys were not involved in any concerted secular opposition of the crown before 1640, and before that date they were accepted as part of the 'gentry community' in their county in spite of their puritanism. It cannot be overemphasised, however, that religious differences were primarily responsible for the polarisation which occurred in their county after 1640. Although the Civil War broke out over immediate issues, such as control of the militia and the King's refusal to allow Parliament a voice in the choice of officers of state, nevertheless long-term religious differences played a significant role in shaping political perspectives and ultimately in dividing local communities in England and Wales in 1642.

The importance of religious feeling in creating the conditions for civil war in England has been recognised in many works. In his *History of the Great Civil War*, S. R. Gardiner wrote: 'above all, it was puritanism which gave to those whose energies were most self-centred the power which always follows upon submission to law. Puritanism not only formed the strength of the opposition to Charles, but the strength of England itself.' The seeming orthodoxy of Gardiner's views has recently been challenged by the so-called 'revisionist' historians, whose views may perhaps best be summarised by Conrad Russell's bold assertion that 'this ideological gulf between "government" and "opposition" is impossible to find in Parliament before 1640', and 'it is remarkable how hard it is to discover a "puritan opposition" in the 1620s'.[41] His masterly study of the Parliaments of the 1620s is part of a debate which has undoubtedly served to refine the concept of 'opposition' in the early Stuart Parliaments.

In a critique of revisionist writings, Theodore Rabb has suggested: 'cannot the term "opposition" be descriptive without necessarily implying a resounding Whig view of English history?' He goes on to demonstrate the significance

[40] Halsall, *Journal of the Siege of Lathom House*, 514.
[41] Gardiner, *Civil War*, I, 9; Russell, 'Parliamentary History in Perspective', 18; Russell, *Parliaments*, 26.

of the 'persistent and rising expression of opposition to official policies from 1604 onward'. Richard Cust has also charted the development and articulation of competing views of government which emerged over the issue of the forced loan in the 1620s. Dr Cust asserts that the loan was 'seen as offering both a religious and a political threat' and has shown how puritan opposition to the loan was effectively assimilated in more general fears that the loan was a challenge both to the authority of Parliament and to the constitution itself.[42] Whilst the importance of the role of Parliament and of principled opposition in the politics of early Stuart England have thus usefully been reassessed, the precise links between puritanism and parliamentary opposition before 1640 still await a full re-examination.

The associations between puritanism and parliamentarianism are, however, well established and were widely commented on by contemporaries who lived through the wars. In his *Reliquiae*, first published in 1696, Richard Baxter commented that

it was principally the differences about religious matter that filled up the Parliament's armies and put the resolution and valour into their soldiers, which carried them on in another manner than mercenary soldiers are carried on. Not that the matter of bishops or no bishops was the main thing (for thousands that wished for good bishops were on the parliament's side) though many called it *bellum episcopale* (and with the Scots that was a greater part of the controversy). But the generality of the people through the land (I say not all, or every one) who were then called puritans, precisians, religious persons, that used to talk of God, and heaven, and scripture, and holiness, and to follow sermons, and read books of devotion, and pray in their families, and spend the Lord's day in religious exercises, and plead for mortification, and serious devotion and strict obedience to God, and speak against swearing, cursing, drunkenness, prophaneness etc. I say, the main body of this sort of men, both preachers and people, adhered to the Parliament. And on the other side, the gentry that were not so precise and strict against an oath, or gaming or plays, or drinking, nor troubled themselves so much about the matters of God and the world to come, and the ministers and people that were for the King's book, for dancing and recreations on the Lord's days, and those that made not so great a matter of every sin, but went to church and heard common prayer, and were glad to hear a sermon which lashed the puritans, and which ordinarily spoke against this strictness and preciseness in religion, and this strict observation of the Lord's day, and following sermons and praying *ex tempore*, and talking so much of scripture and the matters of salvation, and those that hated and derided them that take these courses, the main body of these were against the Parliament.[43]

Numerous county studies have confirmed the connections outlined by Baxter. In his study of the Yorkshire gentry, for example, J. T. Cliffe notes that 'on the parliamentarian side it was the puritans who represented by far the most important element'. Of Lancashire Dr Blackwood has written: 'in

---

[42] T. K. Rabb, 'Revisionism Revised: The Role of the Commons', *Past and Present*, XCII (1981), 66; Cust, *Forced Loan, passim*.

[43] M. Sylvester, ed., *Reliquiae Baxterianae* . . . . (1696), 31.

few counties can puritans have formed such a large proportion of the parliamentarian gentry' and concludes that 'there seems little doubt that religion was the issue which principally divided the two sides in the Civil War'. Professor Underdown has linked the Civil War affiliations of the wider population in the counties of Wiltshire, Somerset and Devon to regional cultural difference, which centred on the patterns of settlement in different farming areas. In arable areas, where villages were 'tightly packed around church and manor-house', mechanisms of social control were more powerful than in the woodland or pasture areas, where the parishes were larger and the inhabitants more scattered. The resulting cultural differences 'reflected fundamentally divergent beliefs about what a community ought to be, which were often expressed in ritual or religious forms' and which helped mould allegiances during the Civil War in those counties.[44] The more general studies produced by Morrill and Fletcher also concur in the finding that many of the parliamentarians were 'puritan activists'. Dr Morrill thus sees the English Civil War not as 'the first European revolution' but as the 'last of the Wars of Religion' and has stated that it was not local or constitutional issues, but religion which 'proved to have the ideological dynamism to drive minorities to arms'.[45]

The pre-eminence of religion as a motivating force for the resort to arms has been repeatedly emphasised in this study of the Harleys. The majority of the parliamentarians who fought and organised the war against King Charles were united in their desire for further Church reforms. The pace of those reforms in Parliament might sometimes slacken, they might even be put aside as the needs of war or of parliamentary tactics would dictate, but they were never abandoned. The demand for the abolition of episcopacy was consistently maintained by Parliament in all of the peace negotiations held from the Treaty of Oxford in 1643 until the abortive attempt to achieve a settlement at Newport at the end of 1648. Parliamentarian MPs might not agree amongst themselves about what should replace episcopacy, indeed some of them even objected to the removal of episcopacy, but they were agreed that the government of the Church by the bishops had to be reformed in some measure.

The slow pace of some of the reforms undertaken by Parliament should not be interpreted as a lack of zeal by its members. The danger of revitalising support for the crown by introducing religious changes was always present, and this undoubtedly influenced Parliament's leaders not to press ahead with

---

[44] Cliffe, *Yorkshire Gentry*, 361; B. G. Blackwood, *The Lancashire Gentry and the Great Rebellion, 1640–60*, Chetham Society, 3rd Series, XXV (Manchester, 1978), 65–6; Underdown, *Revel, Riot and Rebellion*, 5, 278–9.

[45] Morrill, *Revolt of the Provinces*, 50; Fletcher, *Outbreak of the English Civil War*, 405; Morrill, 'The Religious Context of the English Civil War', 178; Morrill, 'The Attack on the Church of England', in Beales and Best, eds., *History, Society and the Churches*, 105.

abolition of episcopacy before the war had been won. Support for episcopacy had been a vital element in the growth of royalism before the war started and any fundamental attack on the bishops might renew or increase sentiment in favour of the King's cause. Nor did the slow pace of reforms dishearten committed reformers such as the Harleys. When Lady Brilliana heard that Harley had carried the bill excluding the bishops from temporal office to the House of Lords in February 1642 she noted: 'I trust the Lord will finish his own work, which he has carried on so beyond our expectation.' As her words indicate, before the meeting of the Long Parliament puritans had little reason to believe that calls for religious reforms would be successful and once changes were under way they far exceeded the earlier expectations of the godly. Moreover, these reforms proceeded at a speed dictated by God; they were the work of the Lord and the men who undertook them were merely his chosen instruments. A similar acceptance on the part of Sir Robert Harley that the course of reform would be painstakingly slow was revealed in Froysell's funeral sermon, where he describes another MP asking Sir Robert why he was 'so earnest for presbytery? You see it is so opposed that it is in vain to seek to settle it.' To which Sir Robert reputedly replied: 'Let us so much rather be earnest for it, though we gain it by inches; what we obtain now with much difficulty and opposition shall be of use one day, when there shall not be heard so much as the sound of a hammer.'[46]

A much-cited speech by Oliver Cromwell is sometimes used to suggest that religion was not the prime cause of the war. Addressing the First Protectorate Parliament in 1655 Cromwell stated that 'religion was not the thing at first contested for'. It is, however, worth quoting the speech at greater length, for he went on to say, 'but God brought it to that issue at last; and gave it unto us by way of redundancy; and at last it proved to be that which was most dear to us. And wherein consisted this more than in obtaining that liberty from the tyranny of the bishops to all species of Protestants to worship God according to their own light and consciences?' This speech was aimed at persuading his hearers of the righteousness of religious toleration for protestants and Cromwell was right to assert that this was not one of the immediate causes of the war. It is perhaps more instructive to look at Cromwell's contemporary utterances, which show that like the Harleys he believed that the parliamentarians were primarily united by their godliness. After his victory at Marston Moor, in July 1644, Cromwell wrote, in a letter to Colonel Walton, 'truly England and the Church of God hath had a great favour from the Lord, in this great victory given unto us, such as the like never was since this war began. It

---

[46] Lady Brilliana to Harley, 11 February 1641/2 BL Loan 29/173 between ff.211 and 212; Froysell, *Beloved Disciple*, 109–10; see also above, pp. 106–7, 110–11.

had all the evidences of an absolute victory obtained by the Lord's blessing upon the godly party principally.'[47]

In her *Memoirs*, Lucy Hutchinson also described 'the godly' as being 'generally . . . the Parliament's friends'. She also stated that although her husband 'was satisfied of the endeavours to reduce [bring back] popery and subvert the true Protestant religion, which was apparent to everyone that impartially considered it, yet he did not think that so clear a ground of the war was the defence of the just English liberties'. Here, writing as she was in retrospect (probably in the mid- to late 1660s), Lucy Hutchinson makes a clear distinction between the religious and the secular causes of the war. This might also appear to be the thrust behind Sir Henry Ludlow's assertion of February 1643 that 'we took up arms for defence of the privileges of Parliament and calling of delinquents to justice', but those who concurred with Ludlow were not necessarily oblivious to the religious dimension of the war.[48] Parliament was seen by its adherents as the bastion of English liberties and right religion was subsumed within those liberties. Since the days of the Henrician Reformation, Parliament had played a significant role in ratifying religious changes in England, and from 1640 onwards that role was extended to press for religious reforms that had previously seemed unattainable. The relationship between true religion and the maintenance of parliamentary liberties was emphasised in a speech to the Short Parliament by John Pym, in which he declared that 'verity in religion receives an influence from the free debates in Parliament and consequently from the privileges in Parliament, without which men will be afraid to speak'. The importance which Pym attached to the freedom to observe true religion was also stressed in a pamphlet published after his death, which claimed that he had said that 'the greatest liberty of our kingdom is religion'. Pym may or may not have used this exact phrase; what matters is that contemporaries believed that he might have done so.[49]

It was a sentiment with which Lady Brilliana and Sir Robert would undoubtedly have agreed. They both believed that they were involved in a war to secure true religion in England and that Parliament was the bulwark which would protect the Church from its enemies. Their belief that they were members of the elect, who were a definable group on earth, also provided the Harleys with a ready formed set of loyalties, which were quite separate from

[47] Ashton, *The English Civil War*, 99; W. C. Abbott, ed., *The Writings and Speeches of Oliver Cromwell* (Cambridge, Mass., 1937–47), III, 586; I, 287; Russell, *Crisis of Parliaments*, 344 n.5 (I am grateful to Professor Russell for drawing this last reference to my attention).
[48] Sutherland, *Lucy Hutchinson's Memoirs*, 60–1, 53, xviii–xix; C. Thompson, ed., *Walter Yonge's Diary of Proceedings in the House of Commons, 1642–1645* (Orchard Press, Essex, 1986), I, 317.
[49] *A Short View of the Life and Actions of the Late Deceased John Pym* (1643), sig. A1v, *TT* E78(13).

their loyalties to the local community, and which proved in the testing ground of civil war to be stronger than their allegiance to either the county or the crown.

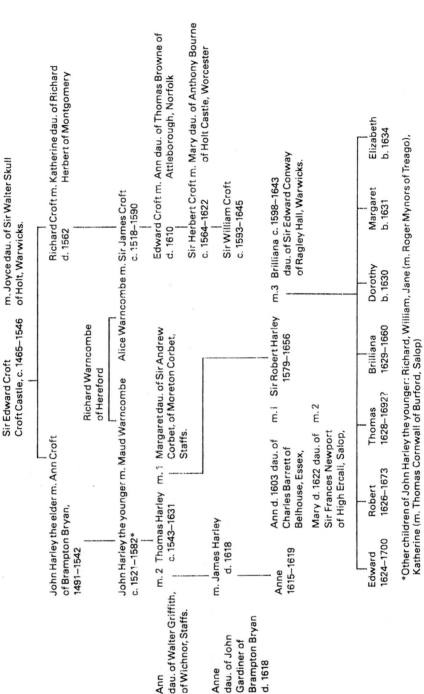

Fig. 2 The Harley and Croft families

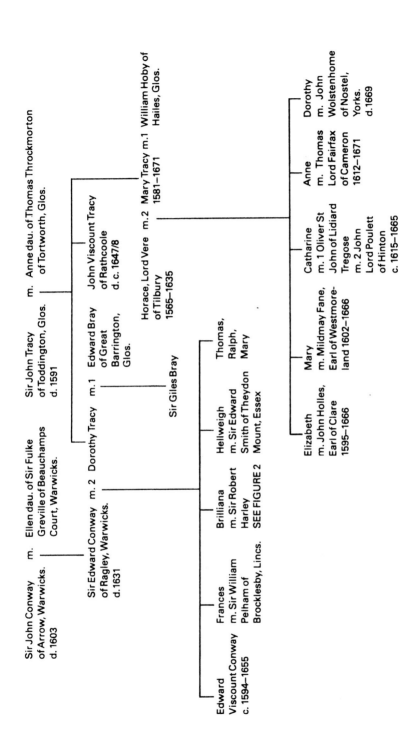

Fig. 3 The Conway, Tracy and Vere families

SELECT BIBLIOGRAPHY OF
MANUSCRIPT AND PRINTED SOURCES

MANUSCRIPT SOURCES: BRITISH DEPOSITORIES

BODLEIAN LIBRARY, OXFORD

Tanner Mss. 303   Defence of Fitzwilliam Coningsby

BRITISH LIBRARY

Additional Mss.
4274–6   Thoresby Papers, vols. 1–3
11041–59   Scudamore Papers, mainly 16th and 17th centuries, vols. 1–19
16178   Order Book of the Herefordshire Committee for Sequestrations
28716   Sir Robert Harley's Notes for the Committee for Elections, 1646
31116   Long Parliament Diary of Lawrence Whitaker, 1642–6
61899   Harley Family Papers, 17th–19th centuries
61989   Harley Family Papers, 17th century

Harleian Mss.
162–6   Long Parliament Diary of Sir Simonds D'Ewes, 1640–1645
478   Long Parliament Diary of John Moore, vol. 4, 1641
1622   *Liber Pacis*, January 1626

Portland Mss.
Loan 29/15   Papers relating to Colonel Birch's regiment and to the estates of
    delinquents in Herefordshire, c. 1646–7
  29/24 part 2   Bills and accounts of Sir Robert Harley and Sir Edward Harley
  29/27 part 1   Miscellaneous papers of Sir Robert Harley and Sir Edward Harley
  29/46   News sheets, broadsides, parliamentary affairs
  29/50   Herefordshire county affairs and Sir Robert Harley's Notes for the Com-
    mittee for Elections, 1647
  29/52   Harley family affairs
  29/72   Letters of Lady Brilliana Harley
  29/78   Letters of Sir Edward Harley
  29/119–21   Letters of Sir Robert Harley
  29/122–4   Miscellaneous papers of Sir Robert Harley
  29/202, 172–7   Harley Papers, General Series, vols. 1–7, 1582–1660

CORPUS CHRISTI COLLEGE, OXFORD

Ms 206   Survey of the Ministry of Herefordshire, 1640/1

DR WILLIAMS' LIBRARY, LONDON

Correspondence of Richard Baxter

HEREFORD AND WORCESTER COUNTY RECORD OFFICE (HEREFORD)

AA.20   Diocese of Hereford Probate Records, Wills Series
S.33   Croft Mss.

HOUSE OF LORDS RECORD OFFICE

Private Bills
3 Jac. I, no. 50   Bill for Naturalising the Children of Sir Edward Conway

NOTTINGHAM UNIVERSITY LIBRARY, MSS. DEPARTMENT

Portland Mss.
Welbeck Collection   Pw2/Hy/1–200   Harley Papers, 17th century
London Collection   Commonplace Book of Brilliana Conway, 1622

NOTTINGHAMSHIRE COUNTY RECORD OFFICE

Portland Mss.
DD.4P, DD.5P   Miscellaneous Papers of Families Related to the Dukes of Portland
including the Harleys and the Veres

PUBLIC RECORD OFFICE

Chancery (C)
C2, C3   Chancery Proceedings
C66   Patent Rolls
C115   Master's Exhibits, Duchess of Norfolk's Deeds (Scudamore Papers)
C181   Crown Office, Entry Books of Commissions
C193/12/2   Commissioners for the Forced Loan
C193/12, 13   Crown Office, *Libri Pacis*
C227   Petty Bag Office, Sheriff Rolls
C231   Crown Office, Docquet Books

Exchequer (E)
E163/18/12   *Liber Pacis*, 1626
E179   Subsidy Rolls
E401/2586   Exchequer of Receipt, Register of Privy Seal Loans, 1625–6

Lord Chamberlain's Office (LC)
LC4   Entry Books of Recognisances

Prerogative Court of Canterbury (PCC)
PCC/PROB 11   Registered Copy Wills, 1384–1858

Star Chamber (STAC)
STAC 8   Star Chamber Proceedings, James I

State Paper Office (SP)
SP12   State Papers, Domestic, Elizabeth I
SP14   State Papers, Domestic, James I
SP16   State Papers, Domestic, Charles I
SP23   Records of the Committee for Compounding with Delinquents
SP28   Commonwealth Exchequer Papers

Miscellaneous
Bishops' Institution Books, Series A   Round Room, 19/59–63, 5 vols., 1556–1660
PRO 30/53   Powis Mss.

SHROPSHIRE RECORD OFFICE

Bridgewater Mss.
212/364   Correspondence, 17th century

MANUSCRIPT SOURCES: FOREIGN DEPOSITORIES

FOLGER LIBRARY, WASHINGTON DC

Vb2, 3   Scudamore Mss.
Xd.140   Letter from the Deputy Lieutenants of Herefordshire to the Lord Treasurer,
2 March 1599/100

HUNTINGTON LIBRARY, CALIFORNIA

Ellesmere Mss.
7350, 7352   Letters from Henry Ecclestone to the Earl of Bridgewater, 1641

PRIVATE COLLECTIONS

Brampton Bryan, Herefordshire
Harley Mss.   Harley Family Papers

Longleat
Portland Mss. Vol. 23, ff. 199r–203r   List of prisoners taken at Brampton Bryan,
1644

PRINTED WORKS

CONTEMPORARY BOOKS AND TRACTS, PUBLISHED IN LONDON

Anonymous. *A Charge Delivered in the Name of the Army . . . June 14 1647*, 1647. *TT* E393(5)

Articles of Impeachment Agreed Upon by the Army, 1647. *TT* E393(12)

The Parliament under the Power of the Sword . . ., 1648. BM 669

A Short View of the Life and Actions of the Late Deceased John Pym, 1643. *TT* E78(13)

A True and Full Relation of the Officers' and Armies' Forcible Seizing of Divers Eminent Members of the Commons House, December 6 and 7 1648, 1648. *TT* E476(14)

Bolton, R. *A Narration of the Grievous Visitation and Dreadful Desertion of Mr Peacock in his Last Sickness*, 1641.

Calvin, *Institutes of the Christian Religion*, 3 vols., 1611.

Clarke, S. *A General Martyrology*, 1651.

The Lives of Ten Eminent Divines, 1662.

The Lives of Sundry Eminent Persons in this Later Age, 1683.

Cole, N. *The Godly Man's Assurance, or a Christian's Certain Resolution of his Own Salvation*, 1615.

Corbet, J. *An Historical Relation of the Military Government of Gloucester*, 1645.

Culmer, R. *Cathedral News from Canterbury Showing the Canterburian Cathedral to be in an Abbey-Like, Corrupt and Rotten Condition, which calls for a Speedy Reformation, or Dissolution . . .*, 1644.

Froysell, T. *The Beloved Disciple, or a Sermon Preached at the Funeral of the Honourable Sir Robert Harley . . . at Brampton Bryan in Herefordshire December 10 1656*, 1658.

The Gale of Opportunity. Or, a Sermon Preached (at Lidbury-North) at the Funeral of the Worshipful Humphrey Walcot, of Walcot, esq; June 8th 1650, 1652.

Gataker, T. *A Wife in Deed*, 1623.

Gower, S., ed., *Eighteen Sermons Preached in Oxford, 1640, by James Ussher, Lord Primate of Ireland*, 1659.

Hardwick, H. *The Saints Gain by Death, and their Assurance Thereof. Sermon Preached at the Funeral of that Worthy Patriot Richard More . . .*, 1664.

Hinde, W. *A Faithful Remonstrance of the Holy Life and Happy Death of John Bruen of Bruen Stapleford in the County of Chester, Esquire*, 1641.

Husbands, E., ed., *An Exact Collection of All Remonstrances, Declarations, Votes, Orders, Ordinances, Proclamations, Petitions, Messages, Answers and Other Remarkable Passages between the King's Most Excellent Majesty, and His High Court of Parliament Beginning at His Majesty's Return From Scotland, Being in December 1641, and Continued until March 21 1643*, 1643.

Ley, J. *A Pattern of Piety, or the Religious Life and Death of . . . Mrs Jane Ratcliffe . . .*, 1640.

Montague, R. *A Gag for the New Gospel? No: A New Gag for an Old Goose*, 1624.

Newsbooks, *Mercurius Aulicus*

Mercurius Pragmaticus

Pierson, T. *The Cure of Hurtful Cares and Fears*, 1636.

Excellent Encouragements Against Afflictions, 1647.

Rushworth, J., ed. *Historical Collections of Private Passages of State*, 7 vols., 1659–1721.

Sylvester, M., ed. *Reliquiae Baxterianae . . .*, 1696.

Symmons, E. *Scripture Vindicated*, Oxford, 1644.

Taylor, T. *The Progress of Saints into Full Holiness*, 1630.

Tombes, J. *Fermentum Pharisaeorum, or, The Leaven of Pharisaicall Wil-Worship: Declared in a Sermon on Matthew 15.9. November 24 1641 at Lemster Herefordshire*, 1643.

LATER EDITIONS AND COMPILATIONS

Abbott, W. C., ed. *The Writings and Speeches of Oliver Cromwell*, 4 vols., Cambridge, Mass., 1937–47.

Bannister, A. T. *Diocese of Hereford: Institutions, AD 1539–1900*, Hereford, 1923.

Bruce, J., W. D. Hamilton and S. C. Lomas, eds. *Calendar of State Papers Domestic of the Reign of Charles I*, 23 vols. London, 1858–1897.

Coates, W. H., ed. *The Journal of Sir Simonds D'Ewes from the First Recess of the Long Parliament to the Withdrawal of King Charles From London*, New Haven, 1942.

Coates, W. H., A. S. Young and V. F. Snow, eds. *The Private Journals of the Long Parliament, 3 January to 5 March 1642*, New Haven and London, 1982.

Cobbet, W., ed. *The Parliamentary History of England*, II, London, 1807.

Cope, E. S. and W. H. Coates, eds. *Proceedings of the Short Parliament of 1640*, Camden Society, 4th Series, XIX, London, 1977.

Duncumb, J. *et al. Collections Towards the History and Antiquities of the County of Hereford*, 6 vols., Hereford, 1804–1915.

Evelyn-White, E. H., ed. *The Journal of William Dowsing*, Ipswich, 1885.

Firth, C. H., ed. *The Clarke Papers*, II, Camden Society, 1894.

Firth, C. H. and R. S. Rait, eds. *Acts and Ordinances of the Interregnum*, 3 vols., London, 1911.

Foster, E., ed. *Proceedings in Parliament 1610*, 2 vols., New Haven, 1966.

Foster, J. *Alumni Oxonienses: The Members of the University of Oxford, 1500–1714*, 4 vols., London, 1891–2.

Gardiner, S. R. *The Constitutional Documents of the Puritan Revolution: 1625–1660*, 3rd edn., revised, Oxford, 1968.

Grazebrook, G. and J. P. Rylands, eds. *The Visitation of Shropshire Taken in the Year 1623*, Harleian Society, XXVIII, XXIX, London, 1889.

Green, M. A. E., ed. *Calendar of the Committee for the Advance of Money, 1643–1656*, 3 vols., London, 1888.

  ed. *Calendar of the Committee for Compounding With Delinquents, 1643–1660*, 5 vols., London, 1888–92.

  ed. *Calendar of State Papers Domestic of the Reign of James I*, 5 vols., London, 1857–72.

Halsall, E. *A Journal of the Siege of Lathom House, in Lancashire . . .*, London, 1902.

Hopwood, C. H. *Middle Temple Records*, 4 vols., London, 1904–5.

Historical Manuscripts Commission, *Fourth Report, Appendix, part I, Manuscripts of the House of Lords*, London, 1874.

  Tenth Report, Appendix, part IV, Manuscripts of the Earl of Powis, London, 1885.

  Thirteenth Report, Appendix, part 4, Dovaston Manuscripts, London, 1892.

Thirteenth Report, Appendix, part 2, Mss. of His Grace the Duke of Portland Preserved at Welbeck Abbey, II, London, 1893.

Fourteenth Report, Appendix, part 2, The Manuscripts of His Grace the Duke of Portland Preserved at Welbeck Abbey, III, London, 1894.

Calendar of the Manuscripts of the Marquess of Bath preserved at Longleat, Wiltshire, I, London, 1904.

HMC, Report on the Mss. of the Duke of Buccleuch and Queensberry K.G., K.T., Preserved at Montagu House, Whitehall, III, London, 1926.

Calendar of the Manuscripts of the most Honourable the Marquess of Salisbury, preserved at Hatfield House, Hertfordshire, XXI, London, 1970.

A Calendar of the Shrewsbury and Talbot Papers, II, London, 1971.

Johnson, R. C., M. F. Keeler, M. J. Cole and W. B. Bidwell, eds. *Proceedings in Parliament, 1628,* 6 vols., New Haven, 1977–83.

Kenyon, J. P. *The Stuart Constitution, 1603–1688, Documents and Commentary,* Cambridge, 1973.

Larkin, J. F. and P. L. Hughes, eds. *Stuart Royal Proclamations: Royal Proclamations of King James I, 1603–1625,* Oxford, 1973.

Lewis, T. T., ed. *Letters of the Lady Brilliana Harley,* Camden Society, 1st Series, LVIII, London, 1854.

Macray, W., ed. *The History of the Rebellion and Civil Wars in England Begun in 1641, by Edward, Earl of Clarendon,* 6 vols., Oxford, 1888.

Maltby, J. D., ed. *The Short Parliament (1640) Diary of Sir Thomas Aston,* Camden Society, 4th Series, XXXV, London, 1988.

Matthews, A. G. *Calamy Revised: Being a Revision of Edmund Calamy's Account of the Ministers and Others Ejected and Silenced 1660–1662,* Oxford, 1932.

Meikle, H. W., ed. *Correspondence of the Scots Commissioners in London 1644–46,* London, 1917.

Mitchell A. F. and J. Struthers, eds. *Minutes of the Sessions of the Westminster Assembly of Divines,* Edinburgh, 1874.

Notestein, W., ed. *The Journal of Sir Simonds D'Ewes from the Beginning of the Long Parliament to the Opening of the Trial of the Earl of Strafford,* New Haven, 1923.

Notestein W. and R. H. Relf, eds. *Commons Debates for 1629,* Minneapolis, 1921.

Pitman, J. R., ed. *The Whole Works of the Rev. John Lightfoot,* XIII, London, 1824.

PRO Lists and Indexes, *List of Sheriffs for England and Wales,* IX, London, 1898.

Return of the Names of Every Member Returned to Serve in Each Parliament, 4 vols., London, 1878–1891.

Sermons or Homilies, Appointed to be Read in Churches in the Time of Queen Elizabeth of Famous Memory: to which are Added the Articles of Religion and the Constitutions and Canons Ecclesiastical, London, 1840.

Shuttleworth, J. M., ed. *The Life of Edward, First Lord Herbert of Cherbury,* Oxford, 1976.

Snow, V. F. and A. S. Young, eds. *The Private Journals of the Long Parliament, 7 March to 1 June 1642,* New Haven, 1987.

Sutherland, J., ed. *Lucy Hutchinson's Memoirs of the Life of Colonel Hutchinson,* Oxford, 1973.

Thompson, C., ed. *The Holles Account of Proceedings in the House of Commons in 1624,* Orchard Press, Essex, 1985.

Walter Yonge's Diary of Proceedings in the House of Commons, 1642–1645, Orchard Press, Essex, 1986.

Venn, J. and Venn, J. A. *Alumni Cantabrigienses*. I: *From the Earliest Times to 1751*, 4 vols., London, 1922–7.
Willis Bund, J., ed. *The Diary of Henry Townshend of Emley Lovett, 1640–1663*, II, London, 1920.
Wood, E. B., ed. *Rowland Vaughan, His Book*, London, 1897.

SECONDARY WORKS

Books
Ashton, R. *The English Civil War: Conservatism and Revolution, 1603–1649*, London, 1978.
Aston, M. *England's Iconoclasts: Laws Against Images*, Oxford, 1988.
Aylmer, G. E. *The King's Servants: The Civil Service of Charles I, 1625–1642*, London, 1974.
Bankes, G. *The Story of Corfe Castle*, London, 1853.
Barnes, T. G. *Somerset 1625–1640: A County's Government During the 'Personal Rule'*, Cambridge, Mass., 1961.
Birch, T. *The Life of Prince Henry of Wales*, Dublin, 1760.
Blackwood, B. G. *The Lancashire Gentry and the Great Rebellion, 1640–60*, Chetham Society, 3rd Series, XXV, Manchester, 1978.
Brunton, D. and D. H. Pennington, *Members of the Long Parliament*, London, 1954.
Calder, I. M. *Activities of the Puritan Faction of the Church of England, 1625–1633*, London, 1957.
Cliffe, J. T. *The Yorkshire Gentry from the Reformation to the Civil War*, London, 1969.
  The Puritan Gentry: The Great Puritan Families of Early Stuart England, London, 1984.
  Puritans in Conflict: The Puritan Gentry During and After the Civil Wars, London, 1988.
Collins, A. *Historical Collection of the Noble Families of Cavendish, Holles, Vere, Harley and Ogle*, London, 1752.
Collinson, P., *The Elizabethan Puritan Movement*, London, 1967.
  The Religion of Protestants: The Church in English Society, 1559–1625, London, 1982.
Cope, E. S., *The Life of a Public Man, Edward, First Baron Montagu of Boughton, 1562–1644*, Philadelphia, 1981.
  Politics Without Parliaments, 1629–1640, London, 1987.
Crawford, P. *Denzil Holles, 1598–1680: A Study of his Political Career*, Royal Historical Society Studies in History, XVI, London, 1979.
Cust, R. P. *The Forced Loan and English Politics, 1626–1628*, Oxford, 1987.
Cust, R. and A. Hughes, eds. *Conflict in Early Stuart England*, London, 1989.
Davies, H. *The Worship of the English Puritans*, Glasgow, 1948.
Donaldson, G. *Scotland: James V–James VII*, Edinburgh, 1978.
Everitt, A. M. *Suffolk and the Great Rebellion, 1640–1660*, Suffolk Record Society, III, Ipswich, 1960.
  The Community of Kent and the Great Rebellion, Leicester, 1966.
  Change in the Provinces: the Seventeenth Century, Leicester, 1969.
Fletcher, A. J. *A County Community in Peace and War: Sussex, 1600–1660*, London, 1975.

The Outbreak of the English Civil War, London, 1981.

Fraser, A. *The Weaker Vessel: Woman's Lot in Seventeenth-Century England*, London, 1984.

Gardiner, S. R. *History of England, 1603–1642*, 10 vols., London, 1883–4.
History of the Great Civil War, 1642–1649, 4 vols., London, 1893.
A History of the Commonwealth and the Protectorate, 1649–1660, 4 vols., London, 1903.

Haller, W. *The Rise of Puritanism*, Philadelphia, 1972.

Ham, R. E. *The County and the Kingdom: Sir Herbert Croft and the Elizabethan State*, Washington, D.C., 1977.

Heath-Agnew, E. *Roundhead to Royalist: A Biography of Colonel John Birch, 1615–1691*, Hereford, 1977.

Hexter, J. *The Reign of King Pym*, Harvard Historical Studies, XLVIII, Cambridge, Mass., 1941.

Hibbard, C. *Charles I and the Popish Plot*, Chapel Hill, 1983.

Hill, C. *Economic Problems of the Church*, Oxford, 1956.
Society and Puritanism in Pre-Revolutionary England, London, 1964.
Intellectual Origins of the English Revolution, Oxford, 1965.
Antichrist in Seventeenth-Century England, Oxford, 1971.
Change and Continuity in 17th Century England, London, 1974.

Hirst, D. *The Representative of the People? Voters and Voting in England Under the Early Stuarts*, Cambridge, 1975.

Holmes, C. *The Eastern Association in the English Civil War*, Cambridge, 1974.
Seventeenth Century Lincolnshire, Lincoln, 1980.

Houlbrooke, R. *The English Family, 1450–1700*, 1984.

Hughes, A. *Politics, Society and Civil War in Warwickshire, 1620–1660*, Cambridge, 1987.

Hunt, W. *The Puritan Moment: The Coming of Revolution to an English County*, Harvard Historical Studies, CII, Cambridge, Mass., 1983.

Hutton, R. *The Royalist War Effort, 1642–1646*, London, 1982.

Keeler, M. F. *The Long Parliament, 1640–1641: A Biographical Study of its Members*, Philadelphia, 1954.

Kendall, R. T. *Calvin and English Calvinism to 1649*, Oxford, 1979.

Kishlansky, M. A. *The Rise of the New Model Army*, Cambridge, 1979.
Parliamentary Selection: Social and Political Choice in Early Modern England, Cambridge, 1986.

Lake, P. G., *Moderate Puritans in the Elizabethan Church*, Cambridge, 1982.

Lockyer, R. *Buckingham: The Life and Political Career of George Villiers, First Duke of Buckingham, 1592–1628*, London, 1981.

Malcolm, J. L. *Caesar's Due: Loyalty and King Charles, 1642–1646*, RHS Studies in History, XXXVIII, London, 1983.

Manning, B. *The English People and the English Revolution*, London, 1976.

Mendle, M. *Dangerous Positions: Mixed Government, the Estates of the Realm, and the Answer to the xix Propositions*, Alabama, 1985.

Mingay, G. E. *The Gentry: The Rise and Fall of a Ruling Class*, London, 1976.

Morrill, J. S. *Cheshire, 1630–1660: County Government and Society during the English Revolution*, Oxford, 1974.
The Revolt of the Provinces: Conservatives and Radicals in the English Civil War, 1630–1650, London, 1976.
ed. *Reactions to the English Civil War, 1642–1649*, London, 1982.

Neale, J. E. *Elizabeth I and her Parliaments, 1584–1601*, London, 1957.
The Elizabethan House of Commons, London, 1949.
Newton, A. P. *The Colonising Activities of the English Puritans*, New Haven, 1914.
Notestein, W. *English Folk: A Book of Characters*, London, 1938.
The House of Commons 1604–1610, New Haven, 1971.
O'Day, R. *The English Clergy: The Emergence and Consolidation of a Profession, 1558–1642*, Leicester, 1979.
Parker, K. L. *The English Sabbath: A Study of Doctrine and Discipline from the Reformation to the Civil War*, Cambridge, 1988.
Paul, R. S. *The Assembly of the Lord: Politics and Religion in the Westminster Assembly and the 'Grand Debate'*, Edinburgh, 1985.
Pevsner, N. *The Buildings of England: Herefordshire*, London, 1963.
Richardson, R. C. *Puritanism in North-West England: A Regional Study of the Diocese of Chester to 1642*, Manchester, 1972.
Robinson, C. J. *A History of the Castles of Herefordshire and Their Lords*, London, 1869.
A History of the Mansions and Manors of Herefordshire, London, 1873.
Rowe, V. *Sir Henry Vane the Younger: A Study in Political and Administrative History*, University of London Historical Studies, XXVIII, London, 1970.
Royal Commission on Historical Monuments, *Herefordshire: An Inventory of the Historical Monuments*, 3 vols., London, 1934–7.
Ruigh, R. E. *The Parliament of 1624*, Cambridge, Mass., 1971.
Russell, C. *The Crisis of Parliaments*, Oxford, 1971.
ed. *The Origins of the English Civil War*, London, 1973.
Parliaments and English Politics, 1621–29, Oxford, 1979.
Seaver, P. *The Puritan Lectureships: The Politics of Religious Dissent, 1560–1662*, London, 1970.
Shaw, W. A. *A History of the English Church During the Civil Wars and Under the Commonwealth, 1640–1660*, 2 vols., London, 1900.
Skeel, C. A. J. *The Council in the Marches of Wales*, London, 1904.
Snow, V. *Essex the Rebel*, University of Nebraska Press, 1970.
Somerville, J. P. *Politics and Ideology in England, 1603–1640*, London, 1986.
Stephen, L. and S. Lee, eds. *Dictionary of National Biography*, 22 vols., London, 1973.
Stone, L. *The Crisis of the Aristocracy, 1558–1641*, Oxford, 1965.
The Family, Sex and Marriage in England, 1500–1800, London, 1977.
Thomas, K. *Religion and the Decline of Magic: Studies in Popular Beliefs in Sixteenth and Seventeenth Century England*, London, 1971.
Tite, G. C. E. *Impeachment and Parliamentary Judicature in Early Stuart England*, London, 1974.
Trevor-Roper, H. R. *Archbishop Laud, 1573–1643*, London, 1940.
Tyacke, N. *Anti-Calvinists: The Rise of English Arminianism, c. 1590–1640*, Oxford, 1987.
Underdown, D. *Pride's Purge: Politics in the Puritan Revolution*, Oxford, 1971.
Somerset in the Civil War and Interregnum, Newton Abbot, 1973.
Revel, Riot and Rebellion, Oxford, 1985.
Webb, J. and T. W. Webb, *Memorials of the Civil War Between King Charles I, and the Parliament of England as it Affected Herefordshire and the Adjacent Counties*, 2 vols., London, 1879.
Wedgwood, C. V. *The King's War*, London, 1958.

Williams, P. *The Council in the Marches of Wales under Elizabeth I*, Cardiff, 1958.
Williams, W. R. *The Parliamentary History of the County of Hereford*, Brecknock, 1896.
Wilson, J. *Fairfax: A Life of Thomas, Lord Fairfax, Captain-General of all the Parliament's Forces in the English Civil War, Creator and Commander of the New Model Army*, New York, 1985.
Woods, T. P. S. *Prelude to Civil War, 1642: Mr Justice Malet and the Kentish Petition*, Salisbury, 1980.
Zagorin, P. *The Court and the Country: The Beginning of the English Revolution*, London, 1969.

Articles

Aylmer, G. E. 'Who Was Ruling in Herefordshire from 1645 to 1661?', *TWNFC*, XL (1970–2).
Betcherman, Lita-Rose. 'The York House Collection and its Keeper', *Apollo*, 92 (October, 1970).
Christianson, P. 'The Peers, the People, and Parliamentary Management in the First Six Months of the Long Parliament', *JMH*, XLIX (1977).
'Reformers and the Church of England under Elizabeth I and the Early Stuarts', *JEH*, XXXI (1980).
Clifton, R. 'Fear of Popery', in C. Russell, ed. *The Origins of the English Civil War*, London, 1973.
Collinson, P. 'Lectures by Combination: Structures and Characteristics of Church Life in Seventeenth Century England', *BIHR*, XLVIII (1975).
'Towards a Broader Understanding of the Early Dissenting Tradition', in C. R. Cole and M. E. Moody, eds. *The Dissenting Tradition: Essays for Leland H. Carlson*, Athens, Ohio, 1975.
'A "Magazine of Religious Patterns": An Erasmian Topic Transposed in English Protestantism', in D. Baker, ed. *Renaissance and Renewal in Christian History*, Studies in Church History, XIV, Oxford, 1977.
'A Comment: Concerning the Name Puritan', *JEH*, XXXI (1980).
Cust, R. 'News and Politics in Early Seventeenth-Century England', *Past and Present*, CXII (1986).
'Charles I and a Draft Declaration for the 1628 Parliament', *Historical Research*, forthcoming.
Cust, R. and P. G. Lake, 'Sir Richard Grosvenor and the Rhetoric of Magistracy', *BIHR*, LIV (1981).
Eales, J. S. 'Sir Robert Harley KB (1579–1656) and the "Character" of a Puritan', *British Library Journal*, XV (1989).
Elton, G. R. 'A High Road to Civil War?' in *Studies in Tudor and Stuart Politics and Government: Papers and Reviews, 1946–1972*, II (1974).
Everitt, A. M. 'The Local Community and the Great Rebellion', Historical Association, General Series 70 (1969).
Faraday, M. A. 'Ship Money in Herefordshire', *TWNFC*, XLI (1974).
Fielding, J. 'Opposition to the Personal Rule of Charles I: The Diary of Robert Woodford, 1637–1641', *Historical Journal*, XXXI (1988).
Fletcher, A. J. 'Concern for Renewal in the Root and Branch Debates of 1641', in D. Baker, ed. *Renaissance and Renewal in Christian History*, Studies in Church History, XIV, Oxford, 1977.

'The Coming of War', in J. S. Morrill, ed. *Reactions to the English Civil War, 1642–1649* (London, 1982).

Fletcher, W. D. G. 'Institutions of Shropshire Incumbents', *TSANHS*, 3rd Series, V (1905).

Gordon, M. D. 'The Collection of Ship Money in the Reign of Charles I', *TRHS*, 3rd Series, IV (1910).

Green, E. 'On the Civil War in Somerset', *Somersetshire Archaeological and Natural History Society's Proceedings*, XIV (1867).

Hall, B. 'Puritanism: The Problem of Definition', in G. J. Cuming, ed. *Studies in Church History*, II, London, 1965.

Ham, R. E. 'The Four Shire Controversy', *Welsh History Review*, VIII (1976–77).

Hexter, J. 'The Problem of the Presbyterian Independents', *American History Review*, XLIV (1938–9).

Hill, C. 'Recent Interpretations of the Civil War', *History*, XLI (1956).

'Parliament and People in Seventeenth Century England', *Past and Present*, XCII (1981).

Hirst, D. M. 'Revisionism Revised: The Place of Principle', *Past and Present*, XCII (1981).

Holmes, C. 'The County Community in Stuart Historiography', *JBS*, XIX (1979–80).

Howse, W. H. 'Contest for a Radnorshire Rectory in the Seventeenth Century', *Journal of the Historical Society of the Church in Wales*, VII (1957).

Hoyle, D. 'A Commons Investigation of Arminianism and Popery in Cambridge on the Eve of the Civil War', *Historical Journal*, XXIX (1986).

Jackson, J. N. 'Some Observations upon the Herefordshire Environment of the Seventeenth and Eighteenth Centuries', *TWNFC*, XXXVI (1958–60).

Kishlansky, M. 'The Emergence of Adversary Politics in the Long Parliament', *JMH*, XLIX (1977).

Lake, P. G. 'Matthew Hutton – A Puritan Bishop?', *History*, LXIV (1979).

'The Significance of the Elizabethan Identification of the Pope as Antichrist', *Journal of Ecclesiastical History*, XXXI (1980).

'The Collection of Ship Money in Cheshire During the Sixteen-Thirties: A Case Study of Relations Between Central and Local Government', *Northern History*, XVII (1981).

'Constitutional Consensus and Puritan Opposition in the 1620s: Thomas Scott and the Spanish Match', *Historical Journal*, XXV (1982).

'Calvinism and the English Church, 1570–1635', *Past and Present*, CXIV (1987).

'Feminine Piety and Personal Potency: The "Emancipation" of Mrs Jane Ratcliffe', *The Seventeenth Century*, II (1987).

'Serving God and the Times: The Calvinist Conformity of Robert Sanderson', *JBS*, XXVII (1988).

Langston, J. N. 'John Workman, Puritan Lecturer in Gloucester', *Bristol and Gloucestershire Archaeological Society Transactions*, LXVI (1945).

Lindley, K. J. 'The Impact of the 1641 Rebellion upon England and Wales, 1641–5', *Irish Historical Studies*, XVIII (1972).

'The Part Played by Catholics', in B. S. Manning, ed. *Politics, Religion and the English Civil War*, London, 1973.

McLaren, D. 'Marital Fertility and Lactation', in M. Prior, ed. *Women in English Society, 1500–1800*, London, 1985.

Morrill, J. 'The Northern Gentry and the Great Rebellion', *Northern History*, XV, (1979).

'The Religious Context of the English Civil War', *TRHS*, 5th Series, 34 (1984).

'Sir William Brereton and England's Wars of Religion', *JBS*, XXIV (1985).

'The Attack on the Church of England in the Long Parliament', in D. Beales and G. Best, eds. *History, Society and the Churches: Essays in Honour of Owen Chadwick*, Cambridge, 1985.

Neale, J. E. 'Parliament and the Articles of Religion, 1571', *English Historical Review*, LXVII (1952).

Newman, P. R. 'Catholic Royalists of Northern England, 1642–1645' *Northern History*, XV (1979).

Notestein, W. 'The Winning of the Initiative by the House of Commons', The Raleigh Lecture on History, 1924 (reprint, London, 1971).

Pearl, V., 'Oliver St John and the "middle group" in the Long Parliament: August 1643–May 1644', *English Historical Review*, XXXI (1966).

Rabb, T. K. 'Revisionism Revised: The Role of the Commons', *Past and Present*, XCII (1981).

Roberts, C. 'The Earl of Bedford and the Coming of the English Revolution', *JMH*, XLIX (1977).

Roy, I. 'The Libraries of Edward, 2nd Viscount Conway and Others: An Inventory and Valuation of 1643', *BIHR*, XLI (1968).

Russell, C. 'Arguments for Religious Unity in England, 1530–1650', *Journal of Ecclesiastical History*, XVIII (1967).

'Parliamentary History in Perspective', *History*, LXI (1976).

'The Parliamentary Career of John Pym', in P. Clark, A. G. R. Smith and N. Tyacke, eds. *The English Commonwealth, 1547–1640: Essays in Politics Presented to Joel Hurstfield*, Leicester, 1979.

Schwarz, M. L. 'Lord Saye and Sele's Objections to the Palatinate Benevolence of 1622: Some New Evidence and its Significance', *Albion*, IV (1972).

Smith, T. S. 'Herefordshire Catholics and the Rites of Passage: 1560–1640', *TWNFC*, XLII (1978).

Tawney, R. H. 'The Rise of the Gentry, 1558–1640', *Economic History Review*, 1st Series, XI (1941).

Trevor-Roper, H. R. 'The Gentry, 1540–1640', *Economic History Review Supplements*, 1 (1953).

Tyacke, N. 'Puritanism, Arminianism, and Counter-Revolution', in C. Russell, ed. *The Origins of the English Civil War*, London, 1973.

Underdown, D. 'Party Management; in the Recruiter Elections, 1645–1648', *English Historical Review*, 83 (1968).

Whitebrook, J. C. 'Dr John Stoughton the Elder', *Congregational Historical Society Transactions*, VI (1913–15).

Williams, P. 'The Attack on the Council in the Marches, 1603–1642', *Transactions of the Honourable Society of Cymmrodorion* (1961).

'The Welsh Borderland under Queen Elizabeth', *Welsh History Review*, I (1960–3).

Wormald, J. 'James I and VI: Two Kings or One?', *History*, LXVIII (1983).

Theses

Adams, D. R. L. 'The Parliamentary Representation of Radnor, 1536–1832', Wales MA Thesis, 1970.

Adams, S. L. 'The Protestant Cause: Religious Alliance with the Western European Calvinist Communities as a Political Issue in England, 1585–1630', University of Oxford, D. Phil. Thesis, 1973.

Hughes, A. 'Politics, Society and Civil War in Warwickshire, 1625–1661', University of Liverpool, Ph.D. Thesis, 1979.

Levy, J. S. 'Perceptions and Beliefs: The Harleys of Brampton Bryan and the Origins and Outbreak of the First Civil War', University of London, Ph.D. Thesis, 1983.

McParlin, G. 'The Herefordshire Gentry in County Government, 1625–1661', University College of Wales, Aberystwyth, Ph.D. Thesis, 1981.

Palfrey, I. 'The Royalist War Effort in Devon, 1642–6', University of Birmingham, MA Thesis, 1985.

Shipps, K. W. 'Lay Patronage in East Anglian Clerics in Pre-Revolutionary England', Yale University, Ph.D. Thesis, 1971.

Silcock, R. H. 'County Government in Worcestershire, 1603–1660', University of London, Ph.D. Thesis, 1974.

Smith, G. L. T. 'Gentry Royalism in North Wales: The Sheriff's Letter Book of 1642', University of Birmingham, MA Thesis, 1982.

Tyacke, N. 'Arminianism in England, in Religion and Politics, 1604–40', Oxford University, D.Phil. Thesis, 1968.

Wanklyn, M. D. G. 'Landed Society and Allegiance in Cheshire and Shropshire in the First Civil War', University of Manchester, Ph.D. Thesis, 1976.

Transcripts

Yale Center for Parliamentary History

Transcript of the Parliamentary Diary of Edward Nicholas, 1624, from the Manuscript at the PRO (SP14/166).

Transcript of the Parliamentary Diary of Sir William Spring, 1624, from the manuscript at Harvard University, Houghton Library (Ms. Eng. 980).

Transcript of the Parliamentary Diary of Sir Richard Grosvenor, 1626, from the manuscript at Trinity College, Dublin (Ms. E5/17).

Transcript of the Parliamentary Diary of Bulstrode Whitelocke, 1626, from the manuscript at Cambridge University Library, Dd. (12/20–22).

INDEX

Abbey Dore, 38
Adwalton, battle of, 1643, 178
Aldern, Thomas, sheriff, 98
altar controversy, 40, 44, 57, 67, 96, 106,
    107, 109, 110, 131, 158, 182–3
Ames, William, minister, 42
Antichrist, 89–90, 108, 112, 176
anti-popery, xi, 68, 98, 137–8, 176, 200,
    see also Arminianism, catholics and
    'popish plot'
Armada, 80
Arminianism, 5, 13, 40, 68, 75, 91, 109,
    131
    supposed links with catholicism, 44–5,
    47, 67, 81–2, 92, 119
Arminians, 13, 26, 44, 67, 75, 79, 81, 82,
    83, 89, 92
army, 185, 186–8, 191, 192–3, see also
    New Model Army
Army Plot, first, 114, 118
    second, 121
array, commission of, 124, 125, 127, 146,
    151, 154, 155, 158, see also
    Herefordshire, commissioners of array
    in
Aston, John, 116, 117, 121, 159 n.17
Aubigny, Catherine Howard, Lady d', 170–
    1
aurum potabile, 27, 50
Axton, William, minister, 17
Aylton, 30, 56 n.30
Aymestrey, 115

Ball, John, 140
Ballam, Mr, schoolteacher, 28
Bankes, Lady Mary, 3
Barrett family of Belhouse, Essex, 18
Barrington, Sir Thomas, MP, 111, 179
Bastwicke, John, 64
Baxter, Richard, minister, 112, 197

Bedford, Francis Russell, fourth Earl of, 98,
    101
Benevolences,
    1614, 71
    1622, 85
    1626, 85
Bennet, Robert, Bishop of Hereford, 54–5
Berkshire, 91
billeting, 82, 84, 97
Birch, Col. John, 14, 153, 185, 186
Bishop's Exclusion Bills,
    1641, 113
    1642, 181, 199
bishops' wars, x, 6–7, 72–3, 88, 90–2, 94,
    95, 98, 104, 115, 126
    pressed men in, 90–1, 96–7, 104, 126,
    see also Scotland
Boteler, Sir William, 135
Boughey, Francis, vicar of Stokesay, 152,
    175
Bourne, William, minister, 108, 112
Boys, John, MP, 191
Brabazon, Wallop, JP, 106, 127, 130, 141,
    155, 156–8, 168
Brampton, Margaret, 30
Brampton Bryan, 16, 17, 114, 115, 139,
    141, 146, 158, 162, 164, 165,
    166
    advowson of, 31, 53, 56 n.30
    arms at, 139 n.42
    castle, 121, 144; sieges of, 3–4, 14, 29,
    122, 150–1, 159, 168, 169–73, 175–6,
    178, 179
    estate of, 21, 29–30, 32, 33, 34, 75
    fair of 144–5
    incumbents of, 17, 53–60, 68, 194
Bray, Sir Giles, 35
breastfeeding, 24
Brecknockshire, 9, 97, 106, 150
Brereton, Sir William, MP, 111, 172
Bridgeman, Sir John, 86

Printed in the United Kingdom
by Lightning Source UK Ltd.
116661UKS00001B/224